METHODS OF TEACHING GEOGRAPHY

METHODS OF TEACHING GEOGRAPHY

By

S.A. Salim Basha

M.A., M.Ed.
Lecturer
Crescent College of Education
Ananthapur
Andhra Pradesh

General Editor

Dr. Digumarti Bhaskara Rao

M.Sc., M.A., M.A., M.Ed., Ph.D.
Reader
R.V.R. College of Education
Srinivasa Nagar Colony
Guntur–522 006
Andhra Pradesh
India

DISCOVERY PUBLISHING HOUSE
NEW DELHI-110002

Published by:
Tilak Wasan

DISCOVERY PUBLISHING HOUSE PVT. LTD.
4383/4B, Ansari Road, Darya Ganj
New Delhi-110 002 (India)
Phone : +91-11-23279245, 23253475, 43596065
E-mail : discoverypublishinghouse@gmail.com
sales@discoverypublishinggroup.com
web : www.discoverypublishinggroup.com

First Edition: **2004**

Reprinted: **2020**

ISBN: 978-81-7141-807-7

Methods of Teaching Geography

Printed at:
Infinity Imaging Systems
Delhi

Foreword

Teacher education is quantitatively marching ahead towards quality education. The central and state governments through the NCTE and the Directorates of School/Higher Education are rendering their legitimate service in improving the quality of teacher education by formulating and implementing various academic policies and educational programmes. Along with these policies and programmes, the teacher educators and the prospective teachers teaching and studying in teacher education institutions need good curriculum and quality books.

The methods of teaching each subject play a pivotal role in enhancing the efficiency of their practitioners. Identifying the very importance of the methods of teaching and the quality of books, a series of books on the methods of teaching different subjects have been developed by experienced teacher educators for the benefit of teachers in making in teacher education institutions. Thanks to the authors.

Valuable suggestions for the improvement of these books are welcome from fellow teacher educators, prospective teachers and other academicians involved in the arena of teacher education.

The authors and the editor dedicate this series of books on the methodology of teaching to Mr. Tilak Raj Wasan, Proprietor, Discovery Publishing House, New Delhi, for taking up this commendable task of publication to meet the felt needs of teacher education faculty and clientele.

Dr. Digumarti Bhaskara Rao
Research Director in Education
Nagarjuna University
br_digumarti@rediffmail.com

Preface

The movement of modern education in India is almost two century old. It has come of age now. Over the decades, great educationists have contributed towards the development and evolution of education, as a discipline. Thus, education in India has been enriched a lot.

As a result, the Indian education system can be placed at par with any advanced education system in the modern world. In fact, education is a vast sea and Teachers' Training is a stream in it. So, it makes it essential that the responsibilities of the faculty members are focused on the task of providing better training to the future teachers, for their better learning and proper development. And this responsible exercise can only be undertaken, if the trainers are equipped with all the needed skill and knowledge of the subject, they are supposed to teach. Hence, it becomes essential for making adequate provisions, for each course to the teacher-trainees. Methods of Teaching are very important for the successful training of teachers and for their career in future.

In order to provide all related material in one cover, here is this book, on this important subject. Of course there are several books on the subject in the market, but, every book has its own style and way of presentation. Similarly, the present one, too has its own merits and advantages.

During the course of the preparation of this book, the undersigned has done his best for the accomplishment of the job. He would be pleased and feel contented, if this book is acknowledged, as a textbook and a reference tool for the teachers and students, alike.

Author

Contents

1
Introduction

Every subject that is taught to children has certain basic elements and fundamentals. These basic elements and fundamentals are responsible for the limitation of the subject-matter of any specific subject and these also influence the subject-matter of a specified subject. To understand a subject these fundamentals are essential. Like any other subject, the knowledge of these fundamentals is essential for the teaching of geography. Thus, to have a correct idea of these fundamentals, a proper explanation of the geographical environment of a particular country is essential. The following five are the basic elements of geography.

(i) Natural conditions

(ii) Formation of the surface of earth or land

(iii) Climate

(iv) Vegetation and agricultural products

(v) Human element or human activities

All these five elements taken together are known *as geographical environment* and these elements are mainly responsible for the geographical control. In the following pages an attempt will be made to consider all these elements in detail.

We can say that physical conditions is another name of geographical conditions. Other things are developed on the basis of physical conditions. The physical conditions are governed by the formation of the surface of the earth or land. The creation of atmosphere depends on physical conditions and the atmosphere or environment has a profound influence on the life of the inhabitants. Thus, it becomes of prime importance to have a thorough study of natural conditions. To have a correct and balanced idea about a country it is essential to have a fairly exhaustive idea of natural conditions existing there. In olden days it sufficed to learn the forces and the laws that guided the physical conditions. However in present age it has lost its importance. Modern geography lays more stress to find out the various causes responsible for bringing about different changes in physical conditions. At present it is generally agreed that in the beginning earth was very hot and it was just like a solid mass of fire. Slowly and slowly it cooled and during this process of cooling the surface of earth was formed. Thus, the cooling process had its effect on the surface of earth. These changes were brought about by certain factors.

If a land is situated much more away from the equator (e.g. northern most and southern most part of earth) then it is likely to be covered with snow for the whole of the year and if a land (or country) is situated near the equator then its climate is likely to be very hot. Similarly we can say that deserts are hot and dry throughout the year. If a region is situated near a sea shore then its climate will be temperate.

Formation of Earth

When the earth was cooling down a crust was formed and at certain places wrinkles were formed. These wrinkles had elevations at certain points and were deep at some other points. Those points that had elevations later grew up into mountains and those points which were deep later on became oceans and valleys. In order to maintain itself nature created plains at some places and it gave rise to plateaus at other places. To make any changes in nature is beyond man's capacity, however slight changes in nature can be affected by man but such changes are in consequential.

The formation of surface of earth now forms the part of study of geology but geography cannot altogether ignore it. It has to be studied because the formation of earth is mainly responsible for the climate and produce of that land. In the plains which are formed by rivers we find good agricultural produce and the hilly areas and plateaus are not suitable for agriculture. The old rocks are camparatively richer in mineral wealth such as coal, iron ore, silver, etc. and the newly-formed rocks are richer in oil.

The formation of land has played a vital role even in the development of human race and civilisation. Since human life is influenced by the formation of earth, geography has to take it into consideration. The study of interaction of man and the nature is taken up in geography and such a study is of vital importance.

The various agencies that are responsible for bringing about continuous changes in the surface of the earth can be broadly. classified as (i) External agencies and (ii) internal agencies.

External agencies include wind, rain, flowing water, ice, sun, glaciers, heat of sun, etc. Internal agencies include such phenomenon as earthquack, eruption of volcano, etc.

The changes caused by these agencies became visible only after a long time say after about hundred or thousands of years. There was a time when people of Greece had erected ghats near crete but now the place is very high from sea level. In India the Thar desert appears to be spreading and Government of India is making all-out efforts to check this expansion. A large-scale tree plantation has been undertaken to check the spread of this desert."

It is one of the important factors that influences the geographical conditions. It is one of the basic elements that controls and influences the physical features. It influences agricultural products, living conditions, food habits, traditions and customs. In India we find that Panjab occupies top position in production of wheat. West Bengal in production of rice and tea is produced in Assam. This can easily be explained on the basis of climatic conditions existing in those regions.

The effect of climatic conditions is direct and discernible. 'Various trades and industries have localised and established due to climate and its influence. The factors that influence the climate can be summarised as under:

(a) Distance from the equator.

(b) Distance from the sea shore.

(c) Elevation from the sea level.

(d) Conditions of wind and its direction.

(e) Location of the mountains, their direction and heights.

(f) Rainfall.

(g) Formation of the land.

All these factors are responsible for the climate of a particular place.

The vegetation and agricultural products are influenced to a large extent by the climate of the region. Those areas which have rains all through the year have dense forests and in dry places and deserts there is very little vegetation. Wood industries are most likely to be set up in the forest areas. Some big industries which get their raw materials from forests are also most likely to be established in such areas.

In alluvial soil we get good agricultural produce which is not possible in plateau lands. Thus, we find that natural factors are responsible for the fertility of land. We also find that if the temperature of a place is near about 80° and if the rainfall average of the area is about 80" in year then such a place is suitable for paddy and jute production. Since such favourable factors do not exist in the land formed by river Indus so the production of jute and rice in this area is not possible.

The steel industry was established in Tata Nagar because of the availability of iron ore in that area. Not only mineral wealth, but even the animal wealth is influenced by climatic conditions. The monkeys, beers and deers are found in dense forests and camels in deserts. We do not find tigers and lions in mountain areas because of unsuitability of such a climate to lions and tigers. Yaks are found in Tibet and Reindeers in Tundra because of suitable climatic conditions existing in those regions. Those places where we find good vegetation are also found to have a good number of animals.

Man is a social animal and thus forms part of animal life. The mode of living and food habits and even his lifestyle are influenced by the climatic conditions of the region. He makes use of mules and Yaks in mountains for carrying loads whereas for the same purpose he employs carts and other animals in plains and camels in deserts. Camel is considered more useful in deserts because it requires only a limited quantity of water. Moreover we find that people living in temperate climate are more hard working as compared to those living in warm and hot countries. It is because of favourable climatic conditions that people living in temperate countries have made more progress and people living in very hot or very cold countries could not progress. Science has been able to make certain small changes in the natural conditions but they are only of marginal effect.

The important factors that influence and determine the human life are:

(a) Structure of body.

(b) Home and food habits.

(c) Industries and commercial establishments.

(d) Means of transport and communication.

(e) Population.

(f) Religion and language.

(g) Civilization.

(h) Anxiety to acquire supermacy and control over environment.

Teacher can make use of the following type of chart to explain the effects of geographical conditions on human life.

1. *Physical conditions*

2. *Climate*

(a) External influence

(b) Internal influence

Both the above factors have a profound effect an geographical conditions of a region.

3. *Climate*

   (a) Longitude

   (b) Elevation from sea level

   (c) Distance from equator

   (d) Wind direction

   (e) Direction of mountains

   (f) Rainfall

4. *Vegetation*

   (a) Natural

   (b) Agricultural

   (c) Mineral

   (d) Animal

The vegetation depends on the factors mentioned at 1,2 and 3.

5. *Human Life and Activities*

   (a) Formation of body.

   (b) Food and shelter or housing.

   (c) Trade and industry.

   (d) Transport and communication.

   (e) Population, religion and literature.

   (f) Civilisation and culture.

   (g) Attempt to acquire control over the environment.

Man çan achieve supermacy over nature by proper use of his intelligence and he is making efforts to secure the resources and make use of nature for his own ends. Thus he is influencing the nature.

From the point of view of teaching geography, the subject-matter may be divided into three parts:

(i) Knowledge of the geographical subject-matter.

(ii) Logical use of subject-matter.

(iii) Geographical imagination.

Knowledge of the Geographical subject-matter: Geography deals with rivers, mountains, etc. and we come across a long list of geographical names. A geography teacher will be able to do justice to the students if he is familiar with all these names and thus has a thorough knowledge of the subject-matter.

Logical use of the subject material: In the modem times when the teaching of geography has become more scientific and psychological, it is essential that the geography teacher makes a logical use of the subject-matter and present it in such a manner that student remains interested in it. To achieve it the use of logical method is essential.

Geographical imagination: The geography teacher must use geographical imagination and should be able to use it to impart knowledge of geogrpahy to his students. For teaching of geography both logic and imagination are to be used simultaneously. To tell about the geography of a land never seen by us the teacher has to use imagination so that the subject-matter becomes clear before his eyes. Thus, we find that in teaching of geography we have to use imagination many a time.

There are certain basic elements and fundamentals in each subject. These fundamentals and basic elements are responsble for the limitation of the scope of the subject-matter of a particular subject. It is these elements that influence the subject-matter. These fundamentals are essential for the understanding of a subject. For the teaching of Geography, the knowledge of these fundamentals is also important. In order to have a correct idea of the fundamentals of Geography, it is necessary to have a proper explanation of the geographical environment of a particular country.

Five elements combined together we call geographical environment and it is these elements that are responsible for the whole of the geographical control. Let us now examine these elements a bit in detail.

Physical conditions—The structure of Geography is based on physical conditions. In other words. physical conditions are another name of geographical conditions. It is on the basis of this thing that other things develop. Physical conditions are very much governed by the formation of the surface of the earth or land. It is the physical conditions that create atmosphere and the atmosphere or environment influence the human life. Therefore, the study of physical conditions is very important. Unless we have an idea of the physical conditions of a particular country, it is not possible to know about other things of that country. There was a time when learning of the names and the laws that guided the physical conditions were considered to be all in all. In the present set-up it has lost all its importance. In the modern Geography we try to look at the various causes that are responsible for different changes in the physical conditions. Scientists of today accept that there was a time when this earth was very hot. It was a solid mass of fire. By and by it cooled down. The process of cooling had its effect on the surface of the earth. These changes were caused by certain physical factors.

Location of a particular land or, in other words, its distance from equator makes a lot of difference in the physical conditions. Northernmost and southernmost part of the world are covered with snow for the whole of the year. On the other hand, countries that are situated near the Equator are extremely hot. Deserts are hot and dry throughout the year. Location near the sea shore makes the climate temperate. Countries that are surrounded by sea or ocean have a climate which is temperate.

Land Surface—We have already seen that once there was a time when the earth was a mass of fire. By and by it colled down. In the process of cooling the crust was formed. At certain places wrinkles were formed. These wrinkles have elevation at certain places and at others they became deep. The places where there was elevation later on grew into mountains. On the other hand, the deep places became oceans and valley. Nature, in order to maintain itself, created plains at certain places and at others it gave rise to plateaus. It is not possible for man to make changes in the nature. It is possible for man to make slight changes in the nature. It is possible for man to make slight changes but not of any consequence.

The formation of the surface of the earth or land is essentially a subject of study of Geology. But Geography cannot ignore it. Here we have to study the sediments of the rocks and the formation of the mountains etc. It has to be studied because the formation of the earth is to a great extent responsible for the climate and produce of that land. In the plains formed by the rivers, there is bound to be a rich produce. This is not true of hilly and plateau areas. There produce is meagre. In old rocks we have mineral wealth such as coal, iron ore, gold, silver, etc. In the comparatively newly formed rocks we have oil, which is of vital importance for the economy of any country.

The formation of the land is also responsible for the development of human race and civilization. No doubt, the scientific study of the formation of the surface of earth is made by Geology but Geography does not take into consideration the general principles of the formation of the surface of the earth. Human life is very much influenced by the formation of the surface of the earth and so Geography has to take it into consideration. In Geography we study the interaction of man and the nature and this has a vital importance for subjects. The surface of the earth is changing continuously. This change is caused by certain agencies.

External agencies are those that do not lie within the earth or the surface of the earth. They include agencies like wind, rain, flowing water, ice, sun, glaciers, heat of the sun, etc.

Internal agencies are those that are present within the earth. They include phenomena like earthquake, eruption of volcano, etc.

These internal and external agencies are continual and continuously affecting the surface of the earth. The changes caused by these agencies are not immediately discernible but they are known-after hundreds and thousands of years. Once upon a time people of Greece had erected certain ghats near Crete. Now that place has become very high from the sea surface. In China also this thing is seen. In India the desert of That seems to be spreading. Government of India have made several efforts in order to check this expansion. A number of trees have been planted in order to check this expansion.

Environment—Climate is a very important factor that influences the geographical conditions. It is one of the basic elements that controls and influences the physical features. It has its influence on agricultural products, living conditions of the people; food habits, traditions and customs. If in Bengal we have, the production of rice, in Punjab production of wheat and in Assam there are tea gardens, it is all caused by geographical features and climatic conditions.

The infleuence of the climatic conditions is direct and discernible. In our everyday life we see the influence of the climate on human life. For a person having knowledge of the climate conditions of the world, the study of Geography becomes easy. He knows that vegetation wealth is very much influenced by climatic conditions. Population and its growth is also determined by population. Various industries and trades are localized and established due to climate and its conditions.

All the factors determine the climate of a particular place. If we know about all these things, we shall know why textile mills are situated at Kanpur, Bomboy, Ahmedabad and jute mills are situated at Calcutta while sugar mills are situated in eastern part of India, namely districts of Gorakhpur, Deoria, Champaran, Chhapra etc.

Countries that are situated nearer the Equator have a hot climate while the places that are situated near the Polar regions have a cold climate.

Agricultural products—The land and the climate are very much responsible for the natural vegetation and the agricultural products. Places, where there is rainfall all around the year, have dense forests. It is on account of this reason that Equatorial regions have dense forests. In dry places and deserts there is very little of vegetation. Places where forests are available, have every likelihood of establishment of wood industries. It is quite possible that a big furniture manufacturing factory maybe established at a place which has a good forest behind it. Agricultural products are also governed by climatic conditions and formation of the surface. In the alluvial soil there is a good deal of agricultural product. In plateau lands it is not possible. Natural factors also influence the fertility of the land. It is on account of the influence of the climate that land, at a particular place, becomes fertile while at others, it becomes barren and less productive. If temperature of a particular place continues to be near about 80% and there is rainfall to the extent of 80" in the year, then that place may be paddy and jute producing area. On account of lack of rain, it is not possible to produce jute and rice in the land formed by river Indus.

Vegetation also influences the geographical factors. Vegetation also influences the industrial and geographical life of a particular land or country. In Canada and Sweden there are a good number of Paper Mills. They are there, because in the adjoining places it is possible to get wood out of which paper may be manufactured. Climate is also suitable for it. In Tata Nagar, it has been possible to establish steel industry only because in the nearing places there are deposits of iron are and coal is also not very hard to find.

Animal wealth is also influenced by climatic conditions, formation of surface and vegetation wealth. If a particular place has dense forest, it is possible to get monkeys, bears, deers, etc. there. In deserts only camels can be found. It is very difficult to get lions and tigers in mountain areas because natural conditions are not suited to them. In Tundra, on account of climatic conditions, we have Reindeers and in Tibet we have Yaks. Pets like houses, cows, oxen, etc , are available at places where geographical conditions suit their life and growth. At places where there is 'rich vegetation, a good number of animals are found.

Human activities – Man is also governed by geographical conditions and factors. He is also a part of the animal life. According to geographical conditions and physical factors, man also changes and modifies his life and livelihood. In mountainious regions, he employs mules and yaks for carrying the burden but in plains he uses carts and such other animals that can serve the purpose successfully. In deserts camel is a very useful animal. Here vegetation is of' such a nature that requires a little water. It is in form of thorny bushes and palm trees etc. It is on account of the geographical factors that men has been able to make so much of progress.

Man is, in fact, the centre of geographical study. His way of living, his food habits, his trade and commerce, population, his dress etc. all are governed by geographical factors. People living in temperate climate are more hard working as compared to people living in warm and hot countries. Civilization has developed at places with good climate and good land. People of hot countries and of extremely cold regions have not been able to make so much progress as people of temperate countries have made. Man, in fact, is a creature of geographical conditions. In the modern age, no doubt science has made him the master of nature, yet many of the things remain to be done. He has succeeded in moulding the nature only to a certain extent.

We determine human life on the basis of the factors enumerated above, and so it shall be possible for us to know about the Geography properly if we know about all these factors. Then, it shall be possible for us to reply to the following questions :—

Why did Britain rule over the world for such a long time ? Why do Eskimos of Tundra and such other places lead their life in such a manner ? Why the population in the forests situated in the Equatorial regions is meagre ? Why is it not possible for people to live in deserts ? How is it that Soviet Russia and America have become such important countries of the world ?

It is the duty of the teacher of Geography to explain to the students the various factors that influence the geographical conditions and the human life.

Human life is influenced by natural and physical factors. Man has the element of intelligence and rationality in him. Through this power of intelligence and rationality, it is possible for him to secure power over nature. Man has been so designed that he can achieve supre-macy over nature. He has also been given power to take to activities. By and by he tries to secure the resources and uses nature for his own ends. In this manner he influences the nature.

The teacher of Geography has a very vital role to play. He can play his part successfully-when he knows about the basic element of Geography.

1. Following are the various basic geographical factors and the controlling agencies :—
   (a) Expansion
   (b) The surface—The formation of the surface is continually changing.
   (c) There are two types of agencies : (i) Internal ; and (ii) External, that influence the formation of the surface of earth.
2. Climate conditions determine the life and vegetation. Climate is also an essential geographical factor.
3. Vegetation and natural wealth are governed by geographical factors.
4. Agricultural product is also very much influenced by the climate and the land.
5. Natural vegetation and mineral wealth are responsible for the trade, commerce and industry of the country.
6. Climatic conditions and natural vegetation are responsible for the animal wealth of a particular country.
7. Human life is also governed by all these factors.
8. Man has the elements of intelligence in him and so he can employ these agencies for the benefit of mankind.
9. For the successful teaching of Geography, the following basic factors are to be borne in mind :—
   (a) Through knowledge of the subject-matter.
   (b) Employing the logical method and geographical imagination.

2

Fundamental Issues

Geography is a subject with varied importance and variegated utility. At one end of the subject we have subjects like Biology, Anthropology, Mathematics, Sociology, Economics, Metallurgy and such other sciences while on the other end we have humanities that continue to influence the subject-matter of Geography. Human activities are also influenced and determined by geographical factors. On account of all these reasons, the importance of Geography has grown much. In the subject-matter we have the study of the natural environment of man studied in it on the other hand wé have the study of social and cultural environments. Very few subjects have such a manifold bearing on the scope of study. Geography is, in fact, a link between natural sciences and socio-sciences. It is very helpful in studying various political and social problems of our society.

Geography has the elements of science as well as art in it. It is not possible for us to go without its study. .It is based on cause and effect theory. It tries to put forward answers to various physical phenomena. All its answers are guided by certain reasons and causes.

In this modern age, Geography has helped the development of various subjects. The background to the study of literature, history and other art subjects is provided by Geography. On the other hand, Geography is helpful in the development and flourishing of various science subjects. It, therefore, occupies a very important place in the syllabus of our study.

Relationship with Humanbeings

Human life and its various facets, including thinking, are influenced by Geography. It is the Geography that influenced by cultural development of human race. Without the knowledge of Geography, the knowledge of various subjects shall remain truneated. Today we are living in an age where barriers of land have ceased to exist. Man lives in an international age with a cosmopolitan outlook. We have to understand the like and the culture of other countries. It is the Geography which provides knowledge of all these things.

If, at all, we are anxious and interested to know the history of any country, we shall have to take a lot of help from the knowledge of Geography of that particular country. It is the stage on which the drama of history is enacted. Literature has a lot of description of geographical things. Description of nature, which forms an important and integral part of literature, is nothing but a part of Geography. Geography has, therefore, to find a place in our syllabus and curriculum.

No country can plan its education without having a keen eye on its social objectives. These social objectives are very much governed and guided by the geographical factors. In fact, it is the Geography which, to a very great extent, determines and influences the socio-economic values of a country. Geography has, therefore, to be given an important place in our curriculum.

Significance of the Discipline

Geography finds its place in the educational syllabus because it is very important for human race. Different writers have different viewpoints regarding the importance of Geography. P.E. James is of the opinion that Geography has its importance due to the following reasons :

(1) Geography helps us to have proper picture of man and his environment. It also provides us with the knowledge of various factors connected with our natural life.

(2) Geography provids us with the knowledge of various types of climates, natural conditions, mineral wealth, etc. of various

countries. It also helps us to know about the differences that we find between various countries.

(3) It helps us to read and discern the maps, sketches, diagrams etc.

(4) Geography develops in man the power of observation. When we go to different countries and places we observe human activities and natural conditions. This opportunity of observation develops in us the power of observations.

Fairgrieve has laid down the following two principles which have made the knowledge of Geography important and pertinent:

(1) Two-thirds of our life passed while dealing with our neighbours and countrymen. In other words, two-thirds of our life forms the duties that we owe as citizens. Through Geography we are able to know about the conditions of different countries and their people. This knowledge helps us to discharge our duties successfully.

(2) From the economic point of view also, Knowledge of Geography is important, it helps us to know, about the economic needs of the people of other countries. Through Geography industrialists, politicians, agriculturists, *etc.*, know about their job.

Importace of Geography can be studied under the following heads.

Practical importance of Geography—Geography has an important place in our life. It enables the students to face the various problems of life. Nobody has denied the practical value and importance of Geography. Students of Geography are able to know about the natural conditions of the whole country, its climate, vegetation, natural resources and its mineral wealth. Through Geography it is also possible to have the knowledge of the trade and industry of a particular country. This knowledge enables youngmen to plan the future. Suppose a person is interested in establishing an industry, after completion of the education, he shall not be able to do it unless he has an idea of the natural resources needed for the location of that industry. Through the knowledge of Geography, he shall be able to know the place where those resources are available.

Geography enables us to acquire knowledge about the earth on which we live. It is also helpful in acquiring knowledge about people of other countries with whom we may have social, political and economic relations. This very clearly indicates the practical value of Geography.

Utility and importance of the knowledge of Geography for administrators and politicians—Politicians and administrators cannot run the administration of a particular country without having knowledge of the geographical conditions of that country. Ecocomic, political and social life is very much governed by geographical factors. Through the knowledge of Geography, it is also possible to know about the inter-dependence of the people of various countries. No country can live without taking help from other countries. In order to have proper relationship, it is necessary to have proper knowledge of the geographical factors. Administrators of a country, that is industrially developed, have to find countries where their finished and manufactured goods may find a market. It is the knowledge of Geography which helps them to know about all these things. Unless the administrators of a country know of it, they shall not be able to enjoy, the goodwill of their countrymen. It is with the knowledge of Geography that the politicians and administrators shall be able to establish beneficial mutual relationship with-other countries and their neighbouring world.

Natural curiosity—Man has the natural curiosity to know about other people and other countries. Geography is helpful in meeting this curiosity. Man is also anxious to know about the various factors that influence our life. It is knowledge of Geography that helps us to know about all these things. From this point of view as well, i.e., satisfying the natural curiosity of a man. Geography has its importance.

Economic importance of Geography—Geography has its importance for economic life as well. Through the knowledge of Geography, it is possible to know about the natural resources, the mineral wealth, the vegetation wealth and other things that shall be helpful for our economic life. No individual and no country can progress and flourish unless it is economically sound. In this task knowledge of Geography is very helpful.

Political importance of the knowledge of Geography—No country can have political importance unless it is able to know about the conditions of other countries. This is true of individuals as well. Through the knowledge of Geography, it is possible to know about all these things.

Knowledge of Geography also develops a sympathetic outlook in the people of a particular country. People are able to understand the problem and conditions of other countries and so they understand their difficulties and problems and try to sympathise with them. A man living in fertile country can very well realise the difficulties of the people living in a desert. This would also bring about the world together and its many political problems.

Importance in understanding and acquiring the knowledge of various social sciences such as Political Science, History, Sociology, Theology, etc.—Knowledge of Geography is helpful in understanding and having a proper knowledge of various social sciences. Without proper knowledge of Geography, it is difficult to have proper assessment of History. We have already stated that Geography provides the stage on which the drama of history is enacted. Historical events were governed by geographical factors. If civilization developed first in India and Egypt, it was on account of geographical reasons. All these reasons help us to have proper knowledge of the subject.

"Political life of a nation is very much governed by its geographical importance. People take to a particular political system on .account of the geographical factors. For example, if direct democracy is prevalent in Switzerland even today, it is very much governed by geographical factors. Similarly, if democracy could succeed in England, it was, to a very great extent, on account of its geographical factors. Knowledge of political science can be thoroughly acquired only with the help of the knowledge of Geography.

Our social customs and social life are very much governed by our geographical factors. Our natural resources, to a very great extent, determine the structure of our society. Social stcucture of a country with rich natural resources is bound to be of a rich and cultured type. Sociology can be properly understood only in the background of the knowledge of Geography.

What has been said about History, Political Science and Sociology is also true of Theology. Theology, as we know, is the science of religion. Religion is also governed by geographical factors. Rules. of a religion, that develop in a rich country, are bound to be different from the rules of a country that has developed in a country with difficult conditions. Religion of people living in desert is bound to be of strict and austere type.

Cultural and intellectual importance of Geography – With the knowledge of Geography, it is possible for us to acquire knowledge about the cultural and intellectual life of a particular nation, This knowledge is also helpful in having a proper study of the cultural life of the whole world.

The knowledge of Geography also helps a student to develop his power of imagination. He is also encouraged to know about cause and effect of various phenomena. It also helps the development of power of reasoning. When a student learns about the mountains, rivers, forests, etc., then images of all these things are formed before him. When these things present themselves in actual from before his eyes, then he is able to know them and discern them easily. The knowledge of all these things is also helpful in enabling the student to know about the culture and civilization of different countries.

Intellectual life of a nation is also governed by geographical factors. Thus, the knowledge of Geography has an intellectual importance as well. Fairgrieve has, in this respect, rightly remarked.

"The real value of Geography lies in the fact that it helps man to place himself in the world to learn his true position and duties."

Social importance of Geography – Knowledge of Geography has a social importance as well. It helps a student to develop a social outlook. When the students know about other countries, they try to treat them as their brother. This feeling develops a social outlook. It takes them out of narrow outlook. They do not remain self-centred. They are also able to know about their environment and to realise its importance. Such a feeling may, ultimately, lead to the development of the feeling of brotherhood, and world citizenship.

In this manner, Geography is helpful in developing goodwill for other countries and a social outlook in the individuals.

Importance of Geography in earning our livelihood—Geography is very important so far as earning of livelihood is concerned. Almost one-third of our life is spent in earning our livelihood. Then there is leisure, we have the problem of spending the leisure in a useful and proper manner. It is the leisure which is utilised in acquiring further knowledge which helps us to broaden our outlook and take to things that are not very common. It is not possible to know the means of earning our livelihood without having a proper knowledge of'the things and conditions that prevail around us. Through the knowledge of Geography, we know about the various sources with the help of which we may earn our livelihood.

Help to maintain a balanced outlook—Balance is very necessary in our life. This balance is acquired with the help of the proper knowledge of the things and the conditions around us. Through the knowledge of Geography, we are able to know about the actual circumstances of our environment. When we have acquired knowledge of perspective, we are able to make a correct assessment of our capabilities and our resources. This helps us to acquire a balanced outlook towards life. The knowledge of geography also helps us to have the knowledge of the resources and capabilities of other people. This knowledge is also helpful in acquiring a balanced outlook towards life.

Inculcates patriotism and internationalism—Through Geography we are able to know about the conditions of our motherland. Knowing is loving. When we know about our motherland, we start loving it. Thus, patriotism is generated.

Through Geography, we are also able to know about other countries. This knowlege is helpful in understanding other countries and their people. Such a knowledge is helpful in generating the international outlook.

Importance in vocational and cultural life—No system of the people and their vocation and industry can deny an important place to Geography in the curriculum and syllabus. It is through Geography that we are able to know about our natural conditions and natural resources. This adds to the importance of Geography. On account of this purpose of Geography, it occupies an important place in primary, secondary and higher education.

President Eisenhower of America called Geography the foundation of humanity. It cannot be denied that it helps the understanding of human life and human problems. In order to achieve this objective, the syllabus of Geography has to be selective and purposeful. It must find a place in our syllabus but the topics selected must be drawn up after careful thinking and observation. Such a teaching of geography will help the students to develop a scientific outlook.

Basic Elements

1. Geography occupies an important place not only in our life but in our education as well. It gives a knowledge of the conditions of environment and helps us to develop a balanced outlook.
2. Knowledge of Geography has various uses. It is very important for man.
3. Professor P.E. James has said that Geography is important in the sense that it gives us knowledge of our natural resources, and helps us to know and understand the maps, sketches and diagrams. It also develops in the students the power of observation.
4. According to Fairgrieve, it helps us to acquire knowledege of our neighbours and acquire economic efficiency.
5. Geography has a practical importance for our life. Through it we are able to know things that shall be of use to us in our life.

6. It is useful for politicians and administrators. They are able to know about the conditions and circumstances in which they have to carry out the administration.

7. It satisfies the natural curiosity of man to know about other people and other lands.

8. It has importance for our economic activities. It helps us to know the conditions in which we may adopt a particular method of earning our livelihood or establish a particular industry.

9. Geography is helpful in understanding and acquiring proper knowledge of various social sciences such as History, Sociology, Political Science, Theology etc.

10. Geography is helpful for our cultural and intellectual life. It develops in us certain qualities that are useful for our cultural and intellectual life.

11. It has social importance for us. It develops in the students a social outlook and sympathetic attitude for people of other countries.

12. Knowledge .of Geography is helpful in developing certain good qualities in the citizen.

13. As already stated, it helps us to earn our livelihood properly and aquire a balanced outlook.

14. It is also helpful in solving various social and economic problems of our life.

15. On account of all these reasons, Geography occupies an important place in our curriculum. It must get such a place.

16. It helps us to understand the human life in the proper background and so its importance cannot be denied.

Old values of Teaching of Geography—In past Geography was taught on the basis of political regions. Then the whole of the world was divided into various countries. Each country was taken up one by one and the Geography was taught. There was no scientific basis for the teaching of Geography. It had no practical background. It was taught and learnt as a theoretical subject. It was all based on the political divisions of the world. Probably in those days political divisions had greater values and so they were given priorities.

In those days various physical divisions were carved out on the basis of administrative convenience. They were made on the basis of the states conquered. There was no similarity in the physical conditions, climate, agricultural products, rainfall, mineral, wealth etc. of various countries. Therefore, these countries could not be studied on some common basis.

We have already seen that Geography is nothing but a description of the world in relation to man. It tries to explain the relationship between man and the world. In recent years, on account of this realisation, the values of the teaching of Geography have changed. Now it is believed that physical environment and geographical factors influence various aspects of man's life, such as economic, social, industrial etc. On the other hand, the political divisions of the world are based on political considerations. They have very little to do with natural conditions. In the study of Geography these political divisions are not very material. It is on account of this realisation that greater emphasis is laid on the study of Geography through Regional Method.

Regional method—Today each physical region is taken as an unit and that particular unit is studied under the head of various factors that are responsible for the physical conditions of that particular region. We have already seen that natural conditions, climate, vegetation, human activities and formation of the land are the various factors that are responsible for the geographical factors of a particular physical region.

In this method of teaching of Geography, as we have already seen, the whole of the world is divided into certain physical region. Each physical region is sub-divided into smaller region. Each physical unit has its own importance. It is also different from the other. Human beings living in a particular physical region are organised together in a common manner. Their ways of living, their dress, their food habits, their customs, etc. acquire common features. In fact, the physical factors of a particular region influence the human activities and human life. The difference in the conditions of life of people of two countries is caused by the difference in the physical conditions.

It is the duty of a student of Geography to find out the geographical factors of a particular region. Through his knowledge he can safely develop consciousness in the people of that particular region. Such a thing can go a long way in establishment of common and between people of various regions.

The knowledge of the geographical conditions is also helpful in the proper development of the personality not only of the individuals but also of the society as a whole.

By studying Geography, through Regional Method, we study the various divisions of the world under the following heads :

(a) Formation of the land.

(b) Natural conditions.

(c) Agriculture.

(d) Products.

(e) Political and economic progress.

There is difference between the study of Geography on the basis of political regions and on the basis of physical regions. The division of the world into various political regions is likely to change soon. This change sometimes disturbs the entire knowledge and study. Physical divisions are not likely to change so easily and so quickly.

Utility of the present method of teaching of Geography — The present method of the teaching of Geography has the following qualities and utility in it :

(a) It is supposed to be very scientific. If we think that Geography is the study of action and interaction of man and his geographical environment, then the study of Geography on regional basis is quite scientific. This method also has the likelihood of the study of subject on comparative basis.

(b) This method is very helpful in studying the geographical characteristics of a particular region. Through this method a student can study the physical features quite easily and with convenience. Though no other method is possible to have an idea of the physical characteristics so easily and quickly.

(c) In this method of the study of Geography various aspects of human life—physical, social, economic, historical etc.—are interconnected. Human life and animal life is very much influenced by the climate and the natural conditions and so it is quite proper to study the human life in the background of the natural conditions.

(d) This method has scope for observation and comparative study. The students of Geography develop imagination in them. They also develop the outlook of observation of various natural objects. Interest for natural objects is also created in them.

Now we believe that Geography is the study of man, in the background of his physical and geographical conditions. These two factors continue to influence each other continually and continuously. Regional method of study of Geography justifies this definition.

Drawbacks—This method of the study of Geography has certain drawbacks in it.

(i) In this method it is assumed that students have acquired some geographical knowledge. It is not possible to teach the student through this method, who do not have any background of the geographical principles. It is necessary for the students to know the principles that govern the climate, the direction of the winds and other natural conditions. In lower classes this method may not be very useful.

(ii) It is not possible to have a final division of the world into several physical divisions. Each region sometimes merges into the other. It is also likely that while studying Geography through this method, we may neglect the smaller regions in view of larger regions.

(iii) There are certain regions that have their own separate identity. These regions do not have common features with other regions. Such regions are likely to be neglected in the study through this method.

The modern concept of the teaching of Geography—In fact, the modern concept of the study of Geography has changed with the method of the study of Geography. This concept is very clearly contained in the following lines of James Fairgrieve—

"The function of Geography is to train future citizens to imagine accurately the conditions of the great world stage and so help them to think only political and social problems in the world around."

This definition of Geography is scientific definition given in the background of modern social values. Geography is not limited up to the study of the physical conditions as they exist. It is not a positive science only. It has a normative outlook as well. It teaches the students the ways and the means that they should adopt in order to utilise the physical conditions for the well being of the society. They have to do things so that the world may grow into a better world. Young men are also taught to influence their political conditions and natural activities so that the whole of the world may be a place of worth living. In this manner Geography is not only the study of physical conditions.

The present method of teaching of Geography broadens the outlook of the students. It provides them with an opportunity to study the actions and interactions of various physical features and activities. It also provides an opportunity for the study of human relations and adds to the practical knowledge of them.

In olden days Geography was studied with a view to provide knowledge of natural and physical conditions to men. In those days the travellers used to go over to different parts of the world and gave a description of their travels and journeys. They also provided a description of the natural conditions. This description was very helpful for the sea and water travellers.

In those days the students of Geography had to cram the geographical details. With the development of the principle of evolution, there-came about a development in the method of the study of Geography. Now details of various physical and political regions were given out in the study of Geography.

In the beginning of the 20th century, Geography secured a formal place in the curriculum. In those days its nature was more or less the same as that of the history. The study of Geography was thus neither scientific nor stress was laid on the influence of geographical factors on men. This resulted into simple knowledge of geographical facts to the students. The students could not utilise this knowledge for their personal gain. Geography by that time had neither occupied a social practical and international importance.

Present Scenario

We are living in an age of democracy. Every citizens has his own responsibilities and duties to perform. This responsibility and duty involves independent thinking. Man has to think about his political problems. Today his outlook has broadened and he has to find out the solution of various socio-economic problems in an intelligible and rational manner. This is not an age of monarchy when people have to follow their rules. Every individual has to adapt himself to the environment. This adaptability makes the teaching of Geography easy and useful. The values of the teaching of Geography have broadened the scope of the study of the subject-matter. It is being studied with different aspects in view. Today study of man in the background of his physical conditions is called Geography. This simply means that the values of the teaching of Geography in the modern age have changed much from the past values.

Broadening of the scope of study – Human life has developed a lot. It is constantly growing and developing. Now the knowledge of Geography includes every aspect of knowledge about man. Political, social, economic, intellectual and Geographical factors, such as natural conditions, weather, vegetation, climate, mineral wealth etc. are the various factors that influence the subject of Geography. No doubt, Geography has separated itself from History but even then they are directly related. Even the subject-matter of History has become broad and so it is natural for the subject-matter of Geography, which provides the stage to the drama of History to become broader.

Study of all the changes carried out by man on the surface of the earth—Man is constantly making efforts to change the face of the earth and nature. He is trying to condition the atmosphere according to his needs and requirements. A the changes that have been caused by human efforts in nature are studied under Geography. It also studies the influence of local and regional factors on human life.

Utility of Geography in training human mind—Teaching of Geography has direct practical values. Geography trains the mind of man. Human welfare is possible only when it has been possible to imbibe the knowledge of Geography in a thorough and perfect manner. It trains the mind of the students in a scientific manner. While studying Geography, the students get an opportunity to study various geographical factors in a minute manner. He has also to find the cause and effect relationship between various events and factors. Then he has to convert his knowledge into hard facts and real picture.

While studying Geography, we study various things as they exist. We imagine things as they are. While studying Geography, we are constantly heading towards complete adoption of the regional method of the study of Geography. In this procedure we are moving from the study of the part to the whole. The Geography tells that the world is a complete unit. It is a combination of various units called physical divisions. Natural law works in the same manner everywhere.

Practical knowledge and world brotherhood—Study of Georgaphy has a good deal of practical bearing. It tries to study the practical aspect of human life. It tells the students about various conditions. of life in various parts of the world. Young man, who has the knowledge of Geography, can very easily utilise this knowledge to do things in a realistic manner. He can also achieve success in life. The recent definition and method of study of Geography has provided a new outlook to the field of education. Geography occupies an important place in the curriculum of study. It is now studied as a study of the abode of human life.

Cause and effect relationship and enriching the treasure`of knowledge—We have already seen that Geography is based on the cause and effect relationship. It has assumed a scientific outlook and a mode of study and so cause and effect relationship is found out while studying the subject-matter.

In olden days man looked helpless in the face of vast field of natural conditions. Now it is not so. Man has acquired victory over various phases of nature. With this conquest, he has found new ways and means of scientific study of Geography. Various apparatuses have been discovered and evolved to study Geography in a scientific manner. Through these apparatuses, it is possible to acquire better knowledge about nature and to the treasure of knowledge. Thus Geography has added to the knowledge and utility of human life.

Today Geography studies, the various aspects of human life such as social, political, historical, etc. All these facts of human life are influenced by geographical factors, and so it is proper for Geography to touch them as well. While studying Geography, people of various countries know about the people of other countries. This leads to co-operation and understanding between peoples of different countries. It further leads to goodwill and co-operation and co-existence. Thus, Geography influences the whole of human life.

1. In olden days, Geography was taught on the basis of political regions.
2. It was considered to be the description of nature as it existed.
3. Today Geography is taught through regional method.
4. The whole of the world has been divided into various physical regions and each region has its own utility.
5. The Regional Method of teaching of Geography is quite scientific; it is helpful in the thorough study of Geographical characteristics and then it also studies various aspects of human life.

6. It has certain drawbacks as well. It is possible that we may not have the final division of the world into various regions.
7. New Geography aims at training future citizens properly.
8. In olden days Geography did not have any vital bearing on human life. Now it is not so.
9. Geography studies the various efforts made by man to change the face of the nature.
10. Geography has an importance in the training of one's mind.
11. Geography also leads to world brotherhood and broadening of field of knowledge.
12. The scientific method of study of Geography brings about the cause and effect relationship in this method.
13. It also enriches the treasure of knowledge.

3

Aims and Objectives

For the proper teaching of a subject it is essential to have a knowledge of aims and objectives of the subject. This is also true for the teaching of geography. Various methods of teaching are then evolved according to these aims and objectives. For determining the aims of teaching any subject we have to take into consideration the utility and usefulness of that subject. We have material as well as spiritual aspects in our life. For a successful spiritual life it is essential that we have a well-founded material life.

The aims and objectives of teaching various subjects are normally very similar and they are generally guided by economic and social considerations. The aims and objectives of teaching geography include all the aims and objects of education. Different writers have listed these aims and objectives in different ways.

In this chapter an attempt will be made to discuss these opinions. However, before taking up such a discussion let us take up the criterion used for selecting aims of teaching geography.

The Aims

In the opinion of Prof. Holtz the teaching of geography has following two sets of aims.

(i) Practical aims, and

(ii) Cultural aims.

Prof. Holtz has included the aims under these two heads as under.

Practical aims

(a) Knowledge of land through geography.

(b) To bring about industrial and agricultural development using the knowledge of geography.

(c) To have a proper idea of various geographical factors that influence our lives.

(d) To have a correct idea of references occurring in geography books and newspapers.

(e) To inculcate in pupil a desire for undertaking travelling and tourism.

Cultural aims

(a) To develop a feeling of patriotism.

(b) To develop love for nature and capacity to understand and appreciate the natural beauty, physical forces and such other things.

(c) To develop the ideal of world citizenship universal brotherhood, cooperation and sympathetic outlook for others.

(d) To assess the cultural values in the light of values of the land and the man.

(e) Adjustment of human life according to the geographical circumstances.

In view of Prof. James Fairgrieve the aims of teaching geography can be expressed as under:

"The function of geography is to train future citizens to imagine accurately the conditions of the great world stage and to help them to think about the political and social problems in the world around".

The aim of teaching geography is that it provides mental discipline which means that the subject trains the pupils' whole mode of thought which in its turn influences his intellectual life and studies in the same field.

The Objectives

The objectives are the specific and precise behavioural outcome of teaching a particular topic in geography. Any topic in geography helps in realising some general aim of teaching geography. The characteristics of a good objective are as under:

(i) It should be specific and precise.

(ii) It should be attainable.

Bloom's Taxonomy. Bloom's taxonomy of objectives is a classification of instructional objectives in a hierarchy. According to it the specific objectives have been classified into the following three categories:

(i) Cognitive domain objectives.

(ii) Affective domain objectives.

(iii) Psychomotor domain objectives.

The cognitive domain objectives include knowledge, understandings, applications, analysis, synthesis and evaluation.

The effective domain objectives include the appreciations, values, attitudes, interests and feelings.

The psychomotor domain objectives include skills.

Some of these are discussed here.

Intellectual development. The basic objective of education is to bring about an all-round development of the personality of the child. All round development includes the intellectual development. A proper intellectual development is a must for any proper cultura^ consciousness. To earn a livelihood is not the sole objective of life. One needs leisure after earning his livelihood and one should be able to spend one's leisure time properly and usefully.

This leisure time should be used for intellectual and spiritual development for a balanced growth of human race. It is only through the intellectual development that we can distinguish between good and bad. This power of distinguishing between good and bad is essential to become a successful member of society.

Knowledge of the world and the broadening outlook. Geography teaching provides to the pupil a knowledge of the different people of the world and the contributions made by them for the development of world culture. Such a knowledge broadens our outlook and brings about the development of world brotherhood and world citizenship.

Through the knowledge of geography the pupil realises the interdependence of mankind. He also becomes familiar with the differences in the physical character of the people and understands that such differences are due to variations in physical environments. Thus we find that development of the international outlook is one of the aims and objectives of teaching of geography.

Development of quality of generosity and sympathetic outlook. From the knowledge of geography a pupil realises the interdependence of mankind and develops a sympathetic attitude when he observes a similarity of needs all over the world. Such an attitude helps them to grow not only as good citizens but as good world citizens. This type of feeling, if developed, will boost the idea of world democracy and will help world peace for all times to come.

Quality of adjustment with environment. Since in geography a student is taught about people of different lands, their culture, their mode of living, etc. This knowledge develops in the student the quality to mould and change himself in accordance with the circumstances and he acquires the quality of adjusting with the environment. This type of adjustment is useful for his future life.

Economic efficiency. From the study of the geographical conditions of various lands the student comes to realise that it is not possible to maintain the same standards of comforts all over the world. Geography lays down the foundation for economic, social and political problems.

The advancement of a country is measured by the services it renders to other nations. The knowledge of geography helps the pupil to render any such service and to earn his livelihood. Thus, geography makes a student self-sufficient.

Development of power of reasoning, invention and discovery. Like any other subject the study of geography develops in the pupil certain mental faculties. The pupils have to reason out many things on the basis of data provided. This develops in the pupils the power of reasoning.

In the process of learning geography students many a times come across various secrets of nature which helps them to acquire an outlook of inventions and discoveries. It fits well with the aim of geography teaching which requires development of imagination power. Geography being a science-oriented subject an effort is also made to find a cause and effect relationship which helps to develop the power of reasoning in the student.

Development of balanced personality. The knowledge of physical factors and environment that a student acquires from study of Geography helps him to develop his personality and this allows the individual to grow properly. In this way a pupil can acquire a balanced personality by making proper use of his knowledge of geography.

Love for nature, travels and knowledge about other countries. Geography broadens the mind and stimulates imagination with the information it provides. It encourages travel. The knowledge gained by such travels helps the pupil in meeting many a problem of every-day life.

A student of geography can appreciate the beauty of nature better and thus geography develops in the student a love for nature. When a student of geography is taught about the beauties of nature, such as snow-clad mountains, green forests and the animal wealth, he is bound to be attached towards nature. This attachment towards nature might cultivate in him a sense of responsibility for the care and protection of nature and its beauty. The study of landscape may become a good pastime with him.

A student of geography when told about other countries and their culture gets inspired to take a travel and to know more about those countries. Culture is the sympathetic appreciation of the universal truth expressed in art, literature, philosophy, science and religion. It sharpens man's instinct to know the unknown, to see the unseen and to fathom the unfathomed.

Acquisition of knowledge of natural resources. It is the primary duty of a geography teacher to contribute his mite towards the realisation of primary aim of education by taking such measures which may ensure sound factual knowledge, a clear understanding of factual relationship and a keen development of intellectual powers. Students of today shall be citizens of tomorrow and the knowledge of natural resources and economic conditions gained by him by study of geography will help him to play his part effectively in administration and the economic development of his country.

Development of international understanding. Development of international understanding is one of the important aims of teaching of geography. In one of its publications UNESCO suggests, "Geography demonstrates that throughout the ages none has been able to boast that he can exist". The interdependence of man and nature has increased enormously. From one's study of different people of the world one knows that all nations, large and small, depend upon each other economically, culturally and socially. Such an interdependence imposes certain duties on each man and on each nation. It is the duty of the geography teacher to point out tointernational pacts and international organisations which are busy in solving complex problems of economic interdependence and international solidarity. Knowledge of geography helps to bridge the gap and help in avoiding conflict by bringing about international understanding. This very fact has been corroborated in Norwood report, "curriculum and examinations in secondary schools". In this report it has been emphasized that, "no one can realise more vividly than the trained geographer that the regions of the world are interdependent and no one can base the approach to world harmony on sounder foundations".

Knowledge about influences of geographical factors on man. The knowledge about influences of various geographical factors on man is another important aim of study of geography. From his knowledge of geography a student can better understand the influence of various geographical factors on man. For example the Tundra residents are meteaters because of the compulsions of various geographical factors.

Help development of human civilisation. Civilisation and culture of an area are influenced by various geographical factors. We know that many a civilisation came into existence and many a civilisation vanished because of geographical factors. To make a study of such factors is an important aim of the study of geography.

Such a knowledge can be used by an individual to compare himself and his circumstances with other individuals and their circumstances. Such a comparison is useful in making a proper assessment of one's own self and that of one's own motherland. This assessment will help the individual in proper discharge of his duties towards others.

Development of a nation. The knowledge of geography makes an important contribution towards the development of a country. When each country depends on other the study of geography becomes essentiali In order to create a desire in a child to serve willingly his country and his fellowmen, the teachers should make them understand thoroughly the geography of their country. The pupil should be allowed to feel the political, social and racial ties of his country from the study of books, direct observations and experiences and let the child develop a constructive attitude to all that concerns his country. The teacher should impart him such lessons which arouse his interest in his surroundings.

The Maxims

Once we have known about the importance of Geography. We must have proper idea about objectives and aim of its teaching. Without the knowledge of the aims and objectives of the teaching of Geography, it is not possible for the teacher to teach the subject properly. According to the objectives and aims, various methods of teaching of Geography are evolved. Aims of the teaching of a particular subject are very much determined by the utility and usefulness of that particular subject in our day to day life. Our life has material as well as spiritual aspects. A subject may have importance in any of these two aspects of our life. We cannot have a successful spiritual life unless our material life is well founded. Similarly our material life shall not be properly guided unless we have a proper spiritual life. According to the importance of the subject in our life, its aims and objectives are determined.

Normally every subject has more or less the same aims and objects of the teaching that are the aims and objects of the education. These aims and objects of the education are guided by economic considerations as well as social objects of the society.

Geography has an integral relationship with the elements that influence our ways and means of livelihood. Geography has all those aims and objectives that are aims and objectives of the education at large, and even the society at large. Different writers have enumerated the aims of teaching of Geography from different point of views.

Prof. Holtz is of the opinion that the following two sets of the aims of the teaching of Geography (a) Practical aims; and (b) Cultural Aims.

(a) Under the practical aims of the teaching of Geography Holtz has enumerated the following :–

(1) Knowledge of the land through Geography.

(2) Through the knowledge of Geography, it is possible to bring about agricultural and industrial development.

(3) Through the study of Geography, it is possible to have a proper idea of the Geographical factors that influence our life.

(4) Through the knowledge of Geography, it is possible to have a correct idea of the geographical references that occur in the books and the newspapers.

(5) It inculcates in the students the desire to take to travelling and tourism.

(b) Under the cultural aims Prof. Holtz include the following :

(1) To develop the feeling of patriotism.

(2) To develop love for nature and capacity to understand and appreciate the natural beauty, physical forces and such other things.

(3) To develop the ideals of world citizenship, universal brotherhood, co-operation amongst human beings and sympathetic outlook for others.

(4) To assess the cultural values in the light ot the values of the man and the land.

(5) Adjustment of human life in accordance with the geographical circumstances.

Prof. James Fairgrieve has laid down the aims of teaching of Geography in the following words :—

"The function of Geography is to train future citizen to imagine accurately the conditions of the great world stage and to help them to think about political and social problems in the world around."

Significant Aspects

- Education is intended to bring about an all round development of the personality of the child. This development involves intellectual development as well. Education cannot be successful without proper intellectual development. Without proper intellectual development, we cannot have proper cultural consciousness. Earning livelihood is not the sole objective of life. After earning one's livelihood there is leisure. That leisure has to be properly employed. If this leisure is employed to provide us with spiritual and intellectual development, then the human race shall grow in a balanced manner It is the intellectual development that provides us with the sense of good and bad, which is another name for discretion. Unless man has the power of discriminating between good and bad, he cannot be a successful member of the society. Knowledge of Geography aims at bringing about the intellectual development of a man.

- Knowledge of Geography provides us with the knowledge of the world at large. Once we have acquired the knowledge of the world at large, we have a broad outlook. In Geography we study about the people of different countries. We are able to know about their ways of life and this helps us to develop a sympathetic outlook for them. This brings about the development of world brotherhood and world citizenship. Geography also aims at it.

  Students read about the ways of life and conditions of the people of different countries. They are also able to know about the geographical conditions of these countries. This knowledge helps them to know about the factors that influence their life. This knowledge is responsible for the development of an international outlook in the students. Development of the international outlook is also one of the aims and objectives of the teaching of Geography.

- In Geography we study various types of cultures and industries. Due to this study, we are able to acquire an attitude of understanding in regard to other cultures and people. Thus, Geography helps the students to develop consideration and sympathetic outlook for other cultures and countries. It does not only help the students to grow into good citizens, but also helps to grow into world citizens. It teaches them to acquire the qualities of co-existence, co-operation and generous outlook. If people could acquire these qualities in abundance, the idea of a world democracy of a world government shall blossom forth successfully, and then the world peace shall not remain a dream of the past.

- By reading Geography, people are able to know about different countries and cultures. This develops in the students the quality to mould and change themselves according to circumstances and adjust themselves with the conditions in which they have to live. Such an adjustment is helpful for future life.

- Knowledge of Geography helps the students to acquire economic efficiency and to earn their livelihood in a successful manner. Without economic efficiency, it is not possible to earn livelihood properly and nicely. In this respect Geography makes the students self-sufficient.

- Teaching of Geography aims at development of certain mental faculties in the students. The students have to reason out many things on the basis of the date provided. This develops in them the faculty of reasoning.

  By reading Geography, they come across many secrets of nature. This knowledge helps them to acquire an outlook for inventions and discoveries. We have already said that it aims at the development of the power of imagination. Since Geography is a subject with a scientific outlook, an attempt is made to establish cause and effect relationship. This cause and effect relationship develops in the students the power of reasoning.

- Every individual has his own traits and qualities. Rousseau, the famous social philosopher, once remarked that if you do not allow the individual itself to grow properly, the originality of the individual shall be killed. Geography provides the student with the knowledge of physical factors and environments. This helps him to acquire a balanced personality.

- Geography develops in the student the love for nature. When the student is told and taught about the beauties of nature, such as snow clad mountain peaks, green forests and the animal wealth, he is bound to be attached towards nature. Then he knows about other countries. This inspires him to take to travels and know about those countries. This develops in him a love for travelling and acquiring knowledge of other countries.

- Students of today shall be the citizen of tomorrow. The knowledge of Geography helps him to know about the natural resources and economic conditions of the country. This help him to play his part effectively in the administration and economic development of his motherland.

- Another aim of the teaching of Geography is to develope better international understanding. According to the publication of UNESCO, some suggestions are on the teaching of Geography, "Geography demonstrate that throughout the ages none has been able to boast that he can exist." The inter-dependence of men and nations has increased enormously. Geography shows that all the nations, large and small, depend upon each other economically, culturally and socially. There is no doubt that this inter-dependence imposes duties on each man and, still more, on each nation, and the Geography teacher should point out in passing to international pact and international organisation intended to help in solving complex problems of economic interdependence and international solidarity. The Norwood report– "curriculum and examinations in secondary school" corroborates the fact by emphasizing that "no one can realize more vividly than the trained geographer that the regions of the world are interdependent and no one can base the approach to world harmony on sounder foundations."
- Geography aims at the study of the influence of the geographical factors on man. By the study of Geography, it is possible for person to know the influence of the natural factors and geographical factors on human life. It is through the Geography only that we know that people of Tundra are invariably and compulsorily meateaters. They are not able to have stable family life and they have to put on skin clothes. This knowledge is helpful in life.
- There are certain geographical factors that influence the development of the civilization and culture. It is a known fact that civilizations have grown on account of geograpical reasons and fallen on account of them. Geography aims at the study of these factors.

This knowledge is helpfal to an individual to compare himself and his circumstances with other individuals and their circumstances. This comparison helps the individual to have proper assessment of his own and his country. This also helps him to discharge his duties successfully towards others.

- Through the knowledge acquired by Geography we can contribute towards the development of the country. In the modern age of science no country can afford to remain aloof from the rest of the world. Every country has to depend upon the natural resources or technology of other countries. Under such circumstances the study of Geography is essential for the development of the country.

Thus it is evident that Geography has several cultural, moral, logical and economic aims. Fulfilment of these aims, shall be very useful for the development of human life.

The Foundation

In order to achieve the aims and objects of the teaching of particular subject, certain maxims are laid down. These maxims are the bases on which the teaching is planned and carried out. These maxims are the guiding principles for the teacher. He has to make the knowledge intelligible to his pupils. It cannot be denied that teaching is an art. The success of the teacher lies in making his subject so simple as to make it intelligible for his students. If the teacher fails in this task, he ceases to be teacher. Teaching of Geography involves greater pains on the part of the teacher. He has to perform the task of a science teacher as well as the teacher of a social science. In order to be successful in his task, he has to fall back upon the maxims of the teaching of a subject. Let us now examine the various maxims, on the basis of which the teaching of Geography is conducted and carried out.

Proceeding from simple to complex—It is a well known maxim of teaching that the teacher must provide from simple to complex. This is the natural process of the mind. If the teacher is able to explain the simple things to the students, he can make them understand the difficult things. The students are able to proceed from simple to complex in a psychologically successful manner. If the teacher wants to, give an idea of ths sea or ocean to the students, he can safely do so by showing them a tank or a pond situated in their neighbourhood. Later on, he may explain that ocean or a sea is much bigger than this thing. Similarly, by presenting a model of a mountain, he can give the idea of a real mountain to the students.

The teacher has to proceed very cautiously in this regard. He has to keep in mind that the student do not get bored. He may take recourse to sketches, drawings, etc. As far as possible, he should try to ascertain if they have actually followed the thing. Cramming is not a good practice. It kills the originality of the students, while teaching, the teacher should avoid developing in the students the habit of craming.

Proceeding from known to unknown—It is natural for a student to proceed from something about which he knows towards other things about which he does not know. The previous knowledge has some effect on the mind of the student and so when similar unknown things are taught to him it is possible for him to establish association with the previous knowledge. We have seen that children have the influence of the things of their environment on their mind. It is, therefore, proper for the teacher to proceed from known to unknown. In other words, the teacher should try to establish an association with the already known things and, thus, help the student to acquire further knowledge. By establishing association, it is possible to know and learn things easily. Once the student has known about a thing, it is possible and easy to tell him about the thing which he does not know. While teaching about the forests and their qualities, it is possible to establish association with the gardens that the students have seen. While teaching Geography, the teacher should try to establish association with 'unknown things and with things that exist in the neighbourhood of the students. It is on account of this that regional or local Geography has a great importance in the teaching of Geography.

From concrete to abstract—A concrete object is discernible by eye and so it is easy to understand it. Comparatively it is difficult to point out an abstract thing. An abstract thing is difficult to grasp. It involves imagination and greater stress on our mental power. If we want to explain truth and non-violence, it shall take us time to define these things and make students to understand them. If, on the other hand, examples of truth and non-violent behaviours are presented before the students, they shall be able to know and understand it easily and quickly. It is always, therefore, wise to proceed from concrete to abstract.

In teaching Geography, comparatively, it is difficult to proceed from concrete to abstract. Geographical factors, that are abstract in nature, cannot be displayed in concrete form. However, the teacher of Geography must keep this maxim in view and try to proceed, accordingly. It shall be wise to give an outline of the country whose Geography is to be taught to the students. The teacher should make use of the picture's maps, sketches and diagrams and try to establish the abstract facts in the minds of the students.

From whole to part – Those persons who think that student first have an idea of the part and then of the whole, are sadly mistaken. Really speaking, the correct process is to proceed from whole to part. It is psychological and scientific also. According to the principles of psychology, the child first knows about the whole and then about its parts. For a very long time students were taught Geography of different countries separately. After teaching them the Geography of a particular country, an attempt was made to take them towards the whole. This had an adverse effect and learning of Geography became a tedious task. The modern education lays stress on proceeding from whole to part. First of all, the whole of the region is taken for study and then its various subdivisions are explained. In this method there is no repetition of the process of proceeding from part to whole. This makes the education scientific. Students do not get fed up and bored. Interest in the subject is maintained. Through this method it is possible to acquire knowledge in a more stable manner and more quickly.

From definite to indefinite – It is psychological and scientific for the teacher to present definite things before the students and then try to proceed from definite to indefinite. Though concrete and definite examples, it is possible to have a correct idea of indefinite and, abstract things. The knowledge, which is acquired on the basis of maxim of proceeding from definite to indefinite is scientific and proper. Students have some knowledge of natural things and natural conditions. Now the teacher has to take advantage of this definite knowledge and proceed to indefinite. With the help of maps, charts, pictures, models, etc. he can proceed towards indefinite things and give the students proper foundation.

From particular to general—The teacher should first give a specific example and then try to proceed towards general principles of phenomena. As far as possible, the teacher should try to present certain examples and get the answers from the students. First of all, the teacher should try to give knowledge of certain particular things and facts and then on the basis of that knowledge, he should try to proceed towards general principles and knowledge about general facts. This will help the students to follow things easily and properly. Teaching of Geography in this manner is easy and proper. The teacher of Geography should proceed from the Geography of the region and go over to the Geography of general principles of the whole world.

From psychological to scientific—Education in order to be successful and useful, must be psychologically and scientifically planned. Before the student can have a proper knowledge of the things he must be taught in a psychological manner. The teacher of Geography must keep in mind the mental development of the students. In the beginning, the student should be taught in a very psychological manner. By and by this psychological manner goes on developing into scientific manner. The teaching must be based on psychological fundamentals. The subject-matter should be so planned and divided that the curiosity of the students may be satisfied as well as accentuated. Today Geography is taught on the basis of cause and effect. This cause and effect relationship is a scientific basis. This scientific basis has to be reached through psychological manner. It is these maxims that make the teaching interesting and successful.

1. There are various aims and maxims of the teaching of Geography. These aims and maxims are subject to the aims and maxims of the education and the society at large.

2. Professor S. L. Holtz has laid down two types of aims of the teaching of Geography—

   (1) Practical aims and; (2) Cultural aims.

   Practical aims of the teaching of Geography include the knowledge of the land, agriculture and industrial development and influence of geographical factors on our life and geographical reference etc.

   Cultural aims of the teaching of Geography include the development of the feeling of patriotism, love for nature and development of aesthetic sense; development of the idea of World Citizenship etc.

   Professor James Fairgrieve thinks that training of future citizens is the aim of the teaching of Geography.

3. Geography is taught with the following aims and objects in view.

   (a) Intellectual development.

   (b) Knowledge of the world and broadening of outlook of the children.

   (c) It aims at development of the qualities of co-operation, generosity and sympathetic outlook.

   (d) Geography also aims at the development of the quality of adjustment with the environment.

   (e) It also aims at bringing about economic efficiency in the students.

   (f) Teaching of Geography aims at development of mental faculties like power of reasoning, invention, discovery etc.

   (g) It is also responsible for the development of balanced personality.

   (h) It aims at developing in the students love for nation, travels and knowledge about countries.

(i) It also helps them to acquire knowledge of natural resources.

(j) Teaching of Geography also aims at the study of the influence of geographical factors on man.

(k) It also aims at the study of geographical elements in the development of human civilization.

In order to achieve these aims of teaching of Geography, the following maxims are and should be employed :

(a) The teacher should proceed from simple to complex.

(b) From known to unknown.

(c) From concrete to abstract.

(d) From whole to part.

(e) From definite to indefinite.

(f) From particular to general.

(g) From psychological to scientific.

(h) If Geography is taught on the basis of the objects and maxims enumerated above, it is possible to have a proper and thorough knowledge of the subject

4

Significant Features

Concept and Meaning

Geography forms a part of social sciences and is one of the social sciences which is now heading towards a scientific form. Change is the law of nature and change is the fundamental of development and progress. Geography has passed through many stages and it was only in 1905 that geography was accorded an important place in the curriculum. Prof. A.Z. Herbertson contributed a lot in this development of geography.

Now-a-days geography means description of earth. But since earth is full of various things which could not be studied in isolation and it is quite difficult to describe everything we find on earth. Thus to overcome these difficulties certain principles have been formulated which are quite useful for us in the study of earth with its relevant factors. These days an attempt is made to study earth as the home of man.

Keeping this in view Prof E.A. Macnee has defined geography, *"so, to give more explicit definition. Geography is the study of earth as the home of man or in other words geography is the study of the environment of man; physical, social, particularly in its relation to human actives".*

Prof. J. Fairgrieve defines Geography as, *"The function of geography is to train future citizens to imagine accurately the conditions of the great world stage and so to help them to think safely about political and social problems in the wortd around".* However Prof. Fairgrieve later on revised his definition of geography so as to include the developing subject matter of geography. He then defined geography, "Geography is the science which treats the relation between earth and man, *"Geography is the science which treats the influence on the man of local conditions and space relations."*

According to Prof. L. Dudley stamp, *"Geography is a description of the world and of its inhabitants"*.

In this definition we find that human factor is taken into consideration and thus in geography we not only study physical factors and environment but it also includes the studies of human activities carried out in relation to environment. Thus *"Geography is the study of the changes and the development"*. The changes that occur are well reflected in the face of the nature, formation of human beings and animals. Thus, geography makes a study of various factors that have brought about these changes, development and downfall of the civilisation of the world.

Some other definitions of geography are:

"Geography is the comparative study of Earth regions".

According to Edmund Burke, *"Geography is an earthly subject but a heavenly science"*.

According to E.G. Steal, *"Geography is the science of initiative, for by means of it we establish our relations with the world and without it we may easily lag behind in the march of progress"*.

Prof. Unstead defines geography, *"Geography is the science which investigates macro-organism and space relationships of its component parts"*.

From this definition it becomes quite clear that geography is the science which studies different stages and parts of the living beings of this world in relation to their local relations. It emphasises the local conditions and in view of this, "Geography deals with actions and reactions that occur within the hydrosphere".

However, it is a narrow definition because land is not influenced by water only. Many other factors also influence the life on the earth. Taking all such other factors into consideration L. Dudley stamp stated, *"The old geography worked from effect to cause. Modern Geography works from cause to effect"*.

This clearly brings about a cause effect relationship in study of geography.

It can be said that geography is a science of sciences. Botany deals with the study of plants, zoology deals with the study of animal life. Astronomy is the study of heavenly bodies and geology makes an effort to explain the structure of earth. Geography synthesises all these sciences (viz Botany, Zoology, Astronomy, Geology) as far as the evolution of man in the universe is concerned. In fact, Modern Geography is a combination of art and science. It has certain relationship with other social sciences and its scope of study is quite broad.

Evolution of the Discipline

Geography dates back to mankind. In the olden days people carried out long journey by land route and sea route. These travellers and conquerors on their return from their journey related accounts of their travel in the form of stories or poems. They were also successful in drawing charts and pictures of such travels and they also acquired knowledge about the natural features and physical features of the earth. The description of such journeys always included the description of various rivers, mountains, forests, etc. and the difficulties the travellers had to face during their journey. Geography is a broad-based knowledge of all these things. Some notable personalities who contributed to the study of geography include *Pythagoras* (a great Egyption traveller), *Herodotus* (known as father of geography, who gave the well-known epithet, "Egypt is the gift of Nile"), *Plato, Aristotle, Alexander.* In the early times geography as an independent subject had no place in curriculum. Therefore, geography was defined by these geographers as the description of the earth.

Aristotle explained eclipses and gave a concept of spherical form of the earth. Bacon revived this concept. Marco Polo who accompanied his father Nicolo and his uncle Maffeo in their journey to China was the first traveller to have traced a route across the whole length of Asia. He had also named and described the Kingdoms that he had seen. In the field of cartography and Astronomy Prince Henry (fifth son of King John I) occupies an unparalleled position.

The first scientific volume of Geography was written by N. Carpenter (English Geographer). It was only in 17th century that Geography was included in the school curriculum because of its practical utility in navigation.

Bernhardus Varenius published *Geographic Genaralis* in 1650 in which he pointed out a dualism in geography. Geography deals with a process and a phenomenon which are purely physical in nature and it also considers the'soqal cultural phenomenon. He died at a young age of 28 in 1650 and after him Immanual Kant made an effort to find a foundation for geography within the frame work of other sciences.

He grouped the knowledge on the basis of object of study as (i) systematic sciences (e.g. Botany, geology, sociology etc.) (ii) Historical sciences (e.g. History, Politied science. etc.) and (iii) Geographical sciences.

Geographical sciences dealt with the study of things that are associated in space. A philosophical foundation was provided to geography by Kant. The substance of geography was moulded into a scientific form by Baron Von Humboldt. While giving a description of areas he had given a comparison of these areas with other lands and in this way he set the tone for scientific geography. The invention of 'isotherms' to compare temperatures is recorded in his name Carl Ritter (a German philospher) has divided the earth into natural regions and showed each unit as a whole interrelated area complex of elements. This later on became a model for regional presentation "Geography is the comparative study of Earth Regions". In the subject matter of geography we find a similarity and contrast of the nature study. Various factors of nature are responsible for the development of art, literature, religion, history, philosophy, etc. Study of geography is not therefore limited to inanimate part of the nature. It has to do with the animate beings of this earth.

In the Nineteenth century both views were prevalent, i.e. geography is a pure science and geography as the study of environmental influences. Later on in this century Fairgrieve, while defining geography stated that, the function of geography is to train future citizens to imagine accurately the conditions of the world stage and in this way to help them to think about political and social problems of the world.

The geography with which we are concerned today is modern geography and it is the result of various stages of development. The present day geography is no more confined to cramming of certain things/facts. The element of scientific study has taken full control of the study of geography. Modern geography is now considered to be a separate science requiring a detailed study of the territories of the world. The modern geography is considered as a unifying science, for its study it derives raw material from other sciences.

Different Streams

Broadly speaking geography may be classified as under. This classification is based on the subject matter of geography.

Physical Geography. This branch of geography deals with various physical factors such as the land, the sea and the atmosphere. It also deals with the study of various phenomena connected with these physical factors. The study of laws that governs the movement and formation of earth, the ocean and its waters, the climate and the vegetation are included in physical geography.

Human Geography. Carl Ritter, the German Philosopher emphasised the human experience in regional context. This human factor is thus a recent addition to the subject matter of Geography. In Geography we study human activities in relation to physical and Geographical environment. Man is carrying out different types of activities which influence the physical factors. For example he takes to agriculture, poultry farming, establishing big industries, etc.

Economic Geography. It is also a new branch of geography and it deals with the study of influences of various geographical factors on the economic activities of man. In economic geography we take up the detailed studies of various industrial activities like manufacturing of goods, agricultural production, means of communication and transport, etc. The study of the Mineral Wealth of a country also forms the subject matter of economic Geography. Economic geography is gaining importance because of the importance of economic factors in modern-day world. A careful study of economic geography can be used to bring about a development of economic conditions.

Political Geography. The branch of geography which forms the part of syllabi in higher classes deals with the government of states and countries. The subject matter of this branch of geography is the political divisions within special reference to different physical factors. For this purpose the whole of the world is divided into political divisions known as *countries* or *Lands.* In this branch of geography we make a study of land, sea, progress and development of various industries of a country. It is the least developed branch of geography and there is enough scope for expansion of its horizons.

Historical Geography. In this branch of geography an attempt is made to take up the study of various factors (geographical) that have influenced human beings since ancient times. Thus such a study provides a chronological study of influences of geographical factors on human life. These studies are quite helpful in assessing the influences of physical factors on various human activities. Such a knowledge is quite beneficial to the students.

The Sphere

In the present-day world geography is no more considered as a mere collection of meaningless facts to be memorised and reproduced whenever required. Present-day geography covers a vast field and comprises many branches. The method of scientific study has taken a full control of the scope and study of geography. Now in study of geography we include the process of adjustment of human beings with their physical and natural environment (human geography). Geography today has a social responsibility as well and it tries to create and develop good citizens. The scope of study of geography is growing every day. The scope of geography has become so vast and complex that a need was felt for specialisation. For purpose of specialisation the subject matter of geography has now been divided into various branches such as *physiogeography, glaciology, seismology, hydrology, cliamatology.*

In addition to various branches of geography dealt within previous section (section 1.3) some other important branches of modern geography are:

Cartography. It deals with the conception, design and execution of maps, and the art of drawing maps and charts. It is quite helpful in geodetic and topographic surveys. It is also used in preparing maps on certain selected scales. A working knowledge of cartography is essential for every student of geography because it helps in preparation of maps and also in reading *maps.*

Urban Geography. In this branch of geography emphasis is placed on concepts of location, interaction and accessibility as also the distribution and movement of population. It takes up all the aspects of urban population such as land use patterns, socio-economic composition, age structure, sex structure, housing sites, employment, etc.

Anthropogeography. It deals with the study of distribution of human beings on the earth in relation to their geographical environment. It bears the same relationship to anthropology as biogeography bears to biology and zoogeography bears to zoology.

Agricultural Geography. In this branch of geography emphasis is placed on understanding the particular kinds of farms and farming systems that have been developed in particular areas. An effort is also made to find out the similarities and differences in farms and farming systems of different areas. Such a comparative study is quite helpful in understanding how different kinds of agriculture are distributed over the earth and how they function.

The Effects

The study of geography influences our lives in all its fields. It is quite useful in economic research and the relationship of resources and human activities. It provides a sound basis for techno-economic surveys which are undertaken for estimating the development potentials of resources of different states. These survey utilise the geographical data from various branches of geography.

The knowledge of geography is also helpful to Town and Country planners because the study of past and present trends of urban structure and distribution and their findings serve a useful purpose for providing amenities to city dwellert. In India Geographers are closely associated for preparing master plans for metropolitan cities such as Mumbai, Kalkata, Chennai, Delhi. Keeping in view the pressure of growing population on land resources most of the countries in general and India in particular have undertaken projects for survey of land use in order to avoid the misuse of land and making a proper use of idle land. The land use map of Damoder Valley in India has been prepared on the same pattern as the land use map of Great Britain prepared by Dr. Dudely Stamp.

Another purpose that is being served by geography teaching is that it helps in solving the unemployment problem in countries all over the world. It is also useful to provide solutions to the problems of floods and draughts. Though these problems can not be completely overcome but mitigation due to these problems can be reduced by making proper use of the knowledge of geography.

The knowledge of geography can also be quite helpful to planner while planning the economy of a country on regional basis.

Geography helps in elucidating and reinterpreting the complex relation between the physical'environment and distribution, mode of life and economic and social activities of man.

The knowledge of geography is quite beneficial in the study of other subjects such as history, economics, sociology, commerce, agriculture etc.

Geography also has an *educative value*. It provides to the student a complete knowledge of natural resources of his country and those of other countries and it helps in' broadening the mental attitude of the pupils and enables them to offer a critical attitude to world problems.

The study of geography also develops in the pupils the powers of observation, imagination, thinking and reasoning.

For a successful execution of a war the knowledge of geography is quite essential.

A proper study of geography can lead to a closer cooperation and better understanding among the nations of the world. Geographers have divided the world into four categories on the basis of their economic standards. These are (i) Developed World (ii) Socialist World (iii) Developing World (iv) Third World countries that have become rich due to the exploration and exploitation of mineral wealth resources, particularly oil. In this category are included Gulf countries, Venezuela, etc.

The developed countries are rich countries and they have surpluses which are due to the untiring efforts of its people. The developing countries are poor countries. However this division is more a man made and must be broken as early as possible. For this a sincere effort must be made both by developed as also the developing countries. In this effort geographers can make a contribution by providing right type of geographical knowledge. The knowledge provided by geographers be properly utilised by economists to bridge the gap between the developed and the developing countries.

The Importance

At present geography is one of the important subjects in scho curriculum. Geography derives a lot of material from such subjec as Biology, Anthropology, Sociology, Economics, Mathematic Chemistry and other sciences. The subject matter of geograpl includes study of natural environment of man and also the stuc of social and cultural environment. Thus geography has a ve wide scope unparalleled by any other subject.

Geography is a science and an art. It tries to train and develc good citizens who may be able to solve various social econom and political problems of the country. The importance of geograph can be understood more clearly by considering the effect c geography teaching on man as a human being, as an administratoı as a politician, etc. We shall also have to consider the practical importance of geography. Economic importance geography, political and social importance, cultural and intellectual importance, etc. The importance of geography is discussed under various heads in the following pages.

Importance of Geography for administrators and politicians. To run the administration efficiently it is essential for the administrator to have a thorough knowledge of the geography of the country. In the absence of a knowledge of geographical conditions of a country it becomes difficult to run the administration efficiently. Geographical factors affect the Economic, political and social life of the inhabitants of an area. From a knowledge of geography it becomes easier to know about inter-dependence of people of various countries. In the present age no country can live without taking help fiom other countries and to have a proper and coordial relationship the knowledge of geography is quite helpful. The administrators in a developed country are on the look-out for a country where their finished and manufactured goods may find a good market. In this adventure the knowledge of geographical conditions of a country are quite handy to the administrator. Such knowledge can help the administrator to establish beneficial lationship with other countries and their neighbouring world.

Political importance. To gain in political importance the owledge of geography of other countries is essential for any intry and even for an individual. It is only by the knowledge of ographical conditions that we develop sympathy for any rticular country. For example if you happen to live in a fertile intry it would not be difficult for you to imagine the plight of a low being living in a desert. Thus, the knowledge of geography lps to bring about the world together and in this way it helps to lve a number of political problems. Thus knowledge of ography is of political importance.

Practical importance. A knowledge of geography is quite iandy to prepare the students to face various problems of life. If a student is familiar with the natural conditions of a country, its climate, vegetation, natural resources, mineral wealth, etc., then it becomes easier for him to plan his future. Such a knowledge can be of much help to would-be industrialists of a country and a student of geography interested in setting up an industry after the completion of his education can make a better selection for the location of his industrial unit keeping in mind the natural resources needed. The knowledge of geography is also helpful to an individual in developing social, political and economic relationships with the other countries. Thus we find that the knowledge of geography has a practical utility.

Cultural and intellectual importance of Geography. A knowledge of geography helps us in acquiring the knowledge about cultural and intellectual life of a particular country and in this way it becomes easier to carry out a proper study of the cultural life of whole world.

The knowledge of geography also helps a student in developing his power of imagination and also encourages him to find out cause and effect of various phenomena. When a student of geography learns about the mountains, rivers, forests, etc. then a image of all these things is formed before him. Whenever he actually comes across any of these things he can identify them and discern them easily. Such a knowledge helps the student to know about the cultures and civilisation of different countries.

Geographical factors also influence the intellectual life of a country so we can say that geography has an intellectual importance. In the words of Fairgrieve, *"The real value of geography lies in the fact that it helps man to place himself in the world to learn his true position and duties"*.

Economic importance. Geography has its economical importance as well. Knowledge of geography helps us to know about various natural resources of a country or a region in a country. Such a knowledge can be used for the economic progress of a country or a region. We flourish in the world only if we have economic prosperity.

Social importance. A knowledge of geography helps a student in developing a proper social outlook. A proper social outlook develops a feeling of brotherhood for the nationals of other countries and makes a student broad-minded. He no more remains self-centred and he develops a feeling of world citizenship. Thus a knowledge of geography has a social importance.

Importance for earning a livelihood. We spend a major part of our life in earning our livelihood and tne knowledge of geography can help us to a large extent in this. Such a knowledge is also helpful to us to utilise our leisure time in a beneficial way. It is the knowledge that we gained in geography about the things and conditions prevailing around us that help us in this. The knowledge of .geography has given us the knowledge of various sources, that are available and which could be profitable tapped to earn our livelihood.

Natural curiosity. We have a natural curiosity to know more and more about the lifestyle of people in other lands and countries. The knowledge of geography helps to satisfy this natural curiosity and also throws light on the various factors that influence our lifestyle. Thus geography has an important role in satisfying our natural curiosities.

Importance in understanding other subjects. A knowledge of geography helps us in understanding various other subjects (e.g. Sociology, Economics, Anthropology, Biology, etc.). For example a knowledge of geography helps in understanding history because it provides the proper perspective. Various historical events have been influenced by geographical factors. The development of civilisation began in India and Egypt because of geographical reasons.

Geographical factors also influence the political system in a country. The prevalance of democracy in Switzerland is due to geographical factors.

To acquire a thorough and proper knowledge of political science the knowledge of geography is essential. The social life and structure of society in a country is governed to a large extent by various geographical factors prevailing in that country. A knowledge of geography also helps to properly understand the subject matter of sociology.

Thus, we find that a knowledge of geography is important in understanding and acquiring the knowledge of various social sciences.

Thus we find that geography occupies an important place in various fields of life. A knowledge of geography also inculcates a spirit of patriotism and internationalism. Because of this geography occupies an important place in primary, secondary and higher education.

President Eisenhower of America called Geography the foundation of humanity.

P.E. James gives the following reasons for the importance of geography.

(i) Geography helps us to have a proper picture of man and his environment.

(ii) Geography gives us information about various types of climates, natural conditions, mineral wealth, etc. of the various nations.

(iii) With the knowledge of geography we can read and discern the maps, sketches, diagrams, etc.

(iv) It develops our power of observation.

In view of Fairgrieve the two principles that make the knowledge of geography impertinent and important are as under:

(i) We spend about 2/3rd of our life in dealing with our neighbours and countrymen. In this period we perform the duties as good citizens. The knowledge of geography helps us in performance of these duties.

(ii) A knowledge of geography comes handy to know about the economic needs of the people of other countries and such a knowledge helps the industrialists, agriculturists, politicians, etc. in better performance of their job.

Geography is one of the social sciences which is now heading towards a scientific form. Man, in fact, is a creature of nature which undergoes change constantly. It is the change which is the fundamental of the development and progress. Similarly, Geography has also been a progressive and changing as well as dynamic subject. It was late as 1905 that it came to occupy an important place in the curriculum. It was *Prof. A. Z. Herbertson* who contributed in making the subject interesting and gave it a new scientific outlook. Scientific inventions have made man well aware of the secrets of nature. It has also made him go near the nature which was one dreaded by people at large. Since that day, the scope of the subject of study of Geography has widened and it has become very important. Every day we make use of the knowledge of this subject. It is, therefore, natural to try to know about Geography. It is a natural question to ask—What is Geography ?

What is Geography ? Literally Geography means description of the earth. Earth is full of various things and it is difficult to study it in isolation. In fact, earth in synonymous with world, which is again rich with various things. If we take to describing every thing that we find on earth, it shall be difficult to come out with a definition. We have to take to certain important things and leave out unimportant ones. In order to come to this position, we have to come forward with certain principles which help us to study earth with its relevant factors. In fact, we study earth as the home of man, It shall, therefore, be quite proper to define Geography in the following words *of Prof. E. A. Macnee*—

"So, to give a more explicit definition. Geography is the study of the earth as the home of man, or, in other words, Geography is the study of the environment of man.; physical and social, particularly in its relation to human activities."

Professor J. Fairgrieve has defined Geography as the description of the earth.

At another place he has defined this subject in relation to training of future citizens, in the following words :—

"The function of Geography is to train future citizens to investigate accurately the condition.'; of the grant world stage and so to help them to think simply about political and social problems in the world around."

The definition of J. Fairgrieve which calls Geography "the description of the earth", throws light on those bases which have brought the development of Geography. This definition will also help us to know about the basic principles of the subject. For example, we may see that in olden days people carried out long journey by land route and sea route. They drew up charts and pictures of these travels. They were also successful in acquiring more knowledge about the natural features and physical features of the earth. A literature that deals with all these things gives description of various difficulties that they had to face in reaching those places. It also gives description of various rivers, mountains, forests, deserts and all other things. In short, they presented a description of those things which, later on, formed Geography. Thus, the description of the various parts of hemisphere presents the subject matter of Geography. All this description can be called a part of Geography. But Geography is not limited to this description. Such a description can only do some good to citizens. But Geography is something more than that. It is broad based knowledge of all these things and requires further understanding and description. We shall try to assess to that thing as well.

Limitations of the Subject

Geography in the beginning did not have a very wide scope. It was limited in subject matter. Travellers used to go to various places and met different sorts of persons. They had to cross rivers, climates, mountains and change ways in order to proceed on their journey. Due to this task of travelling, they came across various cities and had a look at them. They had to face the vagaries of weather. Sometimes the rain obstructed their way and sometimes the storm would dislocate their schedule of journey. By and by tendency to travel by waterways developed. This sea journey gave people an opportunity to see various lands and they earned rich dividends by taking to trade. This had an effect on Geography. Knowledge of Geography was based on the description given by travellers. The would describe about the mountains, rivers and the beauty of the lands. All this was included in the subject matter of Geography. This essentially indicates that Geography was descriptive. Descriptive element in Geography, later on, grew into a different aspect.

"Geography is the science of description"—J. Fairgrieve. This definition is more comprehensive. This does include only the •description of the earth. Now Geography started taking into consideration certain other allied factors of knowledge. This thing brought an element of science in it.

Later on, *Fairgrieve* himself had to revise his definition in order to include the developing subject matter of Geography. He desribed it in the following words:—

"Geography is the science which treats the relation between the earth and man."

He further wrote :—

"Geography is the science which treats of the influence on the man of heal conditions and space relations."

These definitions very clearly bring to light the influences that man has of the environment. Man also influences the environment. Thus, there is an inter-section between man and environment. Day-to-day needs of human beings are studied in the subject matter of Geography. Man has innumerable wants and it is the nature that fulfils most of the wants. It can also not be denied that the wants are generated by nature. For example, men living in cold countries have to put on worm and tight clothes, persons living on the sea shore are good navigators. All these factors indicate that the environment has its influence on man. That is why people have said that is the creation of environment. With this aim in view *Prof. L. Dudley Stamp* has defined geography like this—

It is *"a description of the world and of its inhabitants."*

This definition very clearly indicates that Geography takes into consideration the human factor. It is, in fact, not only the study of the physical factors and environment but also study of the human activities carried out in relation to environment. Man is the centre of the activities of the world. Similarly, he is the centre of the study.of the subject matter of Geography.

"Geography is the study of the changes and the development." This definition very correctly takes into consideration the changes and

development that are continuously and continually taking place on the face of the nature. Man and animal have to survive and struggle for their existence against the cruelties of nature. The changes that takes place are well reflected in the face of the nature, formation of human beings and animals. It is, therefore, natural for Geography to study the various factors that have brought about the changes, development and the downfall of the civilizations of the world.

"Geography is the comparative study of Earth Regions." In the subject-matter of Geography, we find the similarity and the contrast of the nature study. Various factors of nature are responsible for the development of art, literature, religion, history, philosophy etc. Study of Geography is not, therefore, limited up to inanimate part of the nature. It has to do with the animate beings of this earth.

"Geography is an earthly subject but a heavenly science."
– Edmund Burke

This definition of Geography also takes into cosideration the element of astronomy or the sun, the moon and other heavenly bodies. It is true that while living on this earth, we do study the movement of the sun, the moon and other planets. In Geography rain, clouds, air, cold, temperature, etc. are also studied. Geography, therefore, includes physical factors as well. It is, therefore, quite natural to call it a science of the study of heavenly bodies.

"We stand on a microscopic island of knowledge, amidst vast ocean of the unknown."

Study of unknwon forms the subject matter of Geography, as well. In other words, it means that in the world there are innumerable things about which man does not have any correct knowledge. With the help of the study of Geography we are, able to know about various unknown things. In other words Geography is helpful in adding to our knowledge. It is on account of this reason that it is called *the study of unknown.* Intact this definition would be equally applicable to other sciences and fields of the study.

"Geography is the science of initiative, for by means of it we establish our relations with the world and without it we may easily lag behind in the march of progress." – E. G. Steal

This definition very clearly indicates that Geography is very helpful in our development. Without the knowledege of Geography it may not be possible for us to make proper development. This definition is narrow in the sense that it does not give us the idea as to how do the social, religious, political, historical and scientific-factors march ahead on the path of progress. However, this definition tries to give us an idea of the progress that we try to make.

"Geography is the science of relationship between physical factors and principles and of organic factors." —*James Fail grieve*

In other words, this definition means that "Geography is the study of inter-action between man and his environment." In our environment we have rain, air, temperature, currents, ebb and tide, mountains, rivers, animals and fowls etc. Inanimate or inorganic factors do influence the living beings or organic factors. Thus influence is sometimes evident and sometimes it remains unnoticed. This is true about man as well. Man is also influenced by inorganic factors. This influence or impact is felt by him in several ways. In Geography we do try to study this thing. But this is only a part of the subject-matter of Geography. There are other things as well that are studied in Geography.

"Geography is the science which deals with form of relief on the earth's crust and the influences which these forms exercise on the distribution of other phenomena."

This definition indicates that certain physical factors continue to influence other physical factors. This confines itself to the study of rain, air, temperature on certain other factors of nature. It is natural for the nature to be dynamic and active. This definition does lay stress on this aspect of the nature. It is quite pertinent for the clouds to strike against the mountains of Himalayas and sprinkle in form of rain. But this definition is not all in all. There are certain other factors that are studied in Geography. Inter-action of various factors of nature is not the only thing that

Geography studies. It has a wider perspective. *Prof. Unstead* has realised this and defined Geography in the following words :—

"Geography is the science which investigates the condition oj macro-organism and the space relations of its component parts."

This definition shows that Geography is the science which explains how physical conditions influence climate, natural phenomena and animal life and all these facts effect the life of man and how man modifies them in return.

The Geography with which we are concerned today is modern Geography. This modern Geography is the result of certain stages of development. In the present set-up Geography does not confine itself to learning by heart certain lists of things. The element of scientific study has taken full control of the study of Geography. In fact. Geography today is a combination of art and science. It has also some relationship with other social sciences. Its scope of study is quite broad. Various natural conditions of the world, planets of the atmosphere and other heavenly bodies are also studied by it. Nature and other natural factors also form the study of subject-matter of Geography. In it, cause and effect relationship is properly maintained. It is the cause which creates an effect and every effect always has a cause behind it. This fact is very well recognised in Geography.

Geography is a social science and art—It tries to train and develop good citizens why may be able to solve various social, economic and political problems of the country. These citizens have to play their role effectively. Thus, the scope of the study of Geography is quite wide. It takes into consideration various facets of nature as well as human life. In the following pages we shall try to talk about the scope and subject-matter of Geography.

Today the scope of study of Geography has widened. It is no more simply the description of the earth and its inhabitants. It is assumed wider dimensions. It has also grown out of its descriptive character. It does not confine itself only to cramming of the names of the rivers and mountains. Now element of scientific study has taken a complete control of the method and scope of study of Geography. Now an attempt is made to establish cause and effect relationship between various factors of Geography. It is now studied as a subject dealing with the process of adjustment of human beings with their physical and natural environment. It also studies various activities of mankind with reference to the physical and the natural environment. There is no human activity which is not influenced by Geographical factors. It is always proper to study human activities and natural factors in relation to each other. Geography today has responsibility towards society as well. It also tries to create and develop good citizens. Human beings have their activities develop constantly. This constant development of the human activities and the constant change in the physical factors has a bearing on the scope of the study of Geography. Every day the scope of the study of Geography is growing wider. It includes the study of the following things :—

Natural environment— In Geography we study various factors concerning physical environment such as the shape of the earth, the formation of the crust of the earth, rivers and their flow, causes of creation of deserts, oceans, mountains, *etc.*

Under Geography we also study various types of rocks, climates, natural resources, soil, land and other things. While studying all these things, we do not forget and leave the human factor.

Human activities in relation to physical environment—In Geography *we* also study human activities in relation to physical and Geographical environment. Physical factors continue to influence the human activities. A person living in cold climate is bound to be laborious and hard working, while a person living in a warm country is likely to be lethargic and lazy. In Geography we have not to study things as they are. We have also to study things and human activities, as they should be. This would help them to grow into ideal citi—zens. In Geography we also learn about those factors which have made people take to hunting or some industrial job. We find that certain countries produce raw materials while others manufacture goods. Human activity is responsible for all these things. In Geography these things are studied in the light of the fact that man is a member of the society.

Social activities of man – Man does not live all alone. He lives as a member of the society and does his activities in that light. All the activities of man, whether they are in relation to the physical environment or some such other environment, are bound to be influenced by social considerations. Man has been able to make the development only on account of this instinct of society. In Geography we look towards all these activities. While talking about the Geographical factors, one should not forget that these Geographical factors are also influenced by human activities and that too of a social being.

Political activities — Political activities and political set-up are very much influenced by Geographical factors. Then Geographical factors are confined within the limits of particular State or country which is nothing but a political delimitation. In Geography these factors are also kept in mind.

1. Geography is the subject that studies about man and his environment and their inter action.

2. It makes comparative study of various regions of earth.

3. Geography is a social science as well as art.

4. It studies natural environment, human activities as well as political activities.

5. Following are the various departments of Geography :– (a) Physical Geography, (b) Human Geography, (c) Economic Geography, (d) Political Geography, and (e) Historical Geography.

5
Teaching Methods

In order to achieve the aims and objectives of the teaching of a particular subject certain maxims are laid down. The teaching of the subject is then planned and carried out keeping these maxims as the guiding principles. No doubt, teaching is an art but the success of a teacher lies in making his subject so simple as to make it intelligible for his students. The moment a teacher fails in this task he ceases to be a teacher. A geography teacher has to take greater pains as he has to act both as a science teacher as also a social science teacher.

Teaching is thus a most difficult task and everybody is not fit to be a teacher. Some persons may have a 'flair' for teaching and some other can improve their teaching if they are fully aware of different methods of teaching. In order to make children learn effectively, the teacher has to adopt the right method of teaching. In this chapter an attempt will be made to discuss some common methods of teaching of geography.

Before taking up the discussion of various methods of teaching of geography it would be better to know about the maxims of the teaching of geography because to be successful in his task, the geography teacher shall have to fall back upon these maxims. Given below are the maxims on the basis, of which geography teaching is conducted and carried out.

Proceed from simple to complex. It is a well-known maxim of teaching and this is the natural process of mind. It is also psychologically successful method. For imparting the knowledge of sea and ocean a geography teacher can show a pond or a tank to his students. Similarly, a model of mountain can be used to explain various things about a mountain.

Proceed from known to unknown. It is always better to proceed from known to unknown. It demands that the teacher should make efforts to establish some association with the previous knowledge of the students while imparting them any knew knowledge. For example while teaching about forests and their qualities the geography teacher can establish association with gardens that the students have seen. Due to this the regional geography is quite important.

Proceed from concrete to abstract. Though it is desirable to proceed from concrete to abstract but it is difficult in teaching of geography. Geographical factors, that are abstract in nature, cannot be displayed in concrete form. However, teacher should try his best to act according to this maxim. The teacher should make use of pictures, maps, sketches and diagrams and try to establish the abstract facts in the minds of the students.

From whole to part. Such a method is more scientific and psychological. Since quite, long we have been teaching the geography of different countries separately and after teaching them geography of a particular country an attempt was made to take them towards whole. This made the lerning of geography quite difficult and now we lay more stress on proceeding from whole to part. In this approach the whole of the region is taken for study first and then its various sub-divisions are explained. This makes the education scientific. The knowledge acquired in this way is more stable.

Proceed from definite to indefinite. Through concrete and definite examples we can have a better idea of abstract and indefinite things. Teacher of geography should take full advantage of the knowledge of students about certain natural things in proceeding from definite to indefinite. He can make use of maps, charts, etc. and give the students proper foundation.

Proceed from particular to general. It is always better to cite some specific example before proceeding to general principles of a phenomenon. It helps the students to follow things easily and properly. The geography teacher should proceed from the Geography of region and then go over to the Geography of the general principles of the whole world.

Proceed from psychological to scientific. In the beginning the geography teacher should teach his students in a psychological manner. He should also keep in mind the mental development of his students. Slowly and slowly he should shift from psychological to scientific method. He should make an effort to divide the syllabus in such a manner that the curiosity of the students be satisfied as well as accentuated. In present age geography is taught on the basis of cause and effect which is a scientific basis. This scientific basis has to be reached through psychological manner.

With the development of the subject-matter and knowledge of geography, various methods have evolved and are used for teaching of geography. The methodological revolution in geography commenced with the introduction of statistical techniques and since then development of different methods has been on the increase. In recent years we have witnessed the great innovation in the field of teaching methods. The four important aspects of geography teaching are:

(i) A point of view built on a distinct method.

(ii) Its philosophy and motivation : know your neighbour and know yourself.

(iii) Its synthetic approach.

(iv) Its regional concept.

The methods of teaching of geography should be one of the chief concerns of the geography teacher. Teacher has to employ these methods keeping in view the psychological requirements of the students. The psychological requirements of students of different ages are different and so we have to modify the method of teaching accordingly. Some of the important methods of teaching geography are:

(i) Socratic Method or Question-Answer Method.

(ii) Inductive Method.

(iii) Deductive Method.

(iv) Lecture Method.

(v) Textbook Method.

(vi) Descriptive Method.

(vii) Observation Method.

(viii) Story-Telling Method.

(ix) Political Method of Teaching of Geography.

(x) Regional Method of Teaching of Geography

(xi) Human Method of Teaching of Geography.

(xii) Comparative Method.

(xiii) Project Method.

(xiv) Dalton Plan Method

(xv) Laboratory Method.

(xvi) Excursion Method.

Some of these methods of teaching of geography are described in details.

Observation Method

Students travel from one place to another during tours and while going about from one place to another they get an opportunity to observe and see things for themselves. A real impression of an object or a place can best be gained through personal observation. Direct experience is an essential step to right understanding. If the students are given an opportunity to acquire knowledge of geography by observing things themselves, the knowledge shall be stable and shall have a practical value. The knowledge acquired through this method is clear, complete and perfect.

It is most desirable that observational work of the pupils be carefully directed and guided by the teacher. The students in lower classes may be asked to observe geographical things in their environment, near their homes, village and such other localities. They may be told to collect the geographical data. This data will help them understand similar conditions in their own provinces extending to other countries of the world. The 'observation method has a very wide range and can be very conveniently employed. It is a very popular method of teaching of geography. This method is found to be more useful in teaching the following branches of geography:

(i) Natural or physical geography.

(ii) Commercial geography.

Some of the important requirements of this method are as under:

(i) The teacher himself should have properly observed and seen those things which he expects his students to see and observe. It is important because in the absence of a thorough knowledge of such a thing/place he will not be able to impart a scientific knowledge to his students.

(ii) Necessary data must be collected during observation.

Difficulties of the Method

(i) While on trips/tours the teacher sometimes has to face the problem of discipline.

(ii) The tours/trips cannot be planned to observe things that are situated far away.

(iii) Some times guardians are reluctant to permit their wards to go out for observation.

Excursion Method

Excursion occupies an important place in teaching of geography. An excursion arranged for the study of a part of the country on the spot is the most useful method of teaching of geography. In excursions and travels students get an opportunity to observe and see things by themselves. Truely-speaking excursions are part and parcel of observartion method. Keeping in view of this educationists have laid down that excursions should form a part of the teaching of geography. Excursions present the object in its natural colours. These excursions also serve a useful purpose of character formation of the student so that he may not be a misfit in society.

In lower classes students have ample time and so it is possible to plan excursions. A good teacher can arrange a number of excursions and can encourage his students to observe carefully the phenomenon (physical, social, industrial, economic, etc.). The excursions should begin from the observation of hills and valleys that are situated in the neighbourhood of school. The easiest and most important thing to observe is the natural objects like landscapes, land formations and different types of soils.

In the higher classes when the students have developed mentally and physically, they may be taken out on long excursions. The importance of excursion method for teaching of geography has been summed up in the following words *by fames Fairgrieve.*

"More Geography is learned by feet rather than head."

To develop the power of expression of his students it is desirable that while an excursion, teacher provides his students with opportunity for expressing their view about places and things seen by them. The excursion should be planned in such a way that they are not very long and an effort be made to make maximum utilisation of time. However this utility of time should not spoil the interest of students in the subject-matter.

For proper utilisation of time the whole class be divided into groups and each group be asked to make observation of a particular aspect of the nature of geographical environment. Then these groups may be asked to exchange notes.

After the excursion the outdoor observation work be closely related with in-door work. The students should be encouraged to study all those things in the maps. This would strengthen their knowledge and encourges them to proceed from concrete to abstract.

This method of teaching geography fosters such social virtues as cooperation, give and take and group feeling. The importance of this method of teaching has been given in the following words by Prof. *E. A.Macnee,* "It is essential that the foundation of geographical knowledge shall be laid in the field. No amount of reading from books can make up for a prctical knowledge gained by looking at earth which the child is studying. It follows that from very early stages expedition should from part ofgeograpgy."

For the success of this method it is essential that teacher himself is very fond of excursions and is willing to arrange such excursions. Teacher should be willing to face the problems and inconveniences likely to come up during such excursions.

A substitute of the journey is to have talks with travellers of other lands like Japanese,English and the Americans.

Still another alternative is to read a book on travels.

Laboratory Method

In this method of teaching of geography subject is taught like a science subject. Certain experiments are carried out in the laboratory like Geography room. The teacher may demonstrate any experiment and the students shall try to follow it. By this method it is possible to easily impart concrete experiences to students during the course of a lesson when the teacher wants to explain some abstract points. This method combines the instructional strategy of'information imparting' and 'showing how'. This method combines the advantages of both the lecture method and the demonstration method.

In this method of teaching teacher performs experiment before the class and simultaneously explains what he is doing. He also asks relevant questions from the class and students are compelled to observe carefully because they have to describe each and every step of experiment accurately and draw inferences. After thorough questioning and cross-questioning the inferences drawn by the students are discussed in the class. In this way the students remain active participants in the process of teaching. The teacher also relates the outcome of experiment to the content of the on-going lesson. The student may be asked to observe the experiment carefully and respect it. The students may also be encouraged to do the work independently.

The knowledge that has been acquired by drawing out conclusions and finding out results is very stable and useful in future life. Students may also be asked to draw charts, maps, prepare models, etc. It is also possible to explain the revolution and rotation of the earth with the help of demonstration.

This method is based on the principle 'truth is that which works' Requirements for a Good Demonstration

For success of any demonstration following points be always kept in mind:

(i) It should be planned and rehearsed by the teacher beforehand.

(ii) The apparatus used for demonstration should be big enough to be seen by the whole class. It would be much better if a large mirror is placed at a suitable angle above the teacher's table which will enable the pupils to have a view of everything that the teacher is doing while performing the experiment.

Alternately, if the class is well disciplined the teacher may allow the students to sit on the stools placed on the benches to enable them to have a better view.

(iii) Adequate lighting arrangements be made on demonstration table and a proper background be provided.

(iv) All the pieces of apparatus be placed in order before starting the demonstration. The apparatus likely to be used should be placed on the left-hand side of the table and it should be arranged in the same order in which it is likely to be used. After an apparatus is used it should be transferred to right-hand side. Only things relevant to the lesson be placed on demonstration table.

(v) Before actually starting the demonstration, a clear statement about the purpose of demonstration be made to the students.

(vi) The teacher must make sure that the demonstration-cum-lecture method leads to active participation of the students in the process of learning. This he can achieve by putting well-structured questions.

(vii) The demonstration should be quick and slick and should not appear to linger on unnecessarily.

(viii) The demonstration should be interesting so that it captures the attention of the students.

(ix) The teacher must be sure of success of the experiment to be demonstrated and for this he should rehears the experiment under the conditions prevailing in the class-room. However even after all the necessary precaution the experiment fails in the class-room due to one reason or the other, the teacher should not get nervous, instead he should make an effort to find the reasons for the failure of the experiment. Sometimes in this process a good teacher may draw very useful conclusions.

(x) No complaints about inadequate and faulty apparatus be made by the teacher. In such a situation a good teacher finds an opportunity to show his skill.

(xi) It would be much better if the teacher demonstrates those experiments which are connected with common things which are seen and handled by students in their every-day life.

(xii) There should be a correlation between the demonstrations and the sequence of experiments performed by the students in their practical classes.

(xiii) For active participation of students, the teacher may call individual student, in turn, to help him in demonstration work.

(xiv) During lecture-cum-demonstration session, teacher must act like a 'showman' and a 'performer'. He should know different ways of arresting the attention of the students.

(xv) He should write a summary of the principles arrived at because of demonstration, on the blackboard. The blackboard can also be used for drawing necessary diagrams.

Demonstration Method

We commonly find science teachers making use of

demonstration method for teaching of geography. The conduct of a demonstration lesson is very difficult and here we will try to discuss some of the essential steps that should be followed in a demonstration lesson.

Planning and Preparation. A great care be taken by the teacher while planning and preparing his demonstration lesson. He should keep the following points in mind while preparing his lesson:

(a) subject matter,

(b) questions to be asked;

(c) apparatus required for the experiment

To achieve the above-stated objective the teacher should thoroughly go through the pages of the test book, relevant to the lesson. After this he should prepare his lesson plan in which he should essentially include the principles to be explained, a list of experiments to be demonstrated and the type of questions to be asked from the students. These questions be arranged in a systematic order that has to be followed in the class. Before actually demonstrating the experiment to a class the experiment be rehearsed under the conditions prevailing in the class-room. In spite of this, something may go wrong at the actual lesson, so reserve apparatus is often useful. The apparatus should be arranged in a systematic order on the demonstration table. Thus for the success of demonstration method a teacher has to prepare himself as thoroughly as a bride prepares herself for the marriage.

Introduction of the Lesson. As in every other subject so also in case of geography the lesson should start with proper motivation of the students. It is always considered more useful to introduce the lesson in a problematic way which would make students realise the importance of the topic. The usual ways in which a teacher could easily introduce his lesson is by telling some personal experience or incident, a simple and interesting experiment, a familiar anecdote or by telling a story.

A good experiment when carefully demonstrated is likely to leave an everlasting impression on the young mind of the pupil and it would set his pupils talking in school and out of it, about the interesting experiment that had been demonstrated to them in the geography class. This should be kept in mind not only to start the lesson but be used, on every suitable occasion, during the lesson.

Presentation. The method of presenting the subject-matter is very important. A good teacher should present his lesson in an interesting manner and not in a boring way. To make the lesson interesting the teacher may not be very rigid to remain within the prescribed course rather he should make the lesson as much broad-based as is possible. For widening of his lesson the teacher may think of various useful applications of the principle taught by him. He is also at liberty to take examples and illustrations from other allied branches to make his lesson interesting. The life history and some interesting facts from the life of the great geographer whose name is associated with the topic under discussion can also be cited/to make the lesson interesting. Thus, every effort be made to present the matter in a lively and interesting manner and a lesson should never be presented as 'dry bones' of an academic course. It is also advisable to make use of pictures, posters, diagrams, slides, films, etc. in addition to experiments to illustrate the topic in hand.

Constant questions and answers should form part of every demonstration lesson. Questions and cross questions are essential for properly illuminating the topic being discussed. Questions be arranged in such a way that their answers form a complete teaching unit. Though an effort be made to encourage the students to answer a large number of questions, if students fails to answer some questions teacher should provide the answers to such questions. It is unwise to expect all the answers from the pupil and a teacher should feel satisfied if he has been able to create a desire in a student to know what he does not know.

The lesson be presented in a clear voice and the teacher should speak slowly and with correct pronunciation. He should avoid the use of any bombastic and ambiguous terms. The continuous talk is likely to lead to monotony and to avoid it experiments be well spaced throughout the lesson.

Performance of Experiments. A good observer has been described as a person who has learned to use his senses of touch, sight, smell and hearing in an intelligent and alert manner. We want children to observe what happens in experiments and to have ample opportunities to state their observations carefully. We also want them to try to explain what happens in reference to their problem, but we want to make certain. There is separation between observations and generalization and conclusions.

The following steps are generally accepted as valuable in developing and concluding science experiments with the children;

1. Write the problems to be solved in simple words so that every one understands.
2. Make a list of activities that will be used to solve problems.
3. Gather material for conducting experiments.
4. Work out a format of the steps in the order of procedure so that every one knows what is to be done.
5. The teacher should always try the experiment himself to become acquainted with the equipment and procedure.
6. Record the findings in ways commensurate with the maturity level and purposes of the student.
7. Assist students in making generalisations from conclusions only after sufficient evidence and experiences.

The demonstration experiment be presented by the teacher in a model way. He should work in a tidy, clean and orderly manner while demonstrating an experiment. Some of the important points to be kept in mind while demonstrating an experiment are as under:

(i) Experiments should be simple and speedy

(ii) The experiments must work and their results should be clear and striking.

(iii) Experiments be properly spaced throughout the lesson.

(iv) Keep some reserve apparatus on the demonstration table.

(v) Keep the demonstration apparatus intact till it has to be used again.

Black-board Summary. A summary of important results and principles be written on the blackboard. Use of blackboard should also be frequently made for drawing necessary sketches and diagrams. The blackboard summary should be written in neat, clean and legible way. Since black board summary is an index to a teacher's ability he should keep the following points in mind while writing on black board.

(i) Proper space be left between different letters and words.

(ii) Always start Writing from left hand corner of the black board.

(iii) Start a new line only when the first one has extended across the black board.

(iv) Take care not to divide the words at the end of a time.

(v) Make all efforts to keep all the paragraphs and similar signs in calculations under one another.

(vi) While drawing sketches and diagrams preferably use 'single lined' diagrams.

(vii) All the diagrams drawn on the board be properly labelled.

Supervision. Students be asked to take the complete notes of the blackboard summary including the sketches and diagrams drawn. Such a record will be quite helpful to the student for learning his lesson. Such a summary will prove beneficial only if it has been copied correctly from the blackboard and to make sure that students are copying the blackboard summary properly the teacher should check it by frequently going to the seats of the students.

A summary of common errors committed while delivering a demonstration lesson is given below:

(i) The apparatus may not be ready for use

(ii) There may not be an apparent relation between the demonstration experiment and the topic under discussion.

(iii) Black-board summary is not upto the mark.

(iv) Teacher may be in a hurry to arrive at generalisation without allowing sufficient time to arrive at these generalisation from facts.

(v) Teacher may sometimes fail to ask right type of questions.

(vi) Teacher sometimes may use a difficult language.

(vii) Teacher sometimes takes to talking more which may mar the enthusiasm of the students.

(viii) Teacher may not have allowed sufficient time for recording data, etc.

(ix) Teacher has not given proper attention to supervision.

Following are the merits of this method

(i) It is an economical method as compared to purely student-centred approaches.

(ii) It is a psychological method and students take active interest in teaching-learning process.

(iii) It leads students from concrete to abstract situations and thus is more psychological.

(iv) It is a suitable method if the apparatus to be handled is costly and sensitive. Such an apparatus is likely to damage if handled by students.

(v) This method is safe.

(vi) In comparison to Heuristic method, project, etc. it is time saving but lecture method is too speedy.

(vii) It can be used successfully for all types of students.

(viii) In this method such experiments which are difficult for students can be included.

(ix) This method can be used to impart manual and manipulative skills to students.

Some of the disadvantages of this method are as under:

(i) It provides no scope for 'learning by doing' for students, as students just observe what the teacher is performing. Thus students fail to relish the joys of direct personal experience.

(ii) Since the teacher performs the experiment in his own pace, many students cannot comprehend the concept being clarified.

(iii) Since the method is not child-centred it makes no provision for individual differences. All types of students including slow leaners and genius have to proceed with the same speed.

(iv) It fails to develop laboratory skills in the students. It cannot work as a substitute for laboratory work by students in which they are required to handle the apparatus themselves.

(v) In this method students many a time fail to observe many finer details of apparatus because they observe it from a distance.

It is thoroughly accepted that success is greater with experiments in elementary schools if they start with real purpose, are simple done with uncomplicated apparatus, are done by children under careful direction of the teacher, and help the children think and draw valid tentative conclusion.

This method is considered to be one of the good methods for teaching of geography to secondary classes.

Lecture Method

Lecture method is the most commonly used method of teaching

geography. This method is most commonly followed in colleges and in schools in big classes. This method is not quite suitable to realise the real aim of teaching geography. In lecture method only the teacher talks and students are passive listners. Since the students do not actively participate in this method of teaching so this method is a teacher-controlled and information-centred and in this method teacher works as a sole resource in class-room instructions. Due to lack of participation students get bored and some of them sometimes may go to sleep. In this method students is provided with ready-made knowledge by the teacher and due to this spoon feeding the students loses interest and his power of reasoning and observation get no stimulus.

In this method the teacher goes ahead with the subject matter at his own speed. The teacher may make use of black board at times may also dictate notes. This teacher oriented method in its extreme fqrm does not expect any question or response from the students.

It has the following advantages:

(i) It is quite economical method. It is possible to handle a large number of students at a time and no laboratory, equipment, aids, materials are required.

(ii) Using this method the knowledge can be imparted to the students quickly and the prescribed syllabus can be coverd in a short time.

(iii) It is quite attractive and easy to follow. Using this method teacher feels secure and satisfied.

(iv) It simplifies the task of the teacher as he dominates the lesson for 70-85% of the lesson time and students just listen to him.

(v) Using this method it is quite easy to impart factual information and historical anecdotes.

(vi) By following this method teacher can develop his own style of teaching and exposition.

(vii) In this method teacher can easily maintain the logical sequence of the subject by planning his lectures in advance. It minimises the chances of any gaps or overlappings.

(viii) Some good lectures delivered by the teacher may motivate, instigate, inspire a student for some creative thinking.

The disadvantages of lecture method can be as under:

(i) In this method the students participation is negligible and students become passive recipients of information.

(ii) In this method we are never sure if the students are concentrating and understanding the subject-matter being taught to them by the teacher.

(iii) In this method knowledge is imparted so rapidly that weak students develop a hatred for learning.

(iv) It does not allow all the faculties of the student to develop.

(v) In this method there is no place of 'learning by doing'.

(vi) It does not take into account the previous knowledge of the student.

(vii) It does not provide for corrective feedback and remedial help to slow learners.

(viii) It does not cater to the individual needs and differences of students.

(ix) It does not keep to inculcate scientific attitudes and training in scientific method among the pupils.

(x) It is an undemocratic and authoritarian method in which students depend only on the authority of the teacher. They cannot challenge or question the verdict of the teacher. This checks the development of power of critical thinking and proper reasoning in the student.

After considering various merits and demerits of method it may be concluded that this method may be suitable for teaching in higher classes (XI,XII) where we aim to cover the prescribed syllabus quickly. In these classes this method can be used successfully for imparting factual knowledge, introducing some new and difficult topics, make generalisation from the facts already known to the students, revision of lessons already learnt, etc.

Teaching by this method these students of classes XI and XII will also help those students who intend to join college so that they can prepare themselves for college where lecture method of teaching is a dominant method of imparting instruction.

This method of teaching can be made more beneficial if the teacher encourages his students to take notes during the lesson. After the lesson teacher can give his students some time for asking questions and answer their queries without any hesitation. While delivering his lesson the teacher may see that the lesson is delivered in good tone, loudly and clearly. He should use only simple and understandable words for delivering his lesson. If teacher can introduce some humour in his lesson, it would keep students interested in his lesson.

Project Method

This method was given by Dewey. The American philospher, psychologist and practical teacher. The project method is a direct outcome of his philosophy. According to Dr. Kilpatrick, "A project is a unit of whole-hearted purposeful activity carried on preferably, in its natural setting." According to Stevenson, "A project is a problematic act carried to" its completion in its natural setting." According to Ballard, "A project is a bit of real life that has been incorporated into the school.

The project method is not totally new. Project equivalents are advocated for the adolescent period by Rousseau in Emile (BK-III). A project plan is a modified form of an old method called "concen-tration-of-studies." The main features of "concentration-of-studies plan" is that some subject is takpn as the core or the entre and all other school subjects as they arise are studied in connection with it.

Project method is based on the following principles:

(i) learning by doing.

(ii) learning by living.

(iii) children learn better through association, cooperation and activity.

Various definitions of project have already been considered. A modified definition of project is given by Tomas and Long. They define it as "a voluntary undertaking which involves constructive effort or thought and eventuates into objective results".

Considering various definitions of project we may consider it as a kind of life experience which is an outcome of a craving or desire of the pupils. This is a method of spontaneous and incidental teaching. "Learning by living" may be a better meaning of project method, because life is full of projects and individuals carry out these projects in their every-day life.

The projects may broadly be classified as:

(i) Individual projects, and

(ii) Social projects.

Individual projects are to be carried out by individuals whereas social projects are carried out by a group of individuals.

For completing a project we have five stages in actual practice. These are

(i) Providing a situation

(ii) Choosing and proposing.

(iii) Planning of the project.

(iv) Executing the project.

(v) Judging the project. Recording the project is also essential.

Providing a situation. A project should arise out of a need felt by pupils and it should never be forced on them. It should be purposeful and significant. It should look important and must be interesting. For this the teacher should always be on the look-out to find situation that arise and discuss them with students to discover their interests. Situations may be provided by different methods. Some such methods may include talking to students on the topics of common interest e.g. how did they spend their holidays, what did they see in Delhi, etc.

Choosing and proposing. From various definitions of an educational project we get the same underlying ideas (a) school tasks are to be as real and as purposeful as the tasks of wider life beyond the school walls (b) they ' are of such a nature that the pupil is genuinely eager to carry them out in order to achieve a desirable and clearly realised aim.

According to Kilpatrick, "the part of the pupil and the part of the teacher, in most of the school work, depends largely on who does the proposing". The teacher should refrain from proposing any project otherwise the whole purpose of the method would be defeated. Teacher should only tempt the students for a particular project by providing a situation but the proposal for the project should finally come from students. The teacher must exercise guidance in selection of the project and if the students make an unwise choice, the teacher should tactfully guide them for a better project. The essentials of a good project are:

(i) It should have evident worth for the individual or the group that undertakes them.

(ii) The project must have a bearing on a great number of subjects and the knowledge acquired through it may be applicable in a variety of ways.

(iii) The project should be timely.

(iv) The project should be challenging.

(v) The project should be feasible.

It is for the teacher to see that the purpose of the project is clearly defined and understood.

Planning. The students be encouraged by the teacher to plan out the details of the project. In the process of planning teacher has to act only as a guide and he should give suggestions at times but actual planning be left to the students.

Execution. Once the project has been chosen and the details of the project have been planned, the teacher should help the students in executing the project according to the plan. Since execution of a project is the longest step in the project method so it needs a lot of patience on the part of the students and the teacher. During this step the teacher should carefully supervise the pupils in manipulative skills to prevent waste of materials and to guard accidents. The teacher should assign work to different students in accordance with their tastes, interests, aptitudes and capabilities. Teacher should see that every member of the group gets a chance to do something. Teacher should constantly check up the relation between the chalkedout plans and the developing project and as far as possible 'at the spot' changes and modification be avoided. However if such changes become unavoidable these should be noted and reasons explained for future guidance.

Evaluation. The evaluation of the project should be done both by the pupils and the teacher. The pupils should estimate the qualities of what they have done before the teacher gives his evaluation. The evaluation of the project has to be done in the light of plans, difficulties in the execution and achieved results. Let the students have self criticism and look through their own failings and findings. This step is very useful because as a result of the project, the pupils can know the values of the information, interest, skills and attitudes that have been modified by the project.

Record. A complete record of the project be kept by the students. The record should include everything about the project. It should include the proposal, plan and its discussion, duties allotted to different students and how far were they carried out by them. It should also include the details of places visited and surveyed, maps, etc. drawn, guidance for future and all other possible details.

(i) In project method of teaching the role.of a teacher is that of a guide, friend and philosopher.

(ii) He helps the students in solving their problems just like an elder brother.

(iii) He encourages his students to work collectively, amicably in the group.

(iv) He also helps his students to avoid mistakes.

(v) He makes it a point that each member of the group contributes something to the completion of the project and in this process helps the shy and weaker students to work along with their class mates.

(vi) If the students face failure during execution of some steps of the project the teacher should not execute any portion of the project but should only explain to his students the reasons of their failure and should suggest them some better methods or techniques that may be used by them next time for the success of the project

(vii) During the execution step teacher also learns something.

(viii) Teacher should always remain alert and active during execution, step and see that the project goes to completion successfully.

(ix) During execution of the project teacher should maintain a democratic atmosphere.

(x) Teacher must be well-read and well-informed so that he can help the students to the successful completion of the project.

The merits of project method can be as under:

(i) It is a method of teaching based on psychological laws of learning. The education is related to child's life and he acquires it through meaningful activity.

(ii) It imbibes the spirit of cooperation as it is a cooperative venture. Teacher and students join in the project.

(iii) It stimulates interest in natural as also man-made situations. Moreover the interest is spontaneous and not under any compulsions.

(iv) The method provides opportunities for pupils of different tastes and aptitudes within the framework of the same scheme.

(v) It upholds the dignity of labour.

(vi) It introduces democracy in education.

(vii) It brings about a close correlation between a particular activity and various subjects.

(viii) It is a problem-solving method and places very less emphasis on cramming or memorising.

(ix) It helps to inculcate social discipline through joint activities of the teacher and the taught.

(x) A project can be used to arouse interest in a particular topic as it blends school life with outside world. It provides situations in which the students come in direct contact with their environment.

(xi) It develops self-confidence and sel-discipline.

(xii) A project tends to illustrate the real nature of the subject.

(xiii) A project affords opportunity to develop keenness and accuracy of observation and produces a spirit of enquiry.

(xiv) It puts a challenge to the student and thus stimulates constructive and creative thinking.

(xv) It provides the students an opportunity for mutual exchange of ideas.

(xvi) This method helps the children to organise their knowledge.

The drawbacks of project method can be as under:

(i) Projects require a lot of time.

(ii) Though the method provides the student superficial knowledge of so many things it provides insufficient knowledge of some fundamental principles.

(iii) In the project planning and execution of the project the teacher is required to put in much more work in comparison to other methods of teaching.

(iv) The teacher has been assumed as master of all subjects which is practically not possible.

(v) Good textbooks on these lines have not yet been produced.

(vi) It is an expensive method it involves tours, excursions, purchase of apparatus and equipment etc.

(vii) The method of organising instructions is unsystematised and thus the regular timetable of work will be upset.

(viii) The method may fit those who cannot listen but it is very questionable if it has the same value for those who can listen.

(ix) The method leaves a gap in pupils knowledge.

(x) It underestimates man's power of imagination which enables him to savour the full experience of another without the necessity of undergoing the experience himself.

(xi) Sometimes the projects may be too ambitious and beyond pupil's capacity to accomplish.

(xii) Larger projects in hands of an unexperienced teacher lead to boredom.

(xiii) The education given by projects is likely to emphasise relationships in breadth than in depth.

The project method provides a practical approach to learning of both theoretical and practical problems. If it is difficult to follow this method of teaching it would be better at least not to ignore the spirit of this method.

This method has been found to be more suitable for primary and middle classes and is of restricted use for high and higher secondary classes. This method may be tried alongwith formal class-room teaching without disturbing the school timetable. With this in view some projects may be undertaken by the students to be completed on certain fixed days of a week. Alternately first half of the day may be devoted to class-room teaching and the project work be carried out in the remaining half day. To help solve the problem of fund's shortage such projects be chosen which are self-supporting. As it is not suitable for drill and continuous and systematic teaching, it is not very desirable to use it freely.

6

More Methods

Here are given some projects for a geography class.

Projects for Middle Class Students

(i) Running a shop (vegetable shop or cloth shop, grocer's shop, stationary shop)

(ii) Ploughing the field.

(iii) Running a post office.

(iv) Prepartion of models of houses, means of transport, etc.

(v) Studying the physical features of some area by making a 3-dimensional map, with the help of sand, paper, mache, etc.

Projects for Secondary

(i) Study of life in various parts of the world.

(ii) Preparing sand or clay models of different sections of the various river valleys. The Indus, The Ganges, etc.

(iii) Some mountaineous region scene showing railway line, bridge, cultivated fields, roads and other important features.

(iv) Preparation of economic and distributional maps of local area.

(v) Setting and running a geographical data museum.

(vi) Organisation of excursions and tours.

Inductive Method

In this method one is led from concrete to abstract, particular to general. In this method we prove a universal law by showing that if it is true in a particular case it is also true in other similar cases. Through these illustrations an attempt is made to elicit the new theory of knowledge from the students. This is a psychological and logical method. In this method the teacher should take the following precautions.

(i) He should not cite many examples otherwise the students feel bored.

(ii) The teacher should act patiently and make all possible efforts to elict the information,rules and theories from the students.

(iii) The teacher should encourage the students so as to develop their power of research and discovery.

This method is very useful for teaching of Geography. We have cause and effect relationship and this can be very easily clarified by use of this method.

Illustrations. Say our aim is to teach that in areas near equator, there is a good deal of heat and warmth. To achieve the aim the students be asked in a circle around the fire and an attempt be made to elicit the principle that on equator the sun rays are straight and therefore there is so much of heat. In the absence of any arrangement of fire in school we may draw a picture on blackboard and then elicit the principle with the help of questions.

Using this method an attempt should be made to elicit the principle that on the equator the sun rays are straight and so the place is hot. In the polar region the sun rays are slanting and so there is less of heat.

(i) It helps understanding.

(ii) It is a scientific method.

(iii) It develops scientific attitude.

(iv) It is a logical method and develops critical thinking and habit of keen observations.

(v) It is a physchological method and provides sample scope for students activities.

(vi) It is based on acutal observations, thinking and experimentation.

(vii) It keeps alive the students interest because they move from known to unknown.

(viii) It curbs the tendency to learn by rote and also reduces homework.

(ix) It develops self-confidence.

(x) It develops the habit of intelligent hardwork.

This method suffers from the following limitations

(i) It is limited in range and cannot be used in solving and understanding all the topics in geography.

(ii) The generalisation obtained from a few observations are not the complete study of the topic, to fix the topic in the mind of the learner a lot of supplementary in work and practice is needed.

(iii) Inductive reasoning is not absolutely conclusive. The generalisation has been done from the study of a few (three or four) cases. The process thus establishes certain degree of probability which can be increased by increasing the number of valid cases.

(iv) This method needs a lot of time and energy and thus it is time-consuming and laborious method.

(v) This method is not found to be suitable in higher classes because some of the unnecessary details and explanations may make teaching dull and boring.

(vi) The use of this method should be restricted and confined to understanding the rules in the early stages.

(vii) This method may be considered complete and prefect only if the generalisation arrived at by induction can be verified through deductive method.

Deductive Method

Deductive method is opposite of inductive method. In this method the learner proceeds from general to particular, from abstract to concrete. Thus in this method facts are deduced or analysed by the application of established formula or experimentation. In this case the formula is accepted by the learner as an established fact.

In this method teacher announces the topics of the day and he also gives the relevant formula/rule/law/principle etc. The law/formula is also explained to the students with the help of certain examples which are solved on the blackboard. From these students get the idea of use or application of the concerned law/principle/formula. Then the problems are given to the students who solve the problems following the same method as explained to them earlier by the teacher. Students also memorise the results for future application

Following example illustrates the procedure.

Suppose the teacher has to explain to the students that in the Equitorial regions, it is very hot throughtout the year and in the polar regions it is very cold. The teacher will tell this thing at the very outset. Then contrary to the Inductive Method, he may put forward certain illustrations and then strengthen the knowledge of the students.

This method is not useful in lower classes but is a useful method for the students of higher classes.

1. It is short and time-saving and so this method is liked by authors and teachers.
2. It is a suitable method for lower classes.
3. It glorifies memory because students are required to memorise a large number of laws, formula, etc.
4. For revision of topic it is an adequate and advantageous method.
5. It supplements inductive method and thus completes the process of inductive-deductive method.

6. It enhances speed and efficiency in solving problem.

Limitations

1. It is not a scientific method.
2. It encourages rote memory because pure deductive work requires some law principle, formula for every type of problem and it demands blind memorisation of large number of such laws/formulas, etc.
3. Being an unscientific method it does not impart any training in scientific method.
4. It causes unnecessary and heavy burden on the brain which may sometimes results in brain fag.
5. In this method memory becomes more inportant than understanding and intelligence which is educationally not sound.
6. It is an unpsychological method because the facts and principles are not found by students themselves.
7. In this method student cannot become active learners.
8. It is not suitable for development of thinking, reasoning and discovery.

A careful consideration of merits and limitations of Inductive Method and Deductive Method leads to conclude that Inductive Method is the forerunner of Deductive Method. For effective teaching of Geography both methods are used because none is complete without the other. Inductive Method leaves the learner at a point where he cannot stop and after work has to be done and completed by deductive method. Deduction is a process that is suitable for final statement and Induction is most suitable for exploration fields. Induction gives the lead and deduction follows.

Socratic Method

In this method of teaching geography an effort is made by the teacher to systematize the previous knowledge of the students. For removal of any doubts in the minds of students they are brought on the proper track. Making use of Question-Answers an attempt is made to organise and systematise the previous knowledge of the students. For this the teacher should keep the following points in mind.

1. The curiosity of the students has to be awakened and the interest of the students has to be created in the subject matter of the lesson.
2. An all-out effort has to be made to associate the previous knowledge of the student with their present knowledge.
3. The mental status of student has to be kept in mind while teaching the new subject-matter. The teaching of subject-matter has to be modified in accordance with the requirements of mental status of students.
4. New knowledge has to be strengthened with the help of description, narration and discussion.

This method is quite useful for teaching of geography. This method is quite useful for big classes. While using this method teacher should take utmost care to put only such questions which help him in keeping up the interest of the students.

Textbook Method

In this method geography is taught with the help of textbooks. The relevant pages of the textbook are read by the teacher or he asks some student to read those pages of the textbook to the class. Teacher simultaneously explains the difficult terms, questions, etc.

This is not a psychological and scientific method because it is not possible to impart knowledge by reading the textbook or making the students to read it. It may create an atmosphere of boredom in the class-room and students lose interest in the subject.

Some of the limitations of this method are as under.

1. This method does not employ or use the maxims and principles of education.
2. This method narrows the out-look of students and they become inactive and lethargic. They do not participate actively in the acquisition of knowledge.

3. In this method the scope of revision is very limited and the knowledge acquired by the students is not permanent.

For teaching of geography, like other social sciences, this method is not useful. This method is not useful for imparting the real knowledge of geography. It develops a habit of cramming in the students which hampers the proper knowledge of geography. It is, therefore, advisable not to use this method.

Descriptive Method

In geography we have many such things whose pictures have to be drawn on the minds of students. It can be achieved by description. For this the description has to be vivid and lively. It is thus essential to make the description interesting and attractive. While making oral description an attempt be made to make use of models, charts, etc.

For presentation of geographical facts and for explaining their casual relationship the teacher has to give vivid description and present illustrations. Such a description is essential for awakening the power of imagination of students.

The description may be given in the form of a story, description of a travel, dialogue, etc. Finally an attempt be made to draw the substance so that the students have a thorough knowledge. While using this method teacher should not try to go very much in detail. Teacher should also encourage his students to actively participate in description and they be given enough opportunities to give vent to their feelings. Description should invariably be in simple language and lucid style. Teacher should never forget his basic aim of description is to draw a picture of the things in the mind of the students.

A list of topics that can be taught easily by descriptive method is given below

(i) Agriculture

(ii) Food habits, dresses, living conditions of people of different countries and geographical regions.

(iii) Water and rivers.

(iv) Living and working conditions of the workers of various industries.

(v) Markets and the description of various products manufactured in different places.

(vi) Geographical description of the discoveries of various regions.

(vii) The life of animals, mineral and natural wealth of different regions.

(viii) Description of mines, etc. and their working conditions.

(ix) Geographical environment.

An effort be made by the teacher to correlate the description with human life because it is only through such a correlation that the real purpose of geography teaching shall be served.

Story-telling Method

It is also known as *Narrative method* or descriptive method. In this method geographical facts are presented in the form of a story. In this method it is not possible to impart the element of character, plot, style, etc. which characterise any literary story. Moreover, it is not possible to present the entire perspective of human life in these stories. Because of these limitations this method is quite descriptive and narrative. Following types of stories may be narrated in teaching of geography.

(i) Stories depicting the life of people of various countries.

(ii) Stories connected with the animals and geographical environment of different countries.

(iii) Stories of different discoveries such as Columbus, Vasco de Gama, etc.

(iv) Stories of travels and excursions.

(v) Stories about conquest of man over nature.

(vi) Stories concerning human activities in the background of geographical factors.

Some educationists are quite apprehensive of the utility of this method for teaching of geography. In their opinion when the undeveloped minds are told the stories connected with the life of foreign countries they may not be able to grasp them entirely. Thus the stories and the knowledge contained them have little or no utility in such a case.

This method is quite useful for students of primary classes where we do not teach the geography of the world or of foreign countries. In lower classes we teach the geography of our country or the state.

Political Method

It is also known *as patriotic or Single country method of* teaching of geography. In this method the teaching of geography of any one particular country is undertaken. All the details of its lands, situations, natural conditions, climate, agricultural products, vegetation, etc. are discussed. The description of all these things is based on geographical factors of that particular country. When the description of one country is completed, we take up the description of another country. Thus, the geography of the whole world is taught in parts and countries.

Some educationists doubt the utility of this method. In their view the knowledge about one country given in isolation has little or no bearing on teaching of geography of the world. Moreover, in this method political condition of a particular country are not stressed. This method is not very psychological and scientific.

(i) This method is expensive.

(ii) This method is time-consuming.

Regional Method

Till the middle of twentieth century geography was taught on the basis of political divisions but now it has been replaced by regional method of teaching of geography. Now we take different countries with common physical features, climate, mineral wealth, economic progress, etc. at a time and study them together. In this method countries with common geographical features are studied together. It was Herbertson who gave impetus to this method by dividing the whole world into broad climatic regions. Now-a-days the natural regions method is more common and has become a universal method of teaching of regional geography of the world or of an individual country or a continent.

For his classification Herbertson used the criterion of climate and vegetation which means that all geographical factors have been taken into eonsideration but there is ample scope for modification of Herbertson's classification.

It is possible that natural regions may be different from political regions. In words of Prof. Macnee, *"The Regional Method of Teaching of geography is then, a method in which the area studied is divided into natural regions, each of which is studied separately".*

The most common procedure of this method is as under:

Location, structure, relief, drainage system and climate are considered first in the serial order and the students are told the biogeography of the region. Later on the distribution of minerals and their exploitation in the development of industries are studied. It is then followed by a study of population distribution, means of transport and communication, location of towns, etc. The region is then studied in comparison to other regions of the world.

Advantages of Regional Method of Teaching Geography. According to Prof. E.A. Macnee, "The chief advantage of Regional Method is that it is the quickest way of getting pupils to grasp the salient features of the geography of any area. No other method can give so quick a start or so sound a basis for furthur study."

Some merits of this method are:

(i) It is scientific, orderly and systematic method.

(ii) It provides a better understanding of geography and economics on time and energy.

(iii) It prepares the child to pursue independent study of geography which is very useful in individual method of teaching.

(iv) It correlates physical, natural, social, economic and other phases of man's life.

(v) It helps the child to understand the environment.

(vi) It helps to develop the power of observation, imagination and reasoning.

(vii) It broadens the vision of the child and helps him to understand the difference between man and man. Such an understanding is very useful for international understanding.

Limitation

(i) The boundaries of natural regions are not very clearly defined and one region therefore merges into another.

(ii) Sometimes we miss the smaller region while paying full attention to the broader regions. In this way a very vital point is neglected.

(iii) It is not possible to have a final division an regional basis.

If the world as a whole is to be studied then it be done through regions and if any part of world is to be studied it then it be studied under various heads such as structure, relief, climate, etc. already discussed.

After reading the regional geography of 2 or 3 countries the students be asked to take up an independent study of some other contries with the help of a good atlas. The regional method lends itself to independent study and it can be resorted to individual methods of teaching.

While studying by this method the following order of regions may be followed:

(i) Arctic regions and hot regions.

(ii) Tropical Forests and monsoon lands.

(iii) Mid-latitude grass lands.

(iv) Regions of Mediterranean climate.

(v) Mid-latitude forests.

Human Method

In this method man and human life occupies a very important place. In human geography we are concerned with the study of the progress made by man through his efforts and labour. This method is based on study of cause and effect relationship. Physical features and physical environments have a profound effect on man. In this method of teaching man is studied in relation to his geographical environment.

We have to allow for concession for freedom of human activities in study of human geography because human activities are not rigidly controlled by cause and effect relationship. The remarks of Prof. Macnee in this regard are quite correct. He remarked, "Geography is not a mere recital of unrelated facts. Most geographical facts are related to other geographical facts and it is the business of geography to elucidate these relations. In geography teaching, therefore cause and effect should be traced whenever possible and in particular the influence of physical and biological factors on human life."

Comparative Method

In this method students are encouraged to compare various geographical features. To start with, students are asked to know about the geographical features of their neighbourhood and then make a comparison with the features of city and village. They may then be asked to make a comparison of geographical features of a country with those of the other country. In this way the knowledge gained gets stabilised and it becomes permanent. In this method teacher is at liberty to proceed from known to unknown. The students, precious knowledge may be compared with the new knowledge acquired by him. This method is quite useful in assimilation of ideas.

The comparison may be carried out not only of the physical features of one region with those of another but for comparison purpose we can include the products and other things of one particular region and make a comparison of these things of the other region. In the words of Prof. Macnee, "Psychologists have emphasised the important part played in the assimilation of new ideas by the existing content of the mind. The mind tends to interpret the new in terms of the old. It is well, therefore, for the teacher, wherever possible to bring the new ideas which he wishes to present into relation with the previous experiences of the pupils; in other words, to track new knowledge on to old. This is the psychological basis for pedagogical maxim; 'proceed from known to unknown':"

While explaining the method he furthur remarked, "prompted by this ideas the framers of geography courses usually begin the primary courses with things that are familiar to the pupils, the school building and grounds, the village, the local river, the nearest railway line. From the pupils' home and from the things that he can see with his own eyes his geographical knowledge is extended outwards of the districts, state country and continent."

This method is not very useful in lower classes but is of great value for teaching geography in higher classes. Writing about the method Prof. B.C. Wallis has rightly remarked, "comparisons and contracts are the essence of geography teaching at senior stage."

This approach along with that of gaming approach have been added recently in the teaching methodology simulation or analogue is different from real world but it presents significant features of real world in order to make a worthwhile study. In this approach the processes or conditions or situations are re-enacted so as to indicate the basic structures and significant features. It motivates the students in the learning process and help him in making decisions. This approach can be usefully employed to teach mineral resources, location of industries, new towns, growth centres, etc.

This approach is quite similar to project method but differs from it in duration, planning and execution.

In view of the modern educationists, assignment is a well-planned learning situation created by the teacher. The objective of an assignment is to provide the pupil a direct, first hand and stimulating learning experience. The timing of assignment, duration and frequency will depend upon the purpose of assignment. An assignment should be specific and flexible. It is possible to classify the assignments under various heads. Some of these are as under:

(i) Assignments that aim at developing basic skills like using a textbook, a reference book, etc.

(ii) Problem-solving assignments. Such assignments aim at development of power of thinking and imagination.

(iii) Assignments on experiments and observations.

(iv) Assignments on making and handling tools.

(v) Assignments on map making, map reading and map interpretation.

(vi) Assignments for development of attitude leading to national integration and international understanding.

In the previous pages a number of methods of teaching geography have been discussed. Some of them have been recommended for use, some have been disapproved and some have been recommended for use with caution. Out of the methods available a choice is not entirely left to the whimes of the teacher but has to be made by the teacher in the light of the facilities available and nature of work to be done. It does not mean that a teacher may select any one method and then cling to it lavisihiy throughout his service or even an entire academic session. This is a great mistake because each method has its own merits. Our preference for any one method deprives us of the merits of other method. A good teacher should therefore try to imbibe the good qualities of all methods instead of depending on any one method. The teacher should keep himself on the right side of every method. The best method of a teacher is his own individualised and personalised method which is the result of his varied and long experience in teaching some of the points which a teacher must keep in mind are as follows:

(i) Heuristic approach be used to start a lesson. Thus the lesson be introduced in a problematic way so that the students feel that they are going to learn something really useful and worth learning.

(ii) He should choose a pupil dominated method in preference to a teacher dominated method.

(iii) He should have a bright manner of presentation and should illustrate his lesson with experiments, pictures, charts, diagrams etc. specimens and models are preferred for illustration.

(iv) Teaching should be made a cooperative enterprise. Teacher should give maximum opportunity of participation to the students so that they feel that their active participation is quite important for the solution of problem and successful growth of the subject.

(v) Teacher should make all possible efforts to properly correlate the topic in hand with other subjects.

(vi) Teacher should avoid the use of difficult phrases, expressions and lengthy definitions.

(vii) Though Heuristic approach dominates yet the historical method of teaching be utilized at places and the lives and achievements of famous geographers be told to the students. These are a source of inspiration to the students.

(viii) Instructional method and plans must be flexible. In a lesson if, in addition to planned illustrations and experiments students want some more experimental evidence then the teacher should make all possible efforts to satisfy the students.

(ix) After a constant use of some method, teacher can break the monotony by using project method and laboratory method.

Thus we conclude that no single method could be the best method and a good teacher will have to evolve his own individual method consisting ,of good points of all the methods. He will never become a slave to any method and will remain a true master of all of them.

With the development of the subject-matter and the knowledge of Geography, various methods have evolved and are being employed to impart its knowledge to the students. Teacher has to employ these methods, keeping in view the psychological requirements of the students. Students of different stages have different psychological requirements and so the method of teaching has to be modified accordingly.

1. Socratic Method or Question-Answer Method.
2. Inductive Method.
3. Deductive Method.
4. Lecture Method.
5. Text-Book Method.
6. Descriptive Method.
7. Observation Method.
8. Story-Telling Method.
9. Political Method of teaching of Geography.
10. Regional Method of teaching of Geography.
11. Human Method of teaching of Geography.
12. Comparative Method of teaching of Geography.
13. Project Method.
14. Dalton (plan) Method of teaching of Geography.
15. Laboratory Method of teaching of Geography.
16. Excursion Method of teaching of Geography.

• In this method of teaching of Geography, the teacher tries to systematize the previous knowledge of the students. The previous knowledge of the students is disorganised and scattered. By removing the doubts of the students, an attempt is made to bring them to the proper track. By questions and answers an attempt is made to organise and systematise knowledge of the students. In this regard, the teacher has to bear the following things in mind :

(a) The curiosity of the students as to be awakened and the interest of the student has to be created in the subject-matter of the lesson.

(b) A serious attempt has to be made to associate the previous knowledge of the student with their present knowledge. In other words, on the basis of the previous knowledge of the student, the new subject-matter has to be taught.

(c) The mental status of the student has to be borne in mind which teaching the new subject-matter. With the requirements of the mental status of the students, the teaching of the subject-matter has to be modified and organised.

(d) By description, narration and discussion, the new knowledge is strengthened.

This method may be useful in Geography, because here, an attempt is made to provide new knowledge to the students in the background of the previous knowledge. This is possible through question-answer method and it is the Socratic Method. In the classes this method can be more useful. While using this method, the teacher has to be very cautious. He has to put only those questions that shall be useful for keeping up the interest of the students.

• In this method, in order to find out a new theory of a new piece of knowledge, certain illustrations are given. Through these illustrations, an attempt is made to elicit-the new theory of knowledge from the students. Here an attempt is made to proceed from particular to general. From this point of view, this theory is quite Psychological and logical.

In order to use this theory successfully and scientifically, the teacher has to take the following precautions :

(a) The teacher should not give many examples. The example should be limited, so that the students may not get bored.

(b) The teacher should try to act patiently and try to elicit the rules and the theories from the students.

(c) The students should be encouraged so that their power of research and discovery may develop. With the help of the question, they may be encouraged to reach the desired goal.

This method is very useful for the teaching of Geography. We have cause and effect relationship. Through this method, this thing can be very easily carried out. An example will clarify it.

Suppose the student are to be taught that in the areas near equator, there is a good deal of heat and warmth. This may be taught with the help of the following examples :

The students should be asked to sit in a circle around the fire. Questions should be asked and attempt should be made to elicit the principle that on the equator the sun rays are straight and therefore there is so much of heat.

It is quite possible that there may not be arrangement of fire in the class room. In that case a picture may be drawn on the blackboard and, with the help of the questions, principle may be elicited. It is easy to draw a chart on the blackboard. This thing will facilitate the teaching.

While employing this method, the psychological requirements of ths students should always be borne in mind. An attempt should be made to elicit the principle that on the Equator the sun rays are straight and so the place is hot. On the other in the Polar regions the sun rays are slanting and so there is less of heat.

• In this method, first of all, the principle is enunciated. Then, on the basis of several illustrations, the principle is clarified. It is quite possible to enunciate various other acts on the basis of these principles. It may be done with the help of the following illustrations :—

Suppose the teacher has to explain to the students that in the Equatorial regions it is very hot throughout the year and in the Polar regions it is very cold. The teacher may tell this thing at the very outset. Then, contrary to the Inductive Method, he may put forward certain illustrations and then strengthen the knowledge of the students.

This method is not useful for the students of the lower classes. But for the students of the higher classes this method is very useful.

• This method is useful for the students of the higher classes. It may be employed in higher secondary, and university classes. In this method, the teacher, by lecture, tries to explain the facts to the students. He encourages the students to acquire knowledge and employ the acquired knowledge in life.

While delivering a lecture the teacher should determine the mental age and psychological requirements of the students. He should use such language which is intelligible to the students. But in practice it is not possible to do this.

This method is considered to be unpsychological. It is not considered scientific either. People have not favoured the use of this method in Junior High School classes and Secondary classes.

• In text book method, an attempt is made; to teach Geography with the help of the text books. The teacher takes to the reading of the text book or asks the students to read the text book. He goes on explaining the difficult and the complicated questions.

This method is also not considered psychological and scientific. It is not possible to impart knowledge by reading the text book or making the students to read it. This creates an atmosphere of boredom in the class room and the students lose interest in the subject-matter.

Text book method bristles with the following drawbacks :—

(a) The maxims and principles of education are not employed and used in this method.

(b) In this method the outlook of the students becomes narrow. They become inactive and lethargic. They do not take active part in the acquisition of knowledge.

(c) In this method there is very little scope for the revision of the subject-matter taught. The knowledge that is acquired by the students does not become permanent. In teaching Geography, like other social sciences, this method is not very useful.

Sometimes teachers try to give a substance of a lesson taught. By this substance, the students try to learn the subject-matter.

This method may be useful for the students in their case, but it is not useful for the real knowledge of Geography. The students develop the habit of cramming. The exercise of *Rote Memory* hampers the proper knowledge of Geography. It is, therefore, advisable not to use this method.

• In Geography, there are many such things whose picture has to be drawn on the minds of the students. This can be done only through description. The description has to be very vivid and lively. Only then the complete picture shall be imprinted. It is, therefore, very necessary, rather essential, to make the description interesting and attractive. While presenting oral illustration, models, charts, etc, may also be employed.

While presenting the geographical facts and trying to explain their causal relationship, the teacher has to present illustrations and give vivid description. With the help of this description, it is possible to awaken the power of imagination of the students.

This description may be in the form of story, description of a travel, dialogue, etc. In the end an attempt should be made to draw the substance so that the students may have a thorough knowledge. While employing descriptive method, the teacher should not try to go very much in detail. An attempt should be made to encourage the students to take part in this description. They should also be given an opportunity to give vent to their own ideas. Description should invariably be in simple language and lucid style. It should always be kept in mind that main aim of the description is to draw a picture of the things in the mind of the students.

The following subjects can be taught easily through descriptive method:—

(a) Agriculture.

(b) The food habits, dress and living conditions of the people-of different countries and geographical regions.

(c) Water and rivers.

(d) Living and working conditions of the workers of various industries.

(e) Market and the description of various things manufactured in different places.

(f) Geographical description of the discoveries of different regions.

(g) The life of the animals, minerals and the natural wealth.

(h) Description of the mines and such other things and their conditions.

(i) Geographical environment.

The teacher should try to connect the description with the human life. Then only the real purpose of the teaching of Geography shall be served.

• While going about to several places, the students get an opportunity to observe and see things for themselves. If the students are given an opportunity to acquire knowledge of Geography by observing things themselves, the knowledge shall be stable and shall have a practical value. The knowledge acquired through this method is complete, clear and perfect. Such a knowledge has practical value as well.

The students in the lower classes may be asked to observe geographical things in their environment, near their homes, villages and such other places. They may be asked to collect the geographical data after observation. This will give the students an opportunity to collect the geographical knowledge and data.

Observation method is useful for the teaching of the following branches of Geography :–

(a) Natural or Physical Geography, which includes mineral wealth, vegetation, production, trade, commerce, industry etc.

(b) Commercial Geography which includes crops, animals, methods of irrigation and such other things.

This method requires the following things :—

(a) The teacher should have properly observed and seen the things that he expects the students to observe. Unless the teacher has a thorough knowledge of it, it shall not be possible for him to impart scientific knowlege to his students.

(b) The observation should be accompanied by the collection of the necessary data.

This method has the following difficulties :—

(a) Sometimes when the teacher takes the students out, he has to tackle the problem of discipline as well. (b) It is not possible to observe things that are situated at a long distance (c) Sometimes it is difficult to get the permission of the guardians to take the students out for observation.

In spite of all these difficulties, the method of observation can be very successful in the teaching of Geography. As and when the circumstances permit, the subject must be taught properly through this method.

• This method is sometimes also called Narrative Method or Descriptive Method. It is based very much on the geographical background. Geographical facts are presented in the form of a story. It is not possible to impart the element of character, plot, style etc, in Story Telling Method of Geography. These elements are the special characteristics of literary stories. It is also not possible to present the entire perspective of human life in these stories, as it is possible in the case of historical stories. On account of these limitations the Story Telling Method of teaching of Geography is very much descriptive and narrative. Stories of Geograptey may be of the following type :—

(a) Stories connected with the life of the people of various countries.

(b) Stories connected with the animals and geographical environment of different countries.

(c) Stories of different discoveries such as Columbus, Vasco-de-Gama etc.

(d) Stories of travels and excursions.

(e) There may be stories about conquest of man over nature.

(f) There may also be stories concerning human activities in the background of geographical factor.

Some educationists have expressed grave doubts about the utility of this method in the teaching of Geography. They are of the view that when undeveloped minds are told the stories connected with the life of foreign countries, then it is not possible for them to grasp them entirely. In the absence of understanding, these stories and the knowledge contained therein is of very little utility.

In spite of all the criticism put forward against this method, it cannot be denied that Story Telling Method is useful for the teaching of Geography in lower classes. In lower classes we do and have to teach Geography of the world or foreign country. In these classes we teach Geography of our own country or the State. Under such circumstances the stories shall not go a waste.

• This is also called the patriotic or single country method of teaching of Geography. In this method we take up one particular country and give a detailed description of its lands, situation, natural condition, climate, agricultural products, vegetation, natural and mineral wealth, industry, means of communication, administration, economic progress, etc. The description of all things is based on geographical factors of that particular country. In this method we take each one by one. Once we have finished description of particular country, we take up another country. Thus the Geography of the whole world is taught in parts and countries.

Some educationists have expressed grave doubts about the utility of this method. They put forward the argument that knowledge of one country when given in isolation has very little bearing on the teaching of Geography of the whole world. It cannot be denied that Geographical features of different countries are sometimes same and similar. In this method of teaching of Geography, very little stress is laid on the political conditions of that particular country. On account of this drawback, this method is not very psychological and scientific.

This method is expensive and time-consuming. While teaching Geography of different countries several things have to be repeated again and again. Things that a student has learned while learning the Geography of a particular country, are repeated again while reading Geography of the other country. This repetition sometimes leads to boredom and the students lose interst in reading.

• Sometimes the Geography was taught on the basis of political division. Now that method has been replaced,by the Regional method of teaching of Geography. Now we take different countries with common physical features, climate, mineral wealth, economic progress etc. at a time and study them together. In this method countries with common geographical features are studied together. Different regions have certain common features and certain contrasting features. It is possible that a natural region may be different from political region. In Regional Method countries with common Geographical features are treated as one unit. In the words of *Prof. Macnee,* "The Regional Method of Teaching of Geography is then, a method in which the area studied is divided into natural regions, each of which is studied separately."

This method of teaching of Geography has certain advantages. Prof. E. A. Macnee has written:—

"The chief advantage of the Regional Method is that it is the quickest way of getting pupils to grasp the salient features of the Geography of any area. No other method can give so quick a start or so sound a basis for further study."

The following are the chief merits of regional method—

1. This method is scientific, orderly and systematic.
2. It gives a better understanding of geography and economics on time and energy.

3. It deals the children to pursue independent study of geography and proves very useful in individual method of teaching.

4. This method correlates the physical, natural, social, economic and other phases of man's life. It helps the children to understand the drama of man being played upon the stage of nature.

5. It helps the child understand the environment, physical as well as natural and social. Therefore, it is uniformity with the modern conception of geography.

6. The method is based on casual relations therefore it develops the facilities of observation, imagination and reasoning. It is educative in itself.

7. It broadens the vision of children. They understand the differences in man and men. Various regions are scattered over the whole world in patches but the life over the whole region is similar inspite of political barriers. This understanding gives international understanding to the children.

This method has certain limitations as well. The boundaries of the natural regions are not very exactly defined and so one region merges into another. Secondly, it is possible that, while paying attention to broader regions, we may miss the smaller regions and neglect a very vital point. Thirdly, it is not possible to have a final division on the regional basis. There may be regions on the basis of different physical features such as climate, land etc.

In order to have a proper study of Geography, it was Herbertson who introduced this method. He divided the whole world into different regions. These regions were based on certain common natural features. Since that time, this method is being used and utilised.

For utilising the method of the teaching of Geography, the whole world is divided into different regions on the basis of the following features—

(a) The region of study.

(b) Its situation and its longitude and latitude.

(c) Area.

(d) Physical features.

(e) Climate.

(f) Vegetation.

(g) Mineral wealth and natural resources.

(h) Human and economic wealth.

• In this method of teaching Geography man and human life occupies a very important places. In Human Geography we study the progress made by man through his efforts and labour. In this method we always have an eye on the cause and effect relationship. Man is very much influenced by Physical features and Physical environment. In dealing with Geography through this method we study man in relation to his Geographical environment. In fact, the human being occupies the central figures in the study of Geography through this method.

While studying Human Geography, we study the contribution made by man in the development of cities, various industries, means of transport and communication, business and other economic activities.

In Human Geography we have to give concession for freedom of human activities. Human activities are not rigidly governed by cause and effect relationship. They have some element of freedom in them. It is quite possible that one group of human beings may act differently in comparison to the other group of human beings. This fact has to be kept in mind while studying causal relationship in Geography. Prof. Macee has, in this regard, very correctly remarked :

"Geography is not a mere recital of unrelated facts. Most geographical facts are related to other geographical facts and it is the business of Geography to elucidate these relations. In Geography teaching, therefore, cause and effect should be traced wherever possible and in particular the influence of physical and biological factors on human life."

• In this method of teaching of Geography, the students are encouraged to compare various Geographical features. In the beginning they are asked to know about the Geographical features of their neighbourhood and then compare these features with the features of city and village. The teacher of Geography may also compare the Geographical features of a particular country with the geographical features of other countries. This Comparative Method is helpful in making the knowledge stable and permanent. In this method the teacher may proceed from known to unknown. The student must be having some knowledge. This knowledge may be compared with the new knowledge and it would provide them with an opportunity to strengthen their experiences. In the words of Prof. Macnee, this method is useful for assimilation of new ideas.

In this method it is possible to compare not only the physical features of one region with the other but also the products and other things of one particular region with that of the other. In the words of Prof. Macnee, "Psychologists have emphasised the important part played in the assimilation of new ideas by the existing content of the mind. The mind tend to interpret the new in terms of the old. It is well, therefore, for the teacher, wherever possible to bring the new ideas which he wishes to present into relation with the previous experiences of the pupils ; in other words, to track new knowledge on to old. This is the psychological basis for the pedagogical maxim ; 'proceed from the known to unknown'."

Explaining the method employed here, he has remarked, "Prompted by this idea the framers of Geography courses usually begin the primary course with things that are familiar to the pupils, the school building and grounds, the village, the local river, the nearest railway line. From the pupil's home and from the things that he can see with his own eyes his geographical knowledge is extended outwards of the districts. State, country and continent."

This Method is not very useful in lower classes but it can be of great use and value for teaching Geography in higher classes. Prof. B. C. Wallis has rightly remarked :

"Comparisons and Contracts are the essence of Geography-teaching at senior stage."

• We all know that in Project Method, the students are given certain projects and problems. They carry out these projects and solve the problems and learn Geography. Students are encouraged to fulfil their projects in the background of natural settings. The teacher has very little to do. He formulates the directions and directs the students to go on that path. He encourages the students to take independent activities. Students have a good deal of freedom to complete this pioject.

The project may be of an individual or collective type. In individual projects the students have to do the work independently but in collective projects it is the group of the students that has to fulfil the task.

In Project Method the teacher has to draw up the project well in advance. He has to be an imaginative and competent sort of person. These projects, have to differ in accordance with the mental status of the students. For the students of the lower classes the projects shall be of a simple nature and for the students of the higher classes the projects shall be difficult ones.

The Project Method has the following advantages—

1. The students have a clear picture of the project and the aims and they continue to work accordingly.
2. In this method, there is a good deal of activity and so the knowledge is founded on solid base.
3. Since the students have to work in realistic circumstances, they develop an attitude of realism.
4. In projects, the students get a pragmatic education. They learn various things with reference to their utility in life and so they acquire a pragmatic attitude towards life.
5. Since the projects have a bearing on life, the students also develop an attitude of interest for life.

6. Students have a good deal of freedom in this method. They continue to work independently and so the originality of the students develops.

Every Project has the following steps to be followed :

1. Dialogue to talking,
2. Manual work or handicraft,
3. Project and study,
4. Drawing of the outline of the project.

A project may deal with any of the aspects of life.

The students may he asked to draw a chart for record of the weather, they may be asked to draw a model of the map of the district or the State, they may also be asked to run the farm of the school successfully and they may also be asked to draw a model of the railway station.

• This is plan of the teaching of Geography which tries to encourage the students to take to self study or independent study. In fact, this method was first introduced by Miss Helen, a teacher ot America. She had the idea of training the students in discipline and co-operation.

In this method the whole lessen is divided into certain parts. The students are supposed to complete certain parts in a specified period. The students are free to divide their time for the study. The teacher is there to direct and guide. He encourages the consultation as and when required.

In this method there are no class-rooms. Class-rooms are like Laboratories and they are also termed so. In these laboratories, the students carry out their work. They are free to carry out the work independently.

Prof. J.E. Parkinson has laid down certain directions and plans in this regard.

(i) In one plan, he expects the students to draw two maps, depicting the climate of India. He expects the students to plot the lines of temperature showing 80°, 75°, 60° and 55° in the month of

January and 90°, 85° and 80° in July. These two lines are to be ploted separately.

(ii) Which parts of India are extremely cold and extremely hot ? Explain with causes.

(iii) What is the temperature of Delhi, Madras, Shikarpur and Lahore in the months of January and July ?

Similarly, other plans may also be drawn and the students may be asked to learn Geography through this method.

• In this method of teaching of Geography, the subject is taught like a science subject. Certain experiments are carried out in a laboratory like Geography room. The teacher may demonstrate any experiment and the students shall try to follow it. The rainfall may be called and measured. The teacher may do so with the help of an apparatus. The students may be asked to observe it and try to repeat the performance. The students may also be encouraged to do the work independently.

The knowledge that is acquired by draw out conclusions and finding out results is really stable and useful in future life. Students may also be asked to draw charts, models, maps etc. They may also be encouraged to find out the direction with the help of the compass. The revolution and the rotation of the earth may also be explained with the help of demonstration.

• In teaching of Geography excursions occupy an important place. In excursions and travels, the students get an opportunity to observe and see things by themselves. In fact, excursions are a part and parcel of observation method. It shall not be improper to call the excursion method a projection of observation method. In excurisions the students acquire the practical knowledge. Educationists have laid down that excursions should be formed a part of the teaching of Geography since the early stages. In lower classes students have a good deal of time and so it is possible to plan excursions. The excursions should begin from the observation of the hills and valleys that are situated in the neighbourhood of the school. This may go on the observation of the things of higher importance.

Excursions have the greatest advantage of breaking the monotony of the class-room. In class-room the students have to read the subject in a monotonous atmosphere for a number of days. Once they come out of the class-room, they find a change and this change is helpful in strengthening the interest of the students in the subject-matter of Geography.

In higher secondary classes when the students have developed mentally and physically and are competent enough to know about the responsibilities, they may be taken out on long excursions. James Fairgrieve has very rightly summed up the importance of this method in the following words—

"More Geography is learned by feet rather than head."

While the students are on excursions, the teacher should provide them with an opportunity to express their views about the things observed. This would also develop their power of expression. Before expressing a thing, a person has to organise his thoughts. Excursions would also help in this direction.

The excursions should not be very long. Excursions should invariably be limited and properly planned. Maximum attempts should be made to make proper use of the time. Utility of the time should not spoil the interest of the students in the subject-matter.

While the students are on excursion, they should be encouraged to take down the notes of the things that they have observed. This is possible in higher classes and higher secondary classes. Students should be encouraged to carry note books and pencils with them.

It may not be possible for the students of lower classes to take down notes but for the students of higher classes it shall not be difficult.

It is advisable to divide the whole class of students into groups. Each group may be asked to observe a particular aspect of nature of geographical environment. Then these groups may be asked to exchange notes. This exchange of notes would encourage the students to acquire knowledge independently and in a more scientific manner.

After having completed the training or excursion, the students should be encouraged of study all those things in the maps. This would strengthen their knowledge and encourage them to proceed from concrete to abstract. Students should also be encouraged to write out in detail what they have seen in excursion.

The students should also be encouraged to make certain collections while on excursion. Those pieces collected by the students should be lodged in the Geography museum. The lot would also enrich the. Geography museum Prof, E. A. Macnee have described the importance of this method of teaching of Geography the following words : –

"It is essential that the foundation of Geographical knowledge shall be laid in the field. No amount of reading from books can' make up for a practical knowledge gained by looking at the earth which the child is studying. It follows that from the very early stages expeditions should form part of Grography."

This method can be successful only when the teacher himself is fond of excursions and is prepared to take out the students on expeditions and excursions in a scientifically planned manner.

The teacher should also be well aware of the requirements and' difficulties of an excursion. He should be prepared to face them. Only them it is possible for him to work out this method sucessfully.

Salient Features

1. Teaching of Geography is carried out through several methods. Following are the important methods that are employed for the successful teaching of Geography.
2. Socratic method, in other words the question-answer method. Here attempt is made to impart new knowledge on the basis of previous knowledge.
3. In Inductive Method certain illustrations are given and then an attempt is made to elicit the new theory or principle out of the students.

4. Descriptive Method of teaching of Geography attempts at presenting a de-scription of the thing before the students. Certain subject-matters of Geography, such as agriculture, market etc., can easily be taught through this method.

5. In Observation Method the students are encouraged to observe things by themselves. This method involves certain difficulties.

6. Lecture Method of teaching of the Geography is useful for the teaching of Geography to higher classes. Here the teacther tells the lectures and the students try to grasp them. This method makes the students inactive.

7. Text Book Method implies that the teacher students shall read the text book and impart to the students the knowledge of Geography. This method is also not very scientific.

8. In Story-telling Method the subject-matter of Geography is presented before the students in form of stories. The stories deal with various aspects of geographical environment.

9. Political Method of teaching of Geography various political divisions or countries of the world are taken up one by one and their Geography is studied. Till very recently this method was very popular.

10. Regional Method of teaching of Geography implies that the countries having common Physical and Geographical features and shall be studied together. The whole of the world has been divided into certain physical regions.

11. Human Method of teaching of Geography keeps human being as the centre of study. This method is more concerned with the human activities than other things.

12. Comparative Method of teaching of Geography provides opportunity to the students to compare things of one particular region or place with the things of other regions or place. This gives a solid foundation to the knowledge of Geography.

13. Project Method of teaching of Geography gives the students certain projects and the students have to fulfil them.

14. In Dalton Plan the Geography is taught like other subjects. The lesson is divided into certain parts and the students are left free to carry out the plan.

15. Laboratory Method of teaching of Geography or Scientific Method of teaching of Geography implies that the Geography shall be taught like a science subject. In this method the Geography room is treated as a laboratory or a science room where practical experiments are carried out and students learn Geography.

16. Excursions form an integral part of the teaching of Geography. Excursion Method not only provides the students with an opportunity to observe things by themselves but it also provides them with an opportunity to organise their knowledge.

Man is constantly acquiring new experiences. With his development in the world, he tries to gain new experiences. In this method of education, the natural experiences of child form the basis of education. Here the teacher has to proceed on the basis of the experiences acquired by the young men in the modern would of education this method occupies an important place. It is supposed to be more scientific and psychological as compared to other methods of education.

In India basic education has acquired the status of national pattern of education, specially at the primary stage. As we all know, it is craft centred method of education. Here the students are encouraged to do things by their own hands and thus acquire knowledge. This method of education is very much akin to basic education. The two can go together to a great extent.

Combination of theoretical knowledge and practical life. In life we acquire theoretical knowledge. This theoretical knowledge shall be of no use if it cannot be put into practical use. In fact, theory and practice have to go together. Learning by doing is the basis of the logical method of teaching. The students are made to learn by practical experiences. They have to work according to a set pattern. A project is drawn and the whole project is divided into smaller projects. The teacher of Geography provides the knowledge of the subject to the students with the help of these projects. These projects are of a varied nature and so the student is able to know about the various aspects of the subject through this method. The project and the working of this method is so evolved that the student does not feel that the work is going on. The student feels at home in the whole set-up. Through his questions and answers he *is* able to organise the whole of his knowledge and ideas.

Environment and experiences. The child lives in the society or the social environment. This social environment is brought with activities. Various types of activities are going on in the society. This society has diverse activities. These activities continue to take place. These activities add to the experience of the child and so he acquires knowledge which is useful in life. This method is based on the following three types of environment :

1. Physical or natural environment;
2. Social environment;
3. Practical work or trade.

Natural or physical environment. Man is born in the free atmosphere of nature. He sees various natural objects all around him. By coming in contact with these natural things, he acquires new knowledge. Every day in the morning he sees the sun rise and in the evening sees its set in. The process of the day and night goes on. He also acquires the knowledge of the fact that sunrise causes warm and heat and in the night there is cold. When at night the child sees the moon and the stars, he feels happy. In the summer the sun shines in such a manner that the sun rays straight and they cause heat and temperature. In the winter season it is not so. During rainy season there is rainfall and in the winter reason the day is short and the night is long. On the other hand, in the summer season the day is long and the night is short. When the rain falls during the rainy season, we see the water flowing. This also gives an idea that the water flows from an elevated place to a lower place. All these natural activities of the environment add to the experience of the child. He also sees the agricultural products of his atmosphere. These agricultural products provide him with some knowledge and new experiences. It is the duty of the teacher to direct all these experiences in the proper manner. These experiences have to be properly organised. In this process, it is possible for the teacher to provide certain new experiences to the students. New things are also known to the young boys and girls. Here in this method, on the basis of the unknown experiences, certain known facts are taught.

Geography is very much related to nature. Therefore, through this method it is possible to teach Geography more successfully. The students may be taught about the things that they do not know, with the help of their known experiences. Thus the students may be encouraged, in a natural manner, to proceed from known to unknown.

Social environment. Man's sociality is a well known fact. It is not possible to separate man from society. He starts with the assumption that the world is confined within society. It is as a member of the society that the performs various activities and takes to new processes. It is in the society that he learns activity. He takes part in various social activities, religious ceremonies, social customs, pilgrimages, etc. He is not only a passive looker of all these social activities and customs but also plays an active part in it. It is through the social environment it is possible to have an idea of the importance of various activities of contemporary value and social importance. In our day-to-day life we use various things that are imported ones. With the help of this practical experience it is possible to have an idea of import. Sometimes we see that people who are agriculturists see that there is surplus of foodgrain. The student sees that his father has sold a surplus grain to some trader. The trader carries this grain away and sells it in ths market. Thus, there is training of import. While learning about export and import, the student also learns about trade and business. He sees several things arranged for several occasions. He also sees that on certain occasions certain things are utilised for decoration. These pieces of decoration are the result of industry of handicraft. This gives him a knowledge about that.

The teacher can utilise various social functions, customs and festivals for teaching of Geography to the students. He may draw a plan and list of all these things and teach the students about all these things. By this method it shall be possible to place many things in the minds of the students in a natural and spontaneous manner.

Industry or practical work or trade. Through this method or Project Method it is possible to teach the students about trade. A detailed plan may be drawn about collecting the raw material and doing many things in this regard. The students may be asked to perform jobs in regard to this. It would provide them with an opportunity to learn about all these things. They shall also have a detailed knowledge of the various aspects of a particular trade or industry.

In this process it shall be possible to have a study of the local conditions and local environment. Students may be asked to take up some work of some small scale industry and acquire a solid knowledge about trade and its working. For example, the students may be shown the process of jaagary making and this may give an idea to the students about the process of preparation of sugar. The students may also be told about the process of carrying the sugarcane to the mills and preparing sugar. They may also be given an idea of export and import of sugar. This would provide them with an opportunity to study about various means of communication and transport and their Georaphical method.

From this thing it is well evident that this method can be very helpful in the study of Geography, Such a knowledge is practical and useful. In future, the student is capable of giving a practical shape to his knowledge. He can have proper ideas of social and natural environment and utilise the knowledge of these things for establishing or running a particular industry or trade. This would be helpful for the future life.

1. Teaching by the method of learning by doing or Project Method can be very useful for the teaching of Geography.
2. In this method there is combination of the theoretical knowledge as well as practical knowledge.

3. This method implifies study of the following types of environment.

   (a) Physical or natural environment.

   (b) Social environment.

   (c) Practical knowledge of trade or some industry,

4. Teaching by this method, which is also called the Project Method, implifies that the student shall learn about natural environment and social environment and try to put the whole knowledge into practical form.

7

Teacher's Role

Teacher occupies a very important place in the scheme of education. Without a well equipped teacher, teaching of a subject cannot go on. It may be possible to continue the teaching of purely literary subject having a scientific bias, it is not possible to go on without a properly equipped teacher. In subjects involving observation and collection of data, direction of a teacher is very necessary. Without his co-operation and direction teaching work cannot go on successfully.

Geography is such a subject which has the qualities of art as well as science. If on the one hand it has the qualities of a literary subject, on the other it has the qualities of a scientific subject. The practical knowledge is required at every step. Students have to be acquainted about the countries about which they do not know anything. Their imagination has to be excited so that they may know things properly.

In teaching of Geography maps, charts, diagrams etc. form an integral part of the scheme of teaching. These things cannot be used without the proper guidance of the teacher.

For the teaching of Geography it is necessary to have direct observation of the environment and the physical conditions. Students have to be encouraged to observe things by themselves and have-proper assessment and knowledge of the subject-matter, this work has to go on in a well-graded and proper manner. Only a successful teacher of Geography can encourage the students to resort to this method. In rural areas various types of crops, such as wheat, maize, jute, etc. are grown. In market we find things made of textile, steel, etc. All these things are produced and grown under certain geographical factors whose knowledge is very necessary and useful for the students. Only the teacher of Geography can help the students to know about all these things.

A teacher of Geography can play his part successfully when he is able to guide the students to acquire knowledge of the subject in a scientific and thorough manner. In order to be able to do this he should have the following qualities in him :

Various Aspects of Knowledge

A teacher of Geography should have a thorough knowledge of the subject. It does not mean that he should have read taxt-books only. It requires that he should have grasped the spirit of the subject and studied it in the proper perspective. On the other hand the teacher of Geography should also be a student sort of person. His reading should not cease after he has completed his education for a particular degree. He should continue to be a student throughout his life.

A teacher of Geography should not have only read the subject he should have grasped it properly. Once the teacher has grasped the subject properly, he can present it before his students in the proper manner. The teacher of Geography should also be upto date-in the knowledge of the subject-matter This does not mean that he should be a specialist. A specialist is useful person for higher education. For secondary classes he should be able to present the fact of Geography in a Psychological manner. This he can do when he is aware of the fact that social sciences are a developing subject.

No teacher can be successful in his task if he does not possess a thorough knowledge of the child psychology. Children of different stages have their own psychological requirements. Teaching of a subject is based on these psychological requirements. Unless the teacher has thorough knowledge of educational psychology and knows the psychological reqirements of the children, he cannot impart the knowledge of the subject in the proper manner.

The knowledge of child of psychology enables the teacher to know what method should be employed for the children of particular age. This knowledge can bring a good deal of success to the teacher.

Along with the knowledge of the psychology, the teacher should also know about the various methods of the teaching of Geography. For different stages, different methods are useful. These methods are employed according to the psychological requirements of the student. When the teacher is aware of the various methods of teaching he can employ them very successfully.

A student at the age of fourteen is fond of excursions and going about. For a student of this age excursions and travels can have a good deal of educational requirement of the child and knows about the importance of travels and excursions in the teaching of Geography, he can very safely co-ordinate the two and make the teaching successfully.

The teacher of Geography should be a keen observer. We have seen it more than once that, excursions and travel form an integral part for the teaching of Geography. While going about the teacher and the students have to observe things and collect suitable material. If the teacher is keen to observe, he can have the students collect things and make proper use of the subject-matter.

Along with keen power of observation the teacher of Geography should also have good power of imagination. Observations coupled with imagination can lead along way to the success of the teaching of the matter.

Natural environment have a good deal of influence on the life of man. This influence can be properly studied through observation and imagination. We observe this influence at one place and on the basis of imagination which visualize its effect in other places. The teacher of Geography has to acquaint his students about all these things. Unless he has power of observation and strong imagination, he cannot present the Geography of foreign countries before his students in a vivid and attractive manner. These two qualities help the teacher to present the subject-matter of Geography in a lively and interesting manner. It is not necessary that all students should have seen desert or a hilly place. With the help of imagination and observation the teacher can make the student visualize and understand the life in desert and hilly place. He can also make them understand about the way of life of all these places. In fact these two qualities help him in making the teaching of the subject-matter interesting.

The teacher of Geography must have the knowledge of the curriculum and syllabus of other subjects. He should know about their developments and requirements of teaching. This is necessary because Geography is a subject which has the element of science as well as the humanities. It has to be taught in both the ways. A teacher who has no knowledge of the subjects of science shall not be able to do justice to the subject. Similary a teacher who has no knowledge of the curriculum and syllabus of humanities shall also not be able to teach the subject successfully. For teaching the physical Geography in a successful manner the teacher must have the knowledge of the principles of science. In higher classes Geography science is an essential part. A teacher who has knowledge of the principles of science can handle various geographical apparatuses such as Thermmometer, Rain Gauge. Barometer, etc. successfully and confidently.

With the help of knowledge of other subjects, it is possible to establish co-relationship of Geography with other subjects. We have already seen that Geography is related to Language, History, Mathematics, Art, Gardening. With the help of the knowledge of these subjects, thes teaching of Geography can be made interesting and lively. Teaching of a particular topic of Geography can be strengthened with the help of the examples from other subjects.

Practical Knowledge

Geography is a subject which is based on cause and effect relationship. In teaching of this subject everything has to be explained on the basis of the cause and effect. In order to explain the cause of various events, the teacher of Geography should be read with the material that may explain the cause. It is with the help of the maps, charts, diagrams etc. that the cause and effect relationship can be properly explained.

On account of the cause and effect relationship, in the teaching of Geography, models, charts, sketches, etc. occupy an important place in the teaching of Geography. In primary classess models are very important. In secondary classes it is charts and the maps that pay a vital role. The teacher of Geography, while explaining a thing or the point has to take help from maps and charts to explain his points fully well to his students. These teaching aids make the teaching of the subject interesting and lively. The teacher of Geography must be skilled in handling these aids. He should also be good at drawing of the charts and maps. Unless he is good at drawing maps and charts, he shall not be able to draw them on the black-board. If a chart is drawn on the black-board it will be possible for the student to understand the subject-matter successfully with the help of those charts and maps. In short, it means that the teacher of Geography should be able to handle and make the charts, maps, models etc. successfully and properly.

If it is possible to arrange the curriculum on the basis ol season and weather, the teaching can be made realistic and interesting. If the teacher wants to teach about rainfall and he can do it during rainy season, the knowledge shall be stable and permanent. Similarly, lesson about crops may be taught in the season when the crops are grown. During winter season the frost, log, etc. may be taught. The teacher must have the capacity to organise and arrange the subject-matter according to season. He should be all along alive to this requirement of the students and try to teach successfully. This thing has a good deal of utility in the teaching of the subject.

The teacher of geography should have a scientific way of thinking. He should be able to impress upon the minds of his pupils the cause and effect relation in the world of geography. He should suggest the children not to take things for granted without scientific verification. Heuristic attitude in Geography will be the most educative for the childern.

Different Skills

In fact geography is a subject of maps. The teacher of geography must be able to draw maps, sketch maps and diagrams on the black-board. Geographical facts can best be brought home to the children with the help of such aids. But ready-made aids of this kind are not available and controllable at every step. Therefore, the teacher should be able to draw maps and sketches freely.

The teacher of Geography should be a good story-teller. He should have the capacity to draw and frame stories connected with various geographical aspects and present them before the students in a successful and interesting manner. The quality of the teacher can be of great use in lower classes. The teacher should be interested in story-telling and writing out stories. A teacher of Geography with this quality can be really successful.

It is necessary to have a good collection and museum of the things of geographical importance. Such a collection makes the teaching interesting and lively. The teacher of Geography should have interest in collecting things of geographical importance. He should also have interest in organising and arranging a museum. If things of geographical importance are presented in their real form before the students, the teaching becomes interesting and lively. Then it becomes possible for the student to know about soil, rocks, stones, etc. These things can be presented before the students if they are lodged in a museum. This museum can be arranged by the teacher only and unless he has interest, he shall not be able to do it. Same is true of maps, charts, coins, etc. Unless the teacher is fond of collecting things of geographical importance he shall not collect the chart showing the inhabitants of different countries and the routes of sea, land, etc.

It is necessary for every teacher to have qualities of leadership and direction. Unless the teacher has these qualities he shall not be able to handle his students successfully. In a subject like, Geography, these things are all the more important. The teacher of Geography has to take his students out for travels and excursions. In these travels and excursions only a successful leader can guide his students properly. He can maintain discipline effectively only if he has these qualities in him. It is, therefore, necessary for the teacher of Geography to have qualities of leadership and direction in him.

Travels and excursions form an integral part of the teaching of Geography. Unless the teacher himself is interested in excursions and travels he shall not be able to take his students out for such jobs. In these travels and excursions the students acquire knowledge directly. They are able to see various things with their own eyes and also observe geographical phenomena. By direct observation the students acquire knowledge successfully, easily and effectively. Direct knowledge is always better than indirect knowledge. Knowledge acquired with the help of the books is not so lasting as the knowledge acquired with the help of the eyes and ears.

Excursions imply keen observation. If the teacher is fond of excursions he shall also be able to guide his students in the observation of geographical things. In this manner he shall be able to do justice to his job.

We have already stated that in Geography cause and effect relationship plays a vital role. The teacher of geography must have the capacity to explain the geographical causes in a clear and food manner. There are also factors that are responsible for the control of geographical events. We have already talked about them. They include geographical conditions, climate, ways of living etc. All these things are influenced by the controlling factors of Geography. The teacher of Geography must know about them and must be able to explain these things to his students successfully and effectively.

Every subject is taught on the basis of certain aims and objects. The teacher has to remain alive to these aims and objects. Unless, he has the aims and objects he shall not be able to teach the subject effectively and in an interesting manner. If the teacher of Geography continues to assess the extent to which he has been able to teach the subjects on the basis of the aims and objects, he shall be able to teach successfully.

The teacher of Geography should be able to infuse regard for the subject and interest in it. This can be done by handling the subject in psychological manner. The teacher may by his personality and method, incite the students to study Geography and take interest in it.

Wisdom and Intellect

In the words of an eminent writer "One of the aims of teaching geography is to produce international understanding in the children. They are to learn how every individual, every country and every community is dependent upon other individuals, countries and communities. They must understand how physical, natural and social environments are invisible effective in binding us all together. But these secrets can be taught effectively only by such a teacher who himself has faith in international ideas and who appreciates world citizenship. The teacher of geography must be able to rise above political boundaries. A natural region is the natural geographical region and not a politically democrated country."

Every teacher has to be idealist. It is equally necessary for the teacher of Geography to be idealistic. His attitude of teaching as a subject should be based on philosophical foundations. Through these bases he can help the students to develop in them the feeling of world brotherhood and world fraternity.

1. The teacher of every subject has to possess certain qualities in order to teach his subject successfully.
2. This is true about the teacher of Geography as well. Since Geography is Art as well as Science. The teacher of Geography must have the qualities to do justice to subjects of both these types.
3. The teacher of Geography must have the following qualities in him :
   (a) He should have a thorough knowledge of the subject.
   (b) He should also have knowledge of child psychology.
   (c) He should have knowledge about various methods of teaching. In this respect the knowledge should be upto date.
   (d) The teacher of Geography must also be a keen observer. He should have the capacity to observe things keenly.

(e) The teacher of Geography must have the knowledge of curriculum and syllabus of other subjects as well. This 'knowledge would help him to do justice to his subject.

(f) The teacher should have the knowledge and practice of handling various teaching aids such as models, charts, sketches, diägrams, etc.

(g) The teacher of Geography should be capable of arranging his curriculum and syllabus with an eye on the season. If a particular thing is taught in the season in which it can be practically seen, the teaching shall be effective and interesting.

(h) The teacher of Geography should be a good story-teller.

(i) The teacher of Geography should have interest in the collection of the things of Geographical importance.

(j) In order to be able to guide the students properly and keep discipline, the teacher of Geography should have the qualities of leadership and direction in him.

(k) Since travels and excursions form an integral part of the teaching of Geography, the teacher of the subject should have love for travels and excursions.

(l) The teacher of Geography should be capable of explaining to the students the geographical causes and the factors control various geographical events.

(m) The teacher of Geography should be alive to the aims and objects of the teaching of the subject and he should also continue to assess the extent to which he has succeeded in achieving these aims and objects.

(n) The teacher of Geography should also have the capacity to inculcate interest and respect for the subject.

(o) Finally, the teacher of Geography should be an idealist and his attitude of teaching the subject should be based on philosophical bases.

New Entrants

Ours is a country of villages and whole of the India live in villages. So, after completing my studies, I would like to be appointed as a geography teacher in a village school. When I would join the school I shall first of all acquaint myself with physical, natural and social environment of that village. I shall visit the surrounding fields and study life of the people inhabiting in the village. I shall also acquaint myself with the trade of village and know what commodities are exported and what are imported.

The students of the college would be mostly from the agricultural class and be studying agriculture as compulsory subject. So, I shall make my teaching of geography on the actual experience of the agriculture. I shall follow the following devices to make my teaching effective :

Rambles in the countryside—I shall take my students to the countryside—Fields, forest and hills. They have already visited these places but their visits were not systematic and well-planned. I shall narrate to the student about the important things and pass over the unimportant ones.

Visits to the centres of trade and industry—I shall also take my students to the centres of trade and industry. I shall tell them that society has exploited geographical resources to the benefit of man. In the industrial centres, the process of exploitation is going on. By visiting the centres of trade and commerce, students shall have actual understanding of the fact that how our daily needs are met.

Exploitation of the experience of children—I shall also make the actual experience of the children the basis of teaching. My whole teaching would be based upon the knowledge of the students that they have gained earlier.

Home-geography the starting point—Home geography shall be the starting point of my teaching. While teaching about the agricultural products of America, I shall base the new knowledge on their already attained knowledge of Home-geography. In this way I shall be able to base their new knowledge on sound footing. My teaching based on the Home-geography shall be interesting for the students and so they would grasp, the subject without difficulty.

Use of project method—Occasionally I shall follow project and problem methods. Such devices will be occasional but well-planned.

Play-way method—I shall dramatise suitable geographical lessons and will use other play-way methods also.

The use of pictures and maps etc.—I shall use illustrative aids of various kind. I shall show them beautiful pictures on various topics such as children and busy people of distant lands, snow-capped mountains, mighty rivers, magnificent buildings, lofty trees and strange animals. These pictures will not be shown at random but will be exhibited in connection with lessons which they are learning.

Geography room—I must have a fully equipped geography room to produce good atmosphere for the subject. The pupils will be encouraged to help in the equipment and upkeep of the geography room.

Library books—I shall provide interesting and well-illustrated library books to the pupils to create interest in the subject. The books will be selected very carefully.

The use of epidiascope, magic-lantern and film strips—I shall provide a projection for the effective teaching of geography. I shall use epidiascope, magic-lantern and film strips regularly to make my teaching interesting and effective.

Other audio-visual aids—I shall exploit radio also for this purpose. There are often broadcasts of useful lessons connected with geography. I shall have a radio-set for the school. Other available audio-visual aids will also be exploited.

Construction of models and maps etc.—I shall encourage the pupils to prepare geographical models, map and illustrative aids themselves. I will satisfy their urge for construction and develop their interest in the subject.

In order to create interest in geography, as a new teacher I shall do the following–

1. I shall take my students to the countryside and teach them systematically.
2. I shall arrange visits to the centres of trade and industry so that student may understand how their daily needs are met.
3. I shall exploit the experience of the children and base my teaching on Home-geography.
4. I shall use Project-Method and Play way-Method for teaching Geography. I shall make proper use of pictures and maps, Geography room, Library books, epidiascope, magic-lantern and nun-strips, audio-visual aids etc. I shall also say the students to make models and sketch maps by themselves.

8
Teaching Aids

Teaching aids should be used to supplement the process of teaching. Most of the teaching aids are sensory aids and their function is to make teaching concrete, effective and interesting. Geographicals aids are the means of modernisation of methods of teaching geography in schools. In the absence of teaching aids geography lesson becomes dry and ineffective. Field work and practical work also form an important part in the teaching of geography. Pictorial illustrations are the most commonly used aids in teaching of geography.

Various types of teaching aids such as optical instruments, models, charts, atlases, etc. are used in teaching of geography. All these aids are important for a geography teacher because he can make his lesson more illustrative and explanatory by making use of one or more of these teaching aids.

(i) These aids help the teacher in getting the attention of his students.

(ii) These aids help in creating the interest of the student in the topic and activate the mental process of the students.

(iii) The student gets an opportunity to get a firsthand experience by visualising some concrete things, living specimens and actual demonstrations, etc.

(iv) Use of teaching aids help to have a clear conception of ideas, information, facts and principles.

(v) It helps the students in understanding some complicated and difficult concepts.

(vi) They provide an opportunity for a change in the monotonous atmosphere that generally prevails in a class-room.

(vii) They provide an opportunity for a better support between the teacher and his pupil.

(viii) They help the students to develop a scientific attitude.

(ix) They provide a training in scientific method.

(x) They can be used in bigger classes.

(xi) Use of such aids is based on the principles of psychology.

Teaching aids should be used properly to make teaching more effective. Teaching can become more effective if such aids are used widely but the use of such aids cannot provide a guarantee of good teaching.Following points are important for use of teaching aids.

(i) Teaching aids should be woven with classroom teaching and these aids should be used only to supplement the oral and written work being done in the class.

(ii) While making use of any teaching aid an effort be made that the teaching aids being used in any class are in corifirmity with the intellectual level of the students and is in accordance with the previous experience of the students.

(iii) Only such aids the preferred which provide a stimulus to the students for greater thinking and activity.

(iv) If possible actual specimens be preferred to a photograph or a slide of a specimen.

(v) The teaching aid used should be exact, accurate and real as far as practicable.

(vi) The Teacher should use a teahing aid only when he is quite sure about handling a specific teaching aid. For handling some aids (e.g. operating a projector, etc.) training is provided by various authorities. For this purpose more information can be obtained from local SCERT or directly from NCERT, New Delhi.

(vii) Teaching aids used, be such as, are closely related to pupils, experiences.

(viii) The teacher should use a teaching aid only after a proper planning so that the aid is used exactly at the point; in the process of teaching, where it best fits in the process of teaching.

(ix) Teacher should see that a follow-up programme follows the lesson wherein a teaching aid has been used.

(x) Teacher should carry out occasional evaluation about the use, function and effect of a teaching aid on the learning process.

Different Kind of Aids

For convenience of discussion the teaching aids in geography may be grouped as under:

(i) Aids used in elementary schools.

(ii) Aids used in secondary schools.

As a matter of fact no clear-cut demarcation is possible but this catagorisation is done only for convenience of study. The aids used in elementary schools may be called *elementary aids* and those more commonly used in secondary schools are referred to as *aids useful for secondary schools.*

The aids generally used in teaching of geography in elementary and junior schools are of the following type.

(i) Clay and its models.

(ii) Pieces of wood.

(iii) Models.

(iv) Maps, and

(v) Pictures.

Clay and its Models. Elementary school children have a creative instinct and they are quite fond of playing with clay. Making use of this instinct they be provided opportunity to play with clay and draw models out of clay. They be taught in a pathway method. Such an approach will help these younger children to know about things more clearly and properly.

Wood and its pieces. In elementary schools teaching of geography can be done by using small pieces of wood which are cut and designed so that when they are joined they form a picture or a form. These wood pieces are most valuable teaching aid to a teacher in elementary school to impart the knowledge of geography to small children.

Models. In teaching of geography models are frequently used. Sometimes it is difficult for teacher to present certain things in real form before students. It is not possible for geography teacher to give an idea of mountain to his students unless he takes recourse to presentation of subject matter with the help of models. Models are preferred to pictures and diagrams because they introduce a third dimension. The models present the things in miniature and so it is possible to teach certain abstract things with the help of models:

Models are very helpful in making the subject clear to the students as they give the student an idea of actual shape/size, etc. of article under discussion. *Scale models* are designed to show the appearance of a real object and *display models to* represent structural characteristics. A model should be large enough so that it can be seen clearly from all sides of a class-room. Models should be simple and should be according to age level of the students. Since commercial models are very expensive so an effort be made to get the models prepared in the class. Moreover the models that fit into a specific situation may not be available in market.

Models used in geography are generally made of clay, plaster of pans, papoer mache or laminated paper. These models are generally prepared by hand and then painted. At present relief models are obtained by moulding with a metal die. In preparing such models, map details are printed and plastic sheets before moulding.

A new technique has been developed in Japan. In this an original model is prepared by transferring exact pattern of a contour from map to a metal sheet which are than cut to the shape of contour patterns and are laminated in correct position. The copies of this original model are then prepared by moulding a plastic sheet with this original.

Clay models which are cheap and handy are also used. Such models are particularly useful for illustrating land forms. Plastics available in different colours can also be used for this purpose. Plaster of paris preferred to clay models because of its versatility.

The teacher may encourage the students to make out certain models. This would develop the instinct of creativeness, activity and power of expression of students e.g. children may prepare models of clay exhibiting some geographical phenomenon. Children may prepare models showing the rotation and revolution of the earth, distance of the earth from the sun, phases of moon, etc. While encouraging the students to draw models the teacher should keep the sense of proportion in mind. This would develop certain qualities in students which would be quite useful to them in their future life.

Maps. Map is the chief instrument of teaching and learning geography. In teaching of geography maps occupy an important place. With the help of a map the geography teacher can present before the students, a region, a village, a district, etc. The map can provide a very clear idea of'the region, district, village, etc. to the students. When the students start drawing out things from the maps their knowledge is strengthened. The *big maps* are known as *wall maps* and are useful for elementary schools.

Actually speaking 99% of geography is taught with the help of a map. Map is a short instrument of giving perfect knowledge of the students. The aim is to enable the child to read a map, write out a map and think in terms of a map. Maps depict the climatic conditions, natural conditions, location, etc. of certain countries and continents whose geography is being taught to the students. These maps can also be used for comparative study. These maps can also be used for revision of a topic.

Requirements. Maps are useful teaching aids in geography both for elementary and secondary schools. These maps should have the following qualities in them:

1. They should be drawn either by the students or the teacher. They may be drawn on a piece of paper or cloth.
2. They should serve *as* a means of teaching of geography which means that these maps be used as a subservient to the subject-matter of geography.
3. Maps should be drawn clearly and neatly. Only relevant data be plotted on maps and no unnecessary detail be shown on it.
4. Map should be drawn on the basis of physical and natural regions. Political divisions should also be shown on them.
5. Maps should be drawn according to the requirement of subject-matter e.g. if we want to teach climatic conditions of a country the map should depict the climatic conditions.
6. Maps should be drawn accurately.
7. The longitude and latitude should be shown correctly on a map.
8. The teacher should use a pointer while making use of maps.

Pictures. To understand the physical and social activities of man in the background of his physical and natural environments pictures are quite useful. The underlying idea of use of pictures was realised by commensus in his book *Orbis Pictus.* In geography the eruption of a volcano can be easily explained with the help of a picture. Making use of a picture we can present abstract things in concrete form. Pictures help the student in strengthening his knowledge. Pictures give a clearer picture of social and cultural background of the people of a particular country.

Pictures are cheap, easy to produce and store. The teacher can seek the cooperation of students in collection of pictures. Pictures show objects in their natural surroundings. They are more useful in individual study than a class study.

Though pictures are quite useful teaching aids it is not possible to present everything in the form of a picture.

Important sources of pictures

(i) Magazines: Educational magazines. Geographical magazines, National geographical magazines.

(ii) Official Publications: Publications of Govt. Offices, meterological and weather reports.

(iii) Newspapers and Periodicals

(iv) Advertising brouchers insured by railways, shipping companies, airlines, etc.

(v) Discarded books and magazines.

(vi) Postage stamps.

We can classify the pictures under various broad heads such as Town, Physical Geography, Natural Vegetation. Minerals and Industries, Animals, etc.

Pictures and Photographs

The pictures used in geography should have the following characteristics.

1. They should be accurately and neatly drawn.
2. They should be attractive and natural.
3. They should be designed in such a way that there may be places for questions to be put by the teacher to the students.
4. They should carry correct headlines and be upto date.
5. An effort be made to draw a picture in natural background.

Principles for use of pictures. The following principles be kept in mind for successful use of pictures for teaching of geography.

1. Keep an index and a file of pictures.
2. Large pictures be got mounted on wooden frame of plywood and small pictures be got mounted on butter muslin. It helps to minimise the wear and tear of pictures.
3. Use some projecting machine when you want to display a small-size picture.

4. The teacher should explain to the students the things to be studied in a picture.
5. Students be allowed free access to the pictures.
6. After showing a picture the teacher should ask questions which would help to strengthen the knowledge of students and would also sharpen their memory and enrich their imagination.
7. Pictures should be bold, direct and sufficiently large.
8. Pictures should not be overloaded with information rather they should stick to the maximum *'one picture', one idea'.*

In addition to the teaching aids given in article 6,5, there are certain other teaching aids which are used for teaching of geography in secondary schools. There aids are:

(i) Sketches
(ii) Atlas
(iii) Globe
(iv) Meterological equipments
(v) Blackboard
(vi) Radio
(vii) Museum
(viii) Cinema slides and films
(ix) Episcope
(x) Epidiascope, etc.

Sketches. They are of great use in teaching of geography as they help the teacher to give proper idea of the subject-matter to the students. Students can strengthen their knowledge by drawing sketches and it can also be used to revise the topic. When the students learn to draw sketches they find an opportunity for expression.

Sketches provide an idea of natural conditions of a particular place, dress, conditions of life of people, occupation, mineral wealth, etc. Sketches can also be drawn to indicate the route and means of communications in an area.

Characteristics of Sketches

(i) Sketches should be very clearly drawn.

(ii) They should show only thte relevant data.

(iii) The geography teacher should draw sketches on blackboard in a geography class and should also encourage his students to draw them on blackboard and also in their exercise books.

(iv) The sketches be drawn in a manner so as to establish a coordination between mind, eye and hand of the students.

This type of training will be quite helpful to the student in his future life.

Atlas. Atlas is an important teaching aid in teaching of geography. The knowledge of a geography student will remain incomplete without the use of an atlas. Atlas is like a dictionary of geography. Student can make use of an atlas to have a correct idea of anything. Atlas can also be used for comparative study.

Frankly speaking atlas is nothing but a collection of certain maps and charts which depict the different geographical and natural conditions of a particular country, certain sub-continents or continents and the world at large. In 1909 the first comprehensive atlas was published as a part of the Imperial Gazetteer and it was revised in 1931. Later on in March 1949 a specialised atlas was published in the publications of S.P. Chatterjee's "Bengal in Maps" A statistical atlas of Madras was published by state Government in 1949. Another publication "Bihar in Maps" was published by P. Dayal in 1953., In 1950 *'India in Maps'* was published by Government of India. It contained maps on the scale of 1:15 M. The first national Hindi Atlas appeared in 1957. Presently we have a number of atlases that depict different things. The National Atlas organisation has prepared 11 plates of transport and tourism maps on scale 1:1 M in addition to physical maps of India an scale 1:6 M. Many an atlas on census has been published by Registrar

General, Census ofindia. The Government of India has set up an Advisory Board for National Atlas and Geographical names.

Advantages of use of atlas

(i) It saves strain on power of memorising and provides students a ready knowledge.

(ii) It encourages students for self-study.

(iii) It gives to the students in idea of location, direction, distance, etc. of distant lands.

Characteristics of atlas

(i) Maps and atlas should be such as to be useful for the psychological requirements of the students of the stage for which atlas is meant.

(ii) The map should be accurately, neatly and correctly drawn.

(iii) The maps should be attractive and colourful.

(iv) Maps should be indexed.

(v) In atlas not too many maps showing political divisions be allowed. It should contain more maps showing physical divisions and physical conditions of different countries of the world.

(vi) The maps should be realistic and accurate.

Globe. Globe is indispensabale because it always conveys the impression that the earth is round. Globe is nothing but a replica or presentation of world in its actual form but on a shorter scale. Globe occupies a unique position in teaching of geography. It is desirable if globes of different sizes are available in every school. Each school must have at least one globe drawn on a radius of 12". The state globe may or may not have the outlines of continents drawn on them and these are quite useful for teaching change in weather, season, day and night, etc. In the absence of globe it would not be possible to give a proper idea of hemisphere or to explain to the students the rotation of earth around its axis and around sun. It would be difficult to explain even the current and ebb and tide without a globe. Globe may be placed on the table or may be hung on the roof of geography room. Use of globe is recommended even in primary classes.

Globes and Maps

(i) It should be very accurately drawn.

(ii) It should clearly indicate the latitude, longitude, etc.

(iii) It should be of proper size. Generally a globe on scale of 1" = 500 miles is recommended.

(iv) Globes that are hung should be of metal.

(v) Globe should present everything very correctly and neatly.

Meteorological equipments. In geography we are directly or indirectly interested in the study of meteorological facts. The meteorological facts have a profound effect on world geography. We need certain equipments to carry out the study of meteorological facts and these instruments are known as meteorological equipments.

Some such equipments are:

(i) A compass

(ii) A weather clock

(iii) A maximum and minimum thermometer

(iv) A rain gauze

(v) An Anemometer (An instrument used for recording speed of the wind)

(vi) A Barometer

(vii) A Fahrenheit thermometer

(viii) A Centigrade thermometer

(ix) A wet and dry bulb thermometer

Blackboard. It is one of the most common visual aids in use. Blackboard forms an integral part of classroom. Blackboard is a slightly abrasive writing surface made of wood, ply, hardboard, cement, ground glass, asbestos, state, plastic, etc. with black, green or bluish paint on it. This board is used by the teacher to draw sketches, maps, diagrams, etc. It is also used by the teacher to put down the substance of the chapter or the topic taught. Through blackboard it is possible to develop the chapter of the topic being taught.

A chalkboard is generally installed facing the class which is either built into the wall or fixed and framed on the wall and provided with a ledge to keep the chalksticks and duster. Portable chalkboards are also available these days. Such chalkboards can be placed on a stand with adjustable height. Generally white chalksticks are used for writing on the blackboard or chalkboard but sometimes coloured chalksticks are also used. The coloured chalksticks are used for better illustration.

Characteristics of a good chalkboard. Some of the characteristics of a good chalkboard are as follows:

(i) Its surface should be rough enough so that it is capable of holding the writing on the board.

(ii) Its surface should be dull so that it can eliminate glare.

(iii) Its surface should be such that the writing on the board can be easily removed by making use of a cloth or a foam duster.

(iv) Its height should be so adjusted that it is within the easy reach of the teacher and is easily visible to the students.

Effective use of chalkboard. We find that chalkboard is the most common teaching aid used by the teacher for writing important points, drawing illustrations, solving problems, etc. The teacher should keep the following points in mind to use the chalkboard effectively.

(i) Write in a clear and legible handwriting the important points on the chalkboard but avoid over crowding of information on the chalkboard.

(ii) The size of the words written on black board should be such that they can be seen even by the back-benchers. The letters should not be less than one inch in height. The recommended height of letters on a chalkboard is between 6 cm to 8 cm. For this the teacher should frequently inspect his own chalkboard writing from the view point of the back-bench on a corner seat.

(iii) There should be proper arrangement of light in the class-room so that the chalkboard remains glare free.

(iv) To emphasise some points or parts of a sketch or a diagram coloured chalks be used.

(v) Rub off the information already discussed in the class and noted down by the students.

(vi) Draw a difficult illustration before hand to save the class time.

(vii) Stand on one side of the chalkboard while explaining some points to the students.

(viii) Make use of a pointer for drawing attention to the written material on the chalkboard.

(ix) Students may be allowed to express their ideas on chalkboard, or to make alterations or corrections. Sometimes teacher may intentionally draw some incorrect diagram and ask the students to make necessary correction, alteration, etc.

(x) For maintenance of proper discipline in the class the teacher should always keep an eye on his class while writing on the blackboard.

(xi) For proper writing on chalkboard the chalk stick be broken into two pieces and the broken end of the piece be used to start writing.

(xii) While writing on a chalkboard, keep your fingers and wrist stiff and move your arm freely.

Advantages of chalkboard. Some of the advantages of chalkboard over other visual aids are as follows:

(i) It is a very convenient teaching aid for group teaching.

(ii) It is quite economical and can be used again and again.

(iii) Its use is accompanied by the appropriate actions on the part of the teacher. The illustrations drawn on the blackboard captures students attention.

(iv) It is one of the most valuable supplementary teaching aids.

(v) It can be used as a good visual aid for drill and revision.

(vi) These boards can be used for drawing enlarged illustrations from the textbooks.

(vii) It is a convenient aid for giving lesson notes to the students.

Limitations of the chalkboard. Some of the important itations of a chalkboard are as under:

(i) The use of chalkboard makes students very much dependent on the teacher.

(ii) It makes the lesson teacher paced.

(iii) It makes the lesson dull and of routine nature.

(iv) It gives no attention to the individual needs of the students.

(v) Due to constant use chalkboards become smooth and start glaring.

(vi) While using chalksticks to write on. chalkboard the teacher spreads a lot of chalk powder which is inhaled by teacher and students and it may affect their health.

Bulletin boards. It is a display board on which learning material on some geographical topic is displayed. It is generally of the size of a blackboard but sometimes even bigger depending on the wall space available. It is generally in the form of a framed softboard or strawboard or corkboard or rubber sheets. Such bulletin boards can be specified for individual branches of geography or even for some specified topics e.g. puzzles, news, cartoons etc. such a board can also be used for displaying the best work of students. However, for a all-purpose bulletin board the following type of display material is recommended:

(i) Interesting news.

(ii) Book Jackets of recently published geography books.

(iii) Brochures.

(iv) Cartoons.

(v) Poems.

(vi) Sketches.

(vii) Pictures.

(viii) Photographs.

(ix) Thoughts.

(x) Announcements, etc.

An effort be made to change the material on bulletin board as frequently as is practicable. Whenever the teacher starts a new topic he may ask the students to display the concerned material on the bulletin board and the teacher should specifically mention to the students the display material on the bulletin board while teaching a topic to the class. Students be asked to take the charge of bulletin board by rotation.

How to use a bulletin board. To make use of bulletin board as a useful teaching aid the bulletin board be used for creating interest amongst students on specific topics. For effective use of bulletin board as a teaching-aid following points be kept in mind:

(i) Effort be made jointly by the teacher and the students to procure material from various sources on a given subject or topic.

(ii) Before displaying the material on the board sort out the material relevant to a specific subject or topic.

(iii) Make best use of your aesthetic sense to display the material on the bulletin board.

(iv) Do fix a title for the specific subject/topic of display material on the top centre of the bulletin board.

(v) It is desirable if a brief description about the specific subject or topic is fixed below the title.

(vi) The height of bulletin board from ground level be about 1m.

(vii) The bulletin board be fixed in an area where enough lighting can be provided.

(viii) The material displayed should be large enough and should be provided with suitable headings.

(ix) Overcrowding of material on bulletin board be avoided.

Advantages of bulletin boards. Some of the advantages of bulletin board as a teaching aid are as follows:

(i) It is a good supplement to classroom teaching.

(ii) It helps in arousing the interest of students in a specific subject/topic.

(iii) It can be effectively used as a follow-up of chalkboard.

(iv) Such boards add colour and liveliness and thus also have decorative value in addition to their educational value.

(v) Such boards can be conveniently used for introducing a topic and for its review as well.

Limitations of bulletin board. Some limitations in the use of bulletin boards as teaching aids are as follows:

(i) They cannot be used for all inclusive teaching.

(ii) They can be used only as supplementary aids to some other teaching aid.

(iii) At times it becomes very difficult to make proper selection of the display material for certain topic.

Flannel board. It is also sometimes referred to as flannel graph or board. It is made of wood, cardboard or strawboard covered with coloured flannel or woollen cloth. It is one of the latest devices effectively used for geography teaching. Display materials like cut-outs, pictures, drawings and light objects backed with rough surfaces like sand paper strips, flannel strips, etc. will stick to flannelboard temporarily.

For display purposes a flannelboard of 1.5 x 1.5 m is generally used. It can be fixed next to the blackboard or can be placed on a stand about one metre above the ground.

How to use a flannel board? Following points be kept in mind for effective use of flannel board as a teaching aid:

(i) The teacher should collect a large number of pictures or wall-cut diagrams, etc. and back them with sand paper pieces. He may then make use of these by displaying these on the board one by one, after proper selection.

(ii) Display the material on the flannelboard in a sequence to develop the lesson.

(iii) Make proper use of flannelboard for creating proper scenes and designs relevant to the lesson.

(iv) Change the display material on the board as frequently as required.

(v) Flannel-board can be used quite effectively for showing relationship between different parts or steps of a process.

Advantages of flannel board. Some of the advantages of using flannel board as a teaching aid are as follows:

(i) It is quite economical and easy to handle and operate.

(ii) The pictures or cuttings can be easily fixed and removed when required, without spoiling the material. Thus same material can be used for display many a time.

(iii) Any display material on the board holds the interest of students and arrests their attention.

(iv) Such boards enable a teacher to talk along with changing illustrations to develop a lesson.

Magnetic chalkboard. It is a framed iron sheet having porcelain coating in black or green colour. Such a board can be used either to write with chalksticks, glass-marking pencils and crayons or to display pictures, cut-outs and light objects with disc magnets or magnetic holders.

Thus such a board functions both as a chalkboard and as a flannel-board. We can display visual learning material on such a board while writing key points on it. Such a board provides the flexibility of movement of visual material. It is possible to display even a three-dimensional object on such a board using magnetic holders.

Since the magnetic chalkboard functions both as a chalkboard and as a flannelboard. So various points discussed for the effective use of these boards be kept in mind while using magnetic chalkboard as an effective teaching aid.

Advantages of Magnetic chalkboard. Some of the advantages of magnetic chalkboard are as follows:

(i) It is a versatile teaching aid that combines the advantages of both a chalkboard and a flannelboard.

(ii) It is possible to move visual material by sliding it along the surface of the board such a movement is not possible on a flannelboard.

(iii) It is very light and can be easily taken from one place to another.

(iv) Such a board can be easily got prepared in the school from an iron sheet and painting with some food paint.

Charts. Charts also are an important teaching aids.

Sometimes charts are needed by the teacher to supplement his actual teaching. There are certain charts which represent a statistical diagram for a series of diagram which may be difficult to understand. Charts require less efforts for presentation than slides.

Following points be kept in view while using charts as teaching aids:

(i) An effort be made to use charts prepared by students under the guidance of the teacher, however some charts may be purchased.

(ii) Only such charts be purchased which have bold lines and in which such colours are used as could be seen and distinguished even by the back-benchers.

(iii) Charts should give only the essential details.

(iv) Charts should be properly and clearly labelled in block letters.

Sources for procurement of charts

(i) Charts can be prepared by students and teacher.

(ii) Charts can be purchased.

(iii) Charts can be procured on a very nominal cost from the following sources:

(a) Ministry of Education, Govt. of India, Delhi.

(b) NCERT, New Delhi.

(c) Director, Extension Service of College of Education in the State.

(d) SCERT of the state.

(e) District Public Relation Officer.

Advantages of charts

(i) They can be made quickly.

(ii) They have a better appeal.

(iii) Only bare essentials can be shown in the chart and unnecessary details can be avoided.

(iv) Charts are available from various sources.

Radio. Radio can also serve as an effective aid in teaching of gegraphy. Such lessons may be planned which may be broadcast from the radio and they may provide a background to the knowledge of geography. Special programmes may be designed for students which have a bearing on the subject-matter of geography. It is also possible to listen to the description of towns and other things on radio. Broadcast talks are now a regular feature of All India Radio.

All India Radio has in its regular feature some programmes meant for school children. In such a programme generally talks on educational matters are broadcast. Such a talk is quite useful for students as also for geography teacher. The topic, date and time of broadcast of such talks are given in advance by All India Radio. A school can take benefit of such talks only if it possesses a good radio set and a period is provided in the school timetable for listening such talks. Such an arrangement can be worked out by the school authorities and then teacher can refer to such talks while teaching his class. It is also possible to synchronise the broad- cast talk on some topic with the actual teaching of that topic in a class.

Some handicaps of such broadcast task arc listed here.

(i) Sometimes when the receiving set is not working satisfactorily there prevails a sense of strain in the class-room.

(ii) Some students are poor listeners and may not be benefited by such talks although they benefit by normal teaching through questions, demonstrations and reading.

For the maximum utility of such talks following points be kept in view:

(i) The students with bad hearing be seated on front seats.

(ii) To keep students interest alive in such talks teacher should tell his students in advance a few questions which they have to answer after the talk.

(iii) Only short duration talks be arranged.

Such talks cannot be a substitute to the actual teaching and such a talk is only to help in teaching.

Gramophone lectures and tape recordings. Another teaching aid available to a teacher is records of short talks on interesting topics by eminent persons. Magnetic tapes of such recorded talks are now available and the talk can be easily reproduced in the class-room. These talks provide an inspiration to the students and such a talk once recorded can be used again and again. Such recording can either be used to introduce a topic or to develop a topic. Even the voice of different birds and animals can be recorded and reproduced in the class while teaching about such animals or birds.

Magic lantern. Psychologists have now confirmed that a child grasps abstract facts slowly and can only remember a name which recalls some definite reality. Thus he should be confronted with visual teaching aids to broaden his experience.

A *magic lantern* or *episcope* is a simple device used to project pictures from a glass slide on a screen or wall. Teacher can make use of this device when he intends to show some small figure or illustration to whole class. Many a school has a *magic lantern* in their laboratories as it is not very costly slides are readily available in the market on various science topics. These can also be got prepared on demand and the cost of such a slide is quite reasonable. Such slides can even be prepared by teacher himself after some practical training which can be provided by extension service department of training colleges.

Epidiascope. Epidiascope is a more costly instrument but it can project opaque objects as well as transparent objects. The pictures projected by epidiascope are much brighten and needs a less powerful light so that room need not be absolutely dark. Epidiascope can be used to project any picture, map, diagram, photograph or small object. No slide is needed for projection with an epidiascope.

The name *epidiascope* is given to this machine because of the fact that it works, as an *episcope* when it is used to throw the image of an opaque object. This machine can be used to project slides and this is possible just by moving a lower provided for the purpose. When it is used to project a slide then it serves as a *diascope*. Thus *epidiascope* is a combination of these two *i.e. episcope* and *diascope*.

Advantages of epidiascope. In comparison to other projection machines *epidiascope* has some advantages. Some of these are as follows:

(i) It can be operated in a room which may not be absolutely dark.

(ii) With the help of this machine original colours of the picture or photograph can be projected.

(iii) The projection on the screen can be kept for sometime during which teacher can explain and discuss it in the class.

(iv) It provides teacher an option to handle the lesson according to himself.

Following points provide useful hints for the proper handling of an epidiascope.

(i) The apparatus works well in a dark room.

(ii) While projecting with an epidiascope an effort be made to keep exposed to the head of the lamp for minimum, time delicate pictures, photographs or other such objects.

(iii) The person handling the apparatus must be given some practical training before he is allowed to handle the machine.

Film projector, micro-projector, film-strip projector. These are further improvements on the teaching aids discussed so far. These have brought about a revolution in teaching of geography. Geography films are shown to the students to illustrate various topics as also to supplement the class-room teaching. Both type of films have some basic objectives to serve.

Film strip-projector. It is an improvement on magic lantern and this machine can be used to project many a topic on a single strip. One such strip generally consists of 40-100 separate pictures and such film strips are available on loan from Central Film Library, NCERT, New Delhi. On such a film strip pictures concerning one topic are arranged in a definite order.

This machine can be easily handled by the teacher. The machine is operated by hand and thus can be stopped at the discretion of the teacher whenever he wants to explain some aspect of a topic being shown on machine.

Micro projector. This projector is generally operated in a dark room. The projection can be taken on vertical Screen if whole class is expected to see it. However such a film cannot be distinctly seen by a student if he is sitting at a distance more than 12 feet from the screen.

Film projector. This machine is used for showing geography films. Some good science films on various topics are available and these can be had on loan sometimes even free of charge from the source, given below:

(i) Central Film Library, NCERT, New Delhi.

(ii) U.S. Information Service, New Delhi.

(iii) British High Commission's Office, New Delhi.

(iv) Some Other Embassies, New Delhi.

For projecting the films in school generally 16 mm projector ('RCA', 'Bell and Havell') are used. These 16 mm projectors are less costly and easier to transport as compared to a 35 mm projector.

Advantages of motion pictures. There are some definite advantages of motion pictures to be used as teaching aids, some of these are as follows:

(i) They draw attention of the students.

(ii) They help to bring past to the class-room.

(iii) It is possible to reduce or enlarge the size of the object by using the machine.

(iv) They can be used to show a process which a naked human eye cannot see without its aid.

(v) They can be used to show a record of an event.

(vi) They can serve a large class at a time.

(vii) They provide a good aesthetic experience.

(viii) They help in understanding relationship between things, ideas and events.

Precautions. The teacher should take the following precautions whenever he wants to use a film projection as a teaching aid:

(i) He should satisfy himself about the lighting management and seating arrangement in the room where such a film show is to be given.

(ii) He should himself see the film beforehand.

(iii) He should give a complete background of the film to the students before the actual screening of the film.

(iv) He should see that complete calm and peace is maintained during the screening of the film.

(v) Immediately after the film show, he should invite comments, questions, etc. from the students and try to answer all the quarries of the students.

(vi) He should encourage some of his students to write articles, etc. based on the film show and such articles etc. may be shown on wall magazine, may be printed in school magazine.

Television. The role of television in the presen-day world is becoming more and more important and it is one of the most important teaching aids. It combines the advantages of a radio (broad cast) and of a film. This can be used for mass education and now UGC. programmes are a regular feature on "Door Darshan". The topics of discussion are announced in advance and lesson from well-qualified persons and specialists in their fields are shown on TV. Teacher can easily plan his work accordingly and in this way he can make use of TV as a teaching aid.

Geography museum. A museum ought to be a very valuable part of geography department in school. Though the ideal way to gain knowledge is to observe objects and phenomen in their natural setting, but in the present educational set up there is only a little opportunity for this. A science museum helps in this aspect. Museum not only provides necessary help in teaching but also helps in creating the right type of atmosphere in the school.

A good museum should be scholarly built. An effort be made to avoid exhibiting ready-made articles. Change is the law of nature and it is always good to replace with better objects those exhibits which have become unsatisfactory either because of their age or because of their use.

In a geography museum there should be a collection of pieces of rocks, woods and such other things that form the subject-matter of geography. There may also be lodged charts, maps, designs, etc. There may be certain models depicting various types of animals that are found in different geographical conditions.

The geography teacher must have a thorough knowledge of musuem, moreover he should be interested in building up a museum. A teacher who is interested would collect things that are useful for the museum while he takes out his students on tours and excursions.

Some other important points about museum are:

(i) Systematic arrangement of various exhibits.

(ii) Clear and complete description of various parts of an exhibit.

For this purpose an ideal arrangement will be that a card of suitable size (5" x 4") be attached to each item exhibited in the museum and the following information be typed on this card or written in a good hand writing on the card.

(i) Name of the exhibit.

(ii) Place from where exhibit has been obtained and the relevant information.

(iii) Importance of the exhibit.

The language used to provide above information should be simple and all efforts be made to avoid phrases and technical terms in the description of the exhibit.

Textbooks. Other than the teaching aids enumerated above, Geography room and textbooks are also important teaching aids.

A textbook gives continuity and cohesion to the teaching process. A wellchose textbook forms useful basis in new lesson and affords material for home task. In use of textbooks teacher should take extra precaution to select only modern and recent textbook and reference book.

In the present educational setup the role of textbook is of prime importance. However we find that a little attention is paid to this important aspect of education. Most of the textbooks in geography are not of good standard. They follow the prescribed syllabus too rigidly and no attention is paid to develop topics according to the need and interest of students. A good textbook is one which is a source of knowledge arranged.

Miscellaneous. Systematically it enables the teacher to acquire the needed information quickly. It inspires the student to invent, to discover and to inculcate scientific methods. However teacher should not depend solely even on the best of the textbooks because even such a textbook omits many details which teacher wants to tell to his students.

The use of a textbook is made by the students for completing the preparatory part of an assignment. They also use their textbook for doing revision of course. Some students also consult and use their textbooks to study at home, the demonstration lesson given to them by their teacher in school. In this way textbooks are used to supplement the class work. Textbooks also provide a help to students in correct understanding of basic concepts and principles of geography.

Generally a number of books are prescribed by board or university to be used as textbooks. NCERT prepared text books are available upto class XII. While recommending a textbook to his students the teacher should consider the following points to assess the worth of the book.

(i) Correctness of matter.

(ii) Purity of languages.

(iii) Simplicity of diagrams.

(iv) Quality of printing and binding.

Correctness of matter. In this correction the standing of the author and the reputation of publishers should be considered. The books written by well-known author having a long teaching experience of teaching the subject and possessing requisite qualifications be recommended. It would be much appreciated if certain minimum qualifications and experience for authors is laid down by authorities.

Purity of language. A textbook that presents the subject-matter in a simple, clear and lucid language should be preferred. For textbook in a regional language, the terminology should also be given in English within brackets. In such books only standard terminology evolved by the Central Ministry of Education and State Governments should be used.

Simplicity of diagrams. Only simple and well-labelled diagrams be given in textbooks. Such diagrams are self explanatory and help the student in properly understanding the subject matter.

Quality of Printing and Binding. It is desirable that a textbook makes use of a good quality paper and the quality of printing, and type of letters in fine. It should be so bound that its binding is appealing to the student.

In addition to the above a good textbook is expected to select and arrange the subject-matter in a psychological sequence. The book should follow the aims of teaching geography and should serve as a guide for demonstration lesson as also for individual experiments. Each chapter should start with a brief introduction and a summary of the subject-matter be given at the end of the chapter. Some assignments should also be given at the end of each chapter and the assignments should cover such areas as applications to life situations, numerical questions, suggestions for experimental work and projects, objective type tests, etc. Heading and sub-headings be given in bold type. A table of contents be provided at the beginning and a subject-index be provided at the end. Glossary of some important terms be given at the end of the book.

While evaluating a book the teacher should apply objective tests like the following:

1. The contents should be accurate and adequate for the age level and should conform with the syllabus.
2. The concept should not be difficult or ambiguous.
3. The literary style should encourage the student toread the textbook and vocubulary should be well chosen.
4. Photographs should be well-produced.
5. The quantity and quality of illustration should be reasonably good.
6. The general get-up, binding, size of the book, quality of paper, quality of printing, etc. be also taken into consideration.

Textbooks

Textbooks occupy a very important place in the teaching of Geography. They form part of the traditional teaching aids. In fact, it would be wrong to call them teaching aids. They are a means of important knowledge. It is through textbooks that the knowledge is imparted to students. They serve as a guide and means for the teachers as well as the students. Through the help of the textbooks the teacher can impart knowledge to the students and can help them to revise the lesson learnt in the class-room. With the help of the textbooks it is also possible to give home task to the students. If properly used textbooks can go a long way in the teaching of Geography in a successful manner.

It is possible to teach regional Geography without using textbooks but it is not possible to teach Geography of larger areas, such as country, sub-continent, or the world, without the use of the Geography. These textbooks are written with a specific purpose of serving the needs of the students and so it is very necessary for them to be useful and good. These textbooks should be so designed that they may serve the purpose of the students of the standard for which they are used. They should neither be very bulky nor very small. There should be enough material to serve the purpose of the students.

Utility of textbooks in primary classes. In the primary classes the students are not very matured. They require textbooks that may serve the under developed mind. The fact textbook should not be used a lot in the primary classes. Textbooks should be sparingly used. Students of the primary classes do not require teaching through textbooks. They are more interested in the listening. The teaching here should be oral. The textbooks that are used for the students of these classes should be well illustrated: they should contain a good number of charts and pictures. They should be written in such a manner that they may serve the psychological requirements of the children of this stage of education.

Textbooks in the secondary classes. Here the students require textbooks. Students of this stage of education are properly developed. They try to learn things in a realistic manner. They can benefit a good deal from the textbooks. In fact the method of teaching that should be question-answer method. The students may be asked to read the textbooks silently and the questions may be put on the subject-matter. For some difficult subject-matter, the students may be asked to refer to textbooks.

Characteristics and qualities of textbooks. Textbooks in order to be useful should contain the following qualities :

1. Textbooks that are intended to be used should be useful for the students as well as teachers. They should be so designed that on the one hand they may be written according to the psychological requirements of the students and on the other they should serve the purpose of the teacher who wish to impart knowledge to the students in a successful and interesting manner.

2. The size of the book should be handy. It should be possible for the students to carry them properly. They should not be bulky. This is specially true about books intended for the primary classes.

3. Printing and get-up of the books should be interesting and attractive. They should be printed in the letters that they do not require strain on the eyes of the students. On the other hand they should be correctly and neatly printed.

4. The exterior of the picture should be attractive. If the exterior is attractive, students would like to carry them and keep them. This is true of the books intended for primary classes.

5. They should serve the purpose of the subjectmatter as well as the aims and objects of teaching. They should be written with a view on the aims and objects of the teaching.

6. The textbooks should be accurately written. They should present the subject-matter in such a manner that there is no fault in them. The subject-matter, presented therein should be up-to-date.

7. The style of the books should also serve the psychological requirements of the students of different stages. Textbooks intended for the students of the primary classes should be written in a story form. In the textbooks meant higher classes the author many use the regional method or some other method that'is useful for the students of the stage.

8. The textbooks should continue to keep the interests of the students alive in the subject-matter. The subject-matter should be presented in a simple and lucid style and clear form.

9. The textbooks should contain all the necessary and relative material required for a particular stage of education.

10. The textbooks of different stages should be complimentary to each other. Textbooks that are used in primary classes should have some bearing and connection with the textbooks that shall be used by the students in the Junior High School classes. Similarly textbooks that are to be in mind the books that have been used by the students in the Junior High School classes.

11. Textbooks should be free from prejudice. The presentation of the subject-matter should be unbiased. There should be no material which can injure the susceptibility of any class or category of people. They should contain objective

description of the people and conditions of different countries.

12. The textbooks should contain charts, maps, diagrams etc. as and where required. Without the charts, maps and diagrams etc. the subject-matter of Geography cannot be taught properly. It is, therefore, necessary to give place to all these things in the textbooks.
13. Geography is a developing subject. Every day we find that new researches have been made in the field of Geography. Up-to-date knowledge of Geography must be given place in the textbooks.
14. At the end of every chapter of the textbook there should be certain questions that may be used for the revision of the subject-matter. Without these questions the textbooks shall not be useful.
15. If required the textbooks may give a substance of the chapter at the end of each lesson. Such a provision will help the students to grasp the subject-matter properly.

Other kinds of books. Other than the textbooks we have certain other kinds of books that are also used in the teaching of Geography. They are of the following types:

(a) Help Books, and (b) Reference Books.

Help books. Help books are very necessary for the students as well as teachers. There should be good collection of such books in the library of every school. These books help the students to acquire further knowledge of the subject. They are in fact written in an interesting form of a story or description of the travels. Students read them not as textbooks but as interesting reading material. This interesting reading material encourages them to learn more about geographical facts.

Reference books. Reference books are big standard books that are used by the teachers and grown-up children. Annual Geographical Reports, Government Reports, Dictionaries and Encyclopaedia, Magazines, etc. form this category of books. These books should be kept in the library for the use of the teachers and grown-up students. There should also be rich collection of reference books in the school.

Precautions in regard to use of textbooks. While the teacher is teaching the students in the class he should not use the textbooks very much. Textbooks should be used for revising the lesson or for writing out the home task. The teacher may ask the Students to read the book at home or in the class and then put questions in order to ascertain whether the students have grasped the subject-matter or not. While teaching, the teacher must put down the substance of the chapter taught on the blackboard.

We all know that aids are employed to made the teaching effective and interesting. This is true about Geography as well. Geography is a subject that deals with the human environment available in form of natural conditions and physical features. Geography is as we all know, a subject having characteristics of science as well as art or social sciences. It is therefore, necessary to employ methods of both the types. In order to make the teaching effective and interesting certain aids are employed. These aids are very important. It is through these aids that it is possible to make the teaching of geography realistic. The word is very large and their complex activities are carried out on it. It is not possible to give an idea of this feature unless certain aids are employed in the teaching of Geography. These aids provide a change in the monotonous method of teaching. Monotony once broken, enlivens the interest of the students in the subject. It also helps the concentration of the attention on the subject-matter.

These teaching aids may be categorized into two types—

(a) Aids used in elementary schools, and

(b) Aids used in secondary schools.

Really speaking, it is not possible to bring about any rigid categorization. Even then, from the point of view of convenience of study, it will be useful to categories them. Those aids that are used for teaching students in elementary schools shall be put under elementary aids. On the other hand those aids that are predominantly used to secondary schools, shall be called aids useful for secondary schools.

• Aids that are used for teaching of Geography in elementary and senior basic schools may be of the following types—

(a) Clay and its models, (b) Pieces of wood, (c) Models, (d) Maps, and (e) Pictures.

Clay and Models—In elementary schools small children have to be taught. These children have the creative instinct in them. They are very fond of playing with the clay. In fact they should be given an opportunity to play with the clay and draw models out of clay. Their teaching should be based on Playway method. This will help the small children to know about things more clearly and properly.

Wood and its pieces—The teacher may take certain small pieces of wood and teach the students with their help. These pieces should be so cut and designed that they may be joined into certain pictures and forms. With the help of these wood pieces it shall be possible for the teachers to impart knowledge of Geography to small children.

Models—Sometimes it is difficult for the teachers to present certain things in real form before the students. It is not possible for the teacher of Geography to give an idea of mountain to his students unless he takes recourse to presentation of the subject-matter with the help of models. These models present the things in miniature. It is also possible to teach certain abstract thing with the help of these models.

The teacher may encourage the students to make out certain models. This would develop the instinct of creativeness, activity and power of expression of the students. On the one hand if the students shall learn about the thing, they shall also learn to give expression to their psychological trades.

While encouraging the students to draw models the teacher should keep in mind the sense of proportion. This would develop certain qualities in the students that shall be useful in their future life.

Maps—In the teaching of Geography maps occupy an important place. It is method through which the Region, the State, the Village or the District may he presented before the students. These maps help the students to have a clear idea of the country or the Region whose Geography they are reading. When the students start drawing out things from the maps, their knowledge is strengthened. These maps may be small ones and big ones. The big models are useful for students of the elementary classes. These big maps are also called wall maps.

In fact 99% of Geography is taught with the help of the maps. Map is a short instrument of giving perfect knowledge to the students. These maps depict the climatic conditions, natural conditions, location etc. of certain countries and continents whose Geography the students have to study. Through these maps it is also possible to have comparative study of the subject-matter or Geography. The teacher of Geography can also help the students to revise the subject-matter with the help of the map.

Maps are useful not only for the elementary classes but also for secondary classes. These maps should have the following qualities in them :

(a) They should be drawn either by the students or by the teacher themselves. They may be drawn on a piece of paper or a piece of cloth.

(b) These maps should serve as a means of teaching of Geography. The study of map should not form an end in itself. In other words it means that the map should be used as a subservient to the subject matter of Geography.

(c) Map should be very clearly and neatly drawn. Unnecessary details should not be shown on the maps. Only relevant data should be plotted on it.

(d) Map should be drawn on the basis of physical and natural regions. Political division should also be shown on them.

(e) Map should be drawn according to the requirement of the subject-matter. If the climatic condition of the country has to be taught, the map should depict the climatic condition. Similarly, economic conditions and trade should also be shown on the maps.

(f) For secondary schools the maps may be plain ones and the students may be asked to fill in things by themselves. For elementary schools these maps should be coloured ones.

(g) Maps should be accurately drawn. They should not show anything wrong.

(h) Maps should also show longitudes and latitudes correctly.

(i) The teacher should, while using the map, have a pointer in his hand so that he may show the things exactly.

Picture—In Geography the teacher tries to present the physical and social activities of man in the background of his physical and natural environment. These things can be properly studied with the help of the pictures. In Geography we read about the erruption of volcano. This erruption can be very clearly explained with the help of a picture. Through pictures it is possible to present abstract things into concrete torrid. These pictures are also helpful in strengthening the knowledge and the experiences of the students. They give a clearer picture of the social and cultural background of the people of a particular country.

Although pictures have a lot of utility, but certain limits have to be placed on their use. It is not possible to present everything in form of picture and so only those things that are really presentable, should be presented in form of pictures. If the students have the proper background of the thing they study, the teacher must explain the thing as well.

The pictures that are used in the teaching of Geography should have the following characteristics :

(a) They should be accurately and neatly drawn.

(b) They should be attractive and natural.

(c) They should be so designed that there may be place for questions to be put by the teacher and the students. This provision would enable the students and the teacher to have a proper idea of the subject.

(d) The teacher should carry correct headlines and they should be upto date, and

(e) As far as possible, the pictures should be drawn in the natural background.

• Apart from the aids enumerated above, there are certain other aids as well that are employed for the teaching of Geography in secondary schools. These aids are enumerated below :

(1) Sketches,

(2) Atlas,

(3) Globe,

(4) Meteorological equipments,

(5) Black-board,

(6) Radio,

(7) Museum,

(8) Cinema slides and films,

(9) Episcope, and

(10) Epidiascope.

Sketches—Sketches are of great use in the teaching of Geography. They help the teacher to give proper idea of the subject-matter to the students. Students by drawing the sketches can strengthen their knowledge and revise the subject matter. When the-students learn to draw sketches they find an opportunity for expression.

Through these sketches it is possible to give an idea of the natural conditions of a particular place, dress and the conditions of life of the people of that place, their occupation, mineral wealth etc. Through these sketches it is possible to give an idea to the students that natural conditions influence the life to a very great extent. It is also possible to draw the route and means of communication on the sketches.

Sketches and sketch maps should have the following characteristics in them :

(a) These sketches serve the purpose of shorthand script. They should be very clearly drawn.

(b) Unless they are clearer and accurately drawn they shall not be able to give correct idea of the nature.

(c) Only relevant data should be shown in these sketches.

(d) While teaching Geography, the teacher should draw sketches on the black-board and the students should be encouraged to draw them on the black-board and their answer books.

(e) These sketches should be so drawn that they try to establish co-ordination between mind, eye and hand of the students. Such a training of these vital sense organs is helpful in future life.

Atlas—For the teaching of Geography, atlas is an essential accompaniment. Without atlas it is not possible for the students to have proper idea of the subject-matter. Without the use of atlas knowledge shall be incomplete. It is like a dictionary of Geography. This student may look to the atlas as and when he wants to have a correct idea of anything. Atlas is helpful in having a comparative study of the subject-matter.

In fact atlas is nothing but a collection of certain maps and charts. These maps and charts depict the different geoghirapical and natural conditions of a particular country, certain sub-continents or continents and the world at large. Generally maps collected in the atlas are drawn in colour. Use of atlas has the following advantages:

(a) It saves strain on the power of memorising of the students and provides them with ready knowledge.

(b) It encourages them to have self-study.

(c) It gives them an idea of the location, the direction, distance, etc. of different lands.

An atlas can be useful, for the students knowledge if it has the following characteristics and qualities :

(a) Maps of the atlas should be such as to be useful for the psychological requirements of the students of the stage for which the atlas is meant.

(b) The map should be accurately, neatly and correctly drawn.

(c) These maps should be attractive and colourful. They should also have an index.

(d) In atlas there should not be too many maps showing the political divisions. There should be greater number of maps showing the physical divisions and physical condtions of the countries of the world.

(e) These maps should be realistic as well as accurate.

Globe—Globe is nothing but a replica or presentation of the world in its actual form, of course on a shorter scale. In teaching of Geography, Globe occupies a very important place. It is very necessary to have a Globe in order to give a correct idea of the world to the students. Every school must have globes of different types. There should invariably be a globe drawn on a radius of 12". Teaching of change in weather, season, day and night and other natural processes becomes diifficult without globe. It is also not possible to have proper idea of hemisphere in the absence of globes. It cannot be explained to the students how does the earth rotates on its axis and revolves round the sun, without the help of the globe. Current and ebb and tide cannot also be explained without the help of the globe.

Globes may be placed on the table and they may also be hung on the roof of the Geography class.

Globes should be used in the primary classes as well. The teacher should not wait for its use till the .students have reached the Junior High School or High School classes.

Globes should have the following characteristics and qualities

:

(a) It should be very accurately drawn.

(b) It should be very clearly given the longitudes and latitudes and such other things.

(c) The globe should be very clear. It should be such that the students may read and study things on it. It will be better to have a globe on a scale of l'==500 miles.

(d) Globes that are hung should be of the metal that things may be put down on them.

(e) Globe should present everything very correctly and neatly.

Meteorological equipment—Geography directly or indirectly deals with meteorological facts. These facts influence the world stage as well as the actors as much as the physical facts of the earth. Therefore, study of these facts is necessary. But we cannot pursue this study without the help of the available equipment. The following is the list of such instruments :

1. A compass.
2. A weather clock.
3. Maximum and minimum thermometer.
4. A rain-gauze.
5. A Anenometer (for recording speed of the wind).
6. Fahrenheit thermometer.
7. A barometer.
8. Centigrade thermometer.
9. A wet and dry bulb thermometer.

Blackboard—Blackboard is an integral part of the classroom. Generally it is painted black. Today educationists are of the view that it should be painted green and not black. It is on this board that the teacher draws sketches, maps, diagrams etc. and puts down the substance of the chapter or the topic taught. Through blackboard it is possible to develop the chapter and the subject matter which is to be taught.

The teacher has to use the blackboard in a very correct manner. He should have the capacity to write legibly on the blackboard and draw diagrams accuratety and nicely. In Geography, blackboard should be larger ones. Sometimes the teacher has to teach a subject which requires many diagrams and maps. Only a big blackboard can help in the matter.

Radio—Radio can also serve as an effective aid in the teaching of Geography. Such lessons may be planned that may be broadcast from the radio and they may provide background to the knowledge of Geography. It is also possible to teach one chapter at different places through radio. Special programmes may be designed for the students and in these programmes stories and talks may be arranged. These talks and stories may have a bearing on the subject-matter of Geography. It is also possible to listen to the description of the towns and other things on radio. Such memories and reflections are interesting to the students and they also provide proper background.

This is the latest design and every school cannot afford it. However, in spite of it being costly, it cannot be denied that it is an important aid for the teaching of Geography.

Museum—Every institution should have a Geography museum. In this museum there should be a collection of pieces of rocks, woods and such other things that form the subject-matter of Geography. There may also be lodged charts, maps, designs, etc. There may be certain models depicting various types of animals that are found in different geographical conditions.

These things will make the teaching effective and interesting. The teacher of Geography must have a thorough knowledge of the museum. On the other hand he should also be interested in building of the museum. A teacher who is interested would collect things that are useful for the museum while he takes students out on tours and excursions.

Cinema slides and films—These can also play a very vital role in making the teaching of Geography interesting and effective. Films depicting various geographical factors may be shown to the students either in the class-room or in their free time. These films make the students more interested. They provide reaction as well as knowledge. Through them it is also possible to establish caste and effect relationship more easily and quickly. Cinema and its slides have greater scope for presenting things in a more realistic form. While using the cinema films and slides the following things should be kept in mind :

(a) The films should be real, exact and informative.

(b) They should be such that they may encourage and excite the interest of the students in the subject-matter of Geography.

(c) Film should be realistic and they should have importance for the teaching of Geography.

(d) Only authoritative films should be used and they should be used with a view that they solve various geographical problems.

Films are of two types—documentary and informative. Documentaries are helpful in providing opportunity for revision of the subject-matter already known to the studentt. On the other hand informative documentaries provide further knowledge.

If required, explanation should be provided to the students while the film is being shown. This can be done with a running commentary or by a talk that may accompany the display of the film.

The films that are shown in the class-room should not exceed the duration of 5 to 10 minutes. Projectors and lanterns may be used for the job.

While the films are being shown the teacher should keep his vigilant eye on the students. These opportunities should not be allowed to drift into occasion for indiscipline. Before showing the film the teacher should provide a proper background so that the students may follow the film properly.

Episcope—This is like a lantern, although superior in quality. In this apparatus it is not required to have a slide. Pictures collected from the magazines, books, newspapers etc. may be projected on the screen with the help of episcope. It is also possible to project the maps and the diagrams drawn up the pictures. With the help of this aid, it is also possible to magnify small things, from the point of view of utility it is very handy and effective. The teachers of Geography can alway use it without much difficulty.

Epidiascope—It may be called mixture of lantern or projector and episcope. Through this apparatus it is possible to show the slides as well as the maps and the charts that are shown with the help of episcope.

With the help of epidiascope it is also possible to project the substance of a particular chapter on the black-board or the screen. The substance when magnified would catch the attention of the students more effectively. This would also provide opportunity to the students to have proper knowledge of the subject taught.

This instrument may also provide encouragement to the students. With the help of this instrument it is possible to project the maps and the charts drawn by the students. When the students shall see that their own creations are being projected they shall feel encouraged to draw better charts and maps. Such a thing is really useful for teaching Geography in an effective manner.

Other than the teaching aids enumerated above Geography room and text-books are also important aids. In fact these are traditional aids and require no explanation here. However, they continue to occupy an important place in the list of the teaching aids.

1. Teaching aids are required to make the teaching of the subject interesting and effective.
2. These aids may be divided into two categories :

   (a) Those that are employed for teaching of the subject in the elementary schools, and

   (b) Those that are employed for the teachieg of Geography in the secondary schools.
3. Aids that are useful in elementary schools include :

   (a) Clay and its models,

   (b) Wood and its pieces, and

   (c) Maps, Charts etc.
4. Maps that are used in elementary schools should be big and attractive ones.

5. Diagrams and sketches are also helpful for the teaching of Geography in the secondary schools. These diagrams and charts should be accurately and neatly drawn.

6. Atlas and Globe are also important teaching aids. While atlas provides the student with various types of maps, the globe gives him an idea of the real situation of the earth.

7. Certain meteorological equipments are used in the teaching of Geography, some of them are :

A. A compass, B. A weather clock, C, Maximum and minimum thermometer, D. A rain-gauge, E. An anenometer (for recording speed of the wind); F. Fahrenheit thermometer, G. A barometer, H. Centigrade thermometer and I. A wet and dry bulb thermometer.

8. Blackboard is also an integral part of the teaching aids.

9. Cinema and films. Radio Episcope and Epidiascope arc also important and effective teaching aids. They are the teaching of Geography effective and interesting.

10. Other than these aids Geography room and text-books are also traditional teaching aids. They are also helpful in making the teaching of Geography interesting and effective.

9
Levels of Teaching

There is a lot of diversity in the subject-matter of geography. Different portions of this subject matter are taught at different stages of education. Geography, as already pointed out, is a link between natural sciences and social sciences. As a natural science it lays more stress on certain things that form a part of teaching of natural sciences and as a social science it has to take certain methods that are a part of teaching of social sciences. In natural sciences individual work is emphasised and for this the subject is taught by Experimental Methods, Observation method, etc. Oral work is stressed in case of social sciences and for teaching of social sciences oral work, practical work and method of observation are used directly. The observation method is used in lower classes.

Primary Level

Primary school stage (5-10 years of age) is the formative age and the habits formed during this period are likely to continue for the rest of the life. Thus, the student be properly trained, at this stage keeping in view the student's psychology. At this stage a student can learn better by seeing and acquiring the knowledge through personal experiences. At this stage the formation of curriculum needs a good deal of thought and discretion. Moreover the teacher of geography has to use a lot of discretion and intelligence for teaching at this stage of education.

A primary school child is highly intersted in play and in fact play forms an integral part of the personality of the child at this stage of education. The child is highly interested in making toys, models, charts etc. and in listening to stories. At this stage we can mould the child in any frame according to our liking. An all-out effort be made by the teacher to teach the students at this stage through games, keeping in mind the interest of the students.

Since at this stage of education the child is also highly interested in his environment to the local and neighbouring environment should form the basis of teaching the students in primary schools. The knowledge given to the child should have a direct bearing on his environment. The student be acquainted with rain, wind, sun rise, sun set etc. This helps them to understand various natural phenomenon and helps in awakening their imagination. At this stage it is also desirable to tell the stories, about geographical life of the country, to the students. In these stories they be told about elephants, lions, wild life etc. Tours and excursions may be organised so that students can observe certain facts and get an opportunity to see things themselves. In this way they learn by direct method.

In class I and II no formal method be adopted for teaching geography as a separate subject. In these classes it be taught as a part of nature study. The teaching at this stage be confined to the natural things that lie in between the home and the school. The teaching be based on cause and effect relationship.

Following points if kept in mind will help the teacher in teaching of geography at primary school stage:

(i) All-out efforts be made to make the teaching of geography practical.

(ii) Human element should always occupy an important place in teaching of geography at this stage.

(iii) All possible efforts be made to explain interaction between man and nature.

(iv) Teacher should always keep an eye on the intelligence and power of reasoning of man and should try to generate in his students the power of thinking and reasoning.

(v) All efforts be made to explain the effect of nature.

(vi) An effort be made to teach geographhy in correlation with other subjects.

The teacher should attempt to strengthen the previous knowledge of the student. In this age the power of reasoning is developed and the child becomes curious to know certain things. At this age the instinct of curiosity predominates and teacher should utilise this instinct to develop mormal values property in the child. At the age of 11-12 years the student cares for his self-respect and at this stage teacher should be more careful in handling the child. The guiding principles for teaching of geography at this stage are as under:

(i) An effort be made to develop the curiosity and interest of the child in the subject-matter of geography.

(ii) An effort be made to acquaint the child with the technical subjects connected with geography.

(iii) An effort be made to mould the life of the student in such a way that he grows into a useful and ideal citizen.

The primary stage of education generally covers class I, II, III, IV and V. We have already pointed out that geography be taught as a part of nature study in class I and II. The following topics may be covered in classes III, IV and V.

Classes III & IV. In these classes topics may be covered as under:

(i) Narating stories The students be told stories about the places and things with which they are familiar or which they have seen. To acquaint the students with various things teacher may resort to question-answer method.

(ii) Whatever is told to the students be simultaneously written on the blackboard. It helps to strengthen the knowledge of the students.

(iii) An effort be made not to use textbook method at this stage of education.

(iv) An effort be made to make the teaching interesting so that students may not feel bored.

(v) The oral method of teaching be used at this stage and examination too should be oral. Teacher should not insist upon written work by the child.

(vi) Knowledge should be imparted more on the basis of observation and experience of the child.

Class V. This is the last year at the primary school and an attempt be made to strengthen the knowledge and experiences gained by the child in previous classes. An attempt be made to give a practical bias to the teaching. Students may be asked to draw charts, maps, etc. The use of textbooks may be useful at this stage of education.

More emphasis be laid on observation and practical knowledge in the examination at this stage. In the use of textbooks the teacher should be cautious and though he may use the textbooks, but teaching should not be solely based on textbook method.

The story-telling method is the best method of teaching geography at this stage. The students be encouraged to acquire knowledge of different regions and places with the help of stories. The stories may deal with the following things:

(i) Life of people of other lands.

(ii) Stories about discoveries of different lands.

(iii) Natural vegetation, mineral wealth, animal wealth of various regions and countries.

(iv) Industry and commerce of various regions and countries.

Defects in curriculum. The curriculum in geography at primary school stage suffers from various defects and drawbacks. To remove these defects and drawbacks the curriculum should be framed in a scientific manner and it should be such that students feel interested in it. The curriculum should be environment-centred and should be such that it could be finished by the teacher in the prescribed time.

The present syllabus is not the one framed scientifically and the teacher finds it difficult to finish it up in the prescribed time. The textbooks and syllabus are also not free from being cumbersome. All this leads to loss of interest of the child in the subject of geography. In the present syllabus due emphasis is not given to practical work and observation.

To remove these defects and drawbacks the subjects-matter and textbooks should be organised in such a way that students feel interested because interest is very important for proper learning.

Defects in teaching. In primary schools the teaching aids are not available and it is the basic cause of defective teaching in schools. The teaching of geography is bound to suffer in the absence of teaching aids. The primary school teacher is also at a disadvantage to arrange tours and excursions. Tours and excursions occupy a very important place in teaching of geography. For a teacher to be successful he should have a proper knowledge of the practical aspects of geography and should be trained to handle the students properly. However most of the teachers suffer from this defect which is responsible for the loss of interest of the student in the subject of geography.

To remove this defect tours and excursions be given a proper place in school curriculum. Teacher should but in his best in arranging and planning such tours. He should plan them in such a way that the students feel really interested in the subject

Junior High School Level

At this age (about 12-13) known as the age of preamble of adolescence. At this age the child starts looking things in a realistic manner and they become pragmatic. They can also understand cause and effect relationship and they can analyse the events. At this stage they move from the world of imagination to world of realism. They can draw conclusions.

At this age the child wants to take a leading part in life. Because of these psychological changes taking place in child he requires a change in the methods of teaching. Thus, the method of teaching of geography should be different from the one used at primary stage.

When the student enter a junior high school he is capable of acquiring knowledge with the help of charts, models, etc. He can make generalisations and is interested to know the practical utility of a subject. Thus, at this stage geography be taught to him keeping the above points in mind.

In the light of the above discussion the following guiding principles be used for teaching of geography at junior high school stage.

(i) An effort be made to strengthen the previous knowledge of the students.

(ii) An attempt be made to make the students understand the importance of human life and natural environment.

(iii) Whole things be analysed on cause and effect relationship.

(iv) Teacher should provide opportunities which develop the curiosity, power of imagination, learning, reasoning, etc. in the students.

(v) Students be trained to appreciate the human life under different geographical conditions. For this the students be made to understand the effect of various geographical factors on human life.

(vi) An effort be made to circulate in students a tendency to understand geography in a developed form and a capacity to study geography.

(vii) An effort be made to train the students in the use of charts, models, maps, etc.

(viii) At this stage the student be taught the world geography in addition to the geography of his home country.

For teaching the geography of the world teacher should keep in mind the various physical divisions of the world. An effort be made to explain the geographical conditions of different countries on the basis of this division. Psychological factors must also be kept in view while teaching the geography of the world. Our emphasis should be on those factors which enable the student to understand how geographical factors have influenced life.

Comparative method is better to teach the geography, of the world. Both story-telling method and comparative method are used at this stage of education. In addition to a combination of these two methods, the other methods of teaching like the narrative method or descriptive method may also be used if the situation so demands.

In comparative method a comparison be made about the climate conditions, physical conditions, formation of the surface, vegetation, agricultural products, industry, commerce, etc. of different physical divisions of the world.

If geography teaching is accomplished in this way it helps the students to realise the unity of world. When students find a similarity in geographical features of their country with those of some other country they feel nearness (oneness) with the people of that country. Such a feeling is very important to achieve world brotherhood.

At this stage the student be taught the geography of his country in detail. An effort be made to bring about a relationship between the geography of one's motherland with the geography of the world. It should be correctly explained to the child that this relationship is based on physical conditions, climatic vegitations, mineral wealth, commerce, industry, etc. A comparative study of the geography of one's country with that of the world makes this clear.

To teach all these things, the help of maps, charts etc. be taken freely. Students should also be trained in the use of maps, charts, etc. An attempt be made to give a scientific basis to the teaching of geography. The practical value of geography be explained to the students at this stage of education.

The students at this stage are taught physical, political and human geography of the world. Following things be included in the course of study at this stage:

(i) Upto class VIII students should be acquainted with the general geography of the world.

(ii) The use of charts and maps be emphasised in the study of geography at this stage.

(iii) In class VI, geography be taught regional basis.

(iv) In class VII, the effects of geographical factors on human life and other human activities be emphasised. They should be trained to plot things on an outline map.

(v) In class VIII, the student? be trained to draw maps, charts etc. and colour these maps and charts.

At the junior high school stage (VI, VII, VIII classes) an effort be made to encourage the students to keep a record of weather and seasons. They be taught the geography of different continents and countries on the regional basis and more stress be laid on human geography.

The geography teaching at present suffers from the following defects which should be removed for making the subject interesting the teaching scientific.

Detailed and burdensome courses. The present syllabus of geography is very detailed and burdensome because it has not been planned according to psychological requirements of the child. Students are compelled to read big and bulky textbooks and the students are losing interest in the subject. Subject-matter may be scientifically arranged so that the student feels interested in it.

Lack of scientific method. Geography in school is not being taught in a scientific manner. If it is taught in a scientific manner, students will be also to make a practical use of their knowledge in their actual life. Such a teaching method will also keep the students interested in the subject. We can not lay out any specific method for teaching of geography and teacher is at liberty to choose any method that suits the psychology of the students according to their age groups.

High School and Higher Secondary Level

When the students reach the secondary classes they bacome mature and have also become intelligent. At this maturity and intelligence level they can establish cause and effective relationship. At this age the psychological requirements are different and for them we should give a properly-organised and scientifically-planned syllabus and a good method of teaching be used.

The curriculum at this stage should be complete in itself and it should be such as to be capable of focussing the attention of the child on certain geographical problems. It, must be able to develop the power of imagination, reasoning and judgement in the child. At this stage only such topics, which satisfy the above requirements be included in syllabus. Given below are some of the guiding principles for teaching of geography at the secondary stage.

(i) Teacher should make an attempt to strengthen the previous knowledge of the students.

(ii) Students at this stage be taught principles and facts of geography as also the geographical conditions of the people of various countries. They should also be explained the action and interaction between nature and man.

(iii) They be taught in such a way so as to increase the world brotherhood.

(iv) They should be made interested in geography and be trained to grow into useful citizens.

(v) They be trained in the use of maps, charts, globe, atlas, etc.

Method of Teaching. At present geography is taught in schools on regional basis which is a scientific method and also in accordance with the psychological requirements of the children. Carl Riter known as the 'Father of Modern Geography" introduced this method for the first time. In this method the teacher is always conscious to emphasise the influence of geographical factors on human life. The following two things form the basis of this methods.

(i) Analysis and explanation of cause and effect relationship.

(ii) Study of geography from practical and utilitarian point of view.

Making proper use of this method the students can be taught various natural factors that have a bearing on human life in future life of students.

He understands the influence of various natural factors on human activities and also the extent to which such activities have been influenced by natural factors. The students at this stage also know the method of utilisation of human factor for influencing natural conditions.

Regional Method. In secondary classes we have to, direct our attention to the treatment of continents with increasing stress on the regional method of teaching of geography. The regional method of teaching of geograpghy is perfectly suited for the secondary school. However, before entering upon the teaching of geography of the continents the student must be familiar with the outlines of world geography from the point of view of human and economic geography. Such a step may be considered as the final stage of transition period or the beginning of the regional stage. The regional method of teaching of geography is based on realistic approach which is very much suited to the psychological requirements of adolescence. The students previous knowledge of gcographpy and his interest in subject be given a solid foundation. In the regional method of teaching of geography emphasis be .placed on climatic conditions, rainfall, mineral wealth, natural vegetation, human resources etc. Actually speaking this method of teaching geography is quite different from the political method of teaching of geography.

Order of treatment. For sometimes the following plan which is based on psychological grounds is followed for teaching of continents in secondary schools:

COURSE A

1-4 years	1. The preliminary stage Home district
	2. The transition stage (i) Extention of the home district (ii) Home state
	3. The regional stage
5th class	Introduction to the world and India in relation to world in outlines.
6th class	Southern continents
7th class	North America and Asia

8th class	Europe and Great Britain
9th class	India in detail and.world in outlines
10th class	Study of world as a whole
11th class	Regional approach
12th class	Regional approach

Another plan based on logical ground is also suggested. It is called course B.

COURSE B

1-4	1. The preliminary stage Home district 2. The transition stage (i) Extention of home district (ii) Home State 3. The regional stage
5th class	India in relation to the world in outlines.
6th class	Americas
7th class	Asia and Australia
8th class	Africa and Europe
9th class	India and world
10th class	Study of the above from examination point of view
11th class	Regional approach
12th class	Regional approach Most teachers prefer course B

An international seminar was held at Montreal (Canada)in 1950 to discuss the teaching of geography. In this seminar the following subjects were laid down for the teaching of geography at secondary level of education:

(i) General geography of the world.

(ii) Intensive study of the home country or mother land.

(iii) Special branches and departments of geography, such as physical, economic, political geography, etc. A specialised study of any three branches of geography be taken up.

(iv) Study of various problems of world. This should enable the students to have a coordinated knowledge of History and geography.

(v) In this seminar it was also laid down that certain geographical complexes must also be studied. Such a study involves the study of certain difficult geograpical conditions like study of certain countries with more population that can be supported by the natural resources of that particular country.

The other problems that should be studied in geography at secondary stage are as under:

(i) Means of communication and transportation of the world.

(ii) Study of various geographical, political, economical and social factors which were responsible for the establishment of U.N.O.

(iii) Problem of providing aid by developed countries to developing countries.

(iv) Study of U.N.O. the role of U.N.O. in providing basic necessities of life to the people of different countries.

Defects in Teaching of Geography to secondary classes. Some of the defects in the present system of teaching of geography in secondary classes are given below.

(i) The curriculum and syllabus is not sufficiently planned.

(ii) The books which are available are not scientifically written and drawn up.

(iii) No practical value is attached to the teaching of the subject, i.e. students cannot make a practical use of the subject.

(iv) In the present system of teaching too much stress is laid on narration and description leaving practically no scope for observation and scientific study.

(v) Teachers are not at liberty to make proper use of teaching aids.

Because of these defects teaching remains ineffective and arouses no interest in the students.

Removal of the Defects. For geography to occupy its proper place in education and life we must revise the curriculum and make it more scientific by arranging the subject matter in a systematic way. The curriculum and syllabus be so designed as to provide enough opportunities to the teacher for use of teaching aids. It should also provide for the excursions and tours of the students.

It is the regional method of Geography or the study of geography on the basis of physical divisions of the world that shall be really useful.

Given here is the specimen syllabus for a secondary school

Physical Geography or Physio-geography

(a) Shape and size of the earth.

(b) Movement of the earth and their effect (day and nights, seasons), directions, latitude and longitude, longitude and time.

Lithosphere

(a) rocks

(b) agents of denudation

(c) volcanoes

(d) earth quakes

(e) geysers

Hydrosphere

(i) ocean and its movements

(ii) waves

(iii) currents

(iv) Tides and their effects on climate and trade

Atmosphere

(i) Distribution of temperature

(ii) Pressure and winds

(iii) Land and sea breezes

(iv) Monsoons

(v) Trade winds and westerlies

Practical and Map-work

1. Introduction to scientific apparatus like thermometer (centigrade and Farenheit, maximum and minimum, wet and dry), rain gauze, barometer, etc.
2. To make use of these instruments and to record observations using them.
3. Representation of statistical data with the help of statistical diagrams such as curves, wheels, bar diagrams etc.

Map-work

1. Making a map on a given scale.
2. Contours and section drawings.
3. Introduction to ordinance survey maps and exercises on them.
4. Introduction to simple processes of map making and surveying.
5. Introduction to conventional signs.

Regional Geography

5th class	India and world in outline
6th class	Africa and South America
7th class	Australia and Asia
8th class	Europe and North America

9th class	India in relation to world emphasising political and economic developments
10th class	Revision and study from the examination point of view
11th class	Regional approach
12th class	Revision of world geography study for examination.

Subject-matter of Geography has a good deal of diversity. Its own scope is quite wide. Out of this vast scope of the subject-matter of Geography certain subjects are selected and presented at various stages of education. As has already been stated, Geography is a link between natural sciences and social sciences. As a natural science Geography has to lay stress on certain things that form a part of the teaching of social sciences. As a social science, it has to take to certain methods that are a part of the teaching of the social sciences.

In natural sciences a good deal of stress is laid on individual Work, Experimental Methods, Observation Method etc. But in social sciences, a good deal of stress is laid on oral work. In the teaching of Geography and its method of teaching oral work, practical work and method of observation have to be used directly, it as the duty of the teacher of Geography to make the teaching lively and interesting.

The Observation Method is used in lower classes. It is here that the foundation is laid for the teaching of Geography through Observation Method. Therefore, it should begin in early classes.

• In the primary schools the age group of the students is between 5 and 10 years. This is called to be the formative period of a student's life. If particular types of habits are formed, they continue to be there in the rest of the life. It is very necessary to train the students properly at this stage of education. The psychology of the students has to be borne in mind while teaching Geography. The psychology of the students at this stage is such that they can learn things by seeing. By looking at them and by trying to acquire knowledge through personal experiences. The teaching of Geography has to be based on those requirements of the psychology of the children. The curriculum has to be laid with a good deal of discretion and thought. The teacher of Geography has to be used a lot of personal discretion and intelligence.

In the primary classes, the students that receive education have a good deal of interest in playing. Play, in fact, forms an integral part of the personality of the children at this stage of education. They are very fond of making clay toys, charts, roaming about in the plains and listening to stories. This is a very tender age which can be moulded into any manner one likes. It will be wise to teach the students through games, various principles and methods of Geography. Their interest should always be borne in mind.

The students of this age group are very much interested in their environment. This local and immediate environment must form the basis of the teaching.

Their knowledge should have a direct bearing on the environment. Sunrise, rain, evening, wind etc, are all the necessary things with which the students must be acquainted at this stage of education. By knowing about all these things, they shall know about various facts of nature. Their imagination shall be awakened. They must be told about the stories, concerning the geographical life of the country. They should be told about the elephants, the lions, wild life etc. With these things they may be given an idea of the physical environment. They may also be taken on excursions and tours and made to understand the things that they observe. This will provide them with an opportunity to see things themselves, and learn by direct method.

In the primary or basic classes, formal method should not be adopted in teaching Geography. In Classes I and II, Geography should not be taught as a separate subject. It should be treated as a part of nature study. The student goes from home to school, in the way he sees various things of nature. The teacher may ask the natural things that he has to pass on his way from home to school. Then he may be asked about the things that he sees in his village. In fact, the teaching of Geography should begin from the surroundings and go up to school. The teaching of the local Geography should be based on cause and effect relationship.

The teacher of Geography must keep in mind the following principles :

(a) The teaching should be made, as far as possible, practical.

(b) The human element should always be kept in the centre. Geography should be taught as a subject dealing with the human life and not as a subject dealing with the human things like mountains, vegetation etc.

(c) As far as possible, the interaction between man and nature should always be explained.

(d) The teacher of Geography should keep an eye on the intelligence and the power of reasoning of man. He should generate in the students the power of thinking and reasoning.

(e) The effect of nature should always be explained.

(f) Geography should not be taught in isolation. It should always be taught in co-relation with other subjects.

At this stage of education, attempt should be made to strengthen the knowledge acquired by the child in the pre-primary stage of education. By this time, the student grows more matured and ripe as compared to the pre-primary stage. He starts taking interest in the things of his neighbourhood. He tries to collect knowledge about his neighbourhood. The power of observation has, by this time, developed in him to understand things in a proper perspective. In other words, the student has, by this time, developed the power of observation and collection of facts. He also tries to apply his power of reasoning and organise the facts in the proper manner. This is the age when the instinct of curiosity predominates. The teacher should try to make use of this instinct in such a way that normal values may develop properly.

At the age of 11 or 12, the self respect starts developing in him. Praise or condemnation of the teacher means a lot for the students. The teacher should handle the child very cautiously at this stage.

The following principles may guide the teacher in imparting knowledge of subject of Geography to his pupils at this stage of education.

(a) The teacher should try to develop the curiosity and the interest of the student in the subject-matter of geogeraphy.

(b) He should try to acquaint the student with the technical subjects connected with Geography.

(c) He should try to mould the life of the student in such a way that he may grow into an useful and ideal citizen.

In fact, this basic stage of education starts from Class I and goes upto Class V. It is the combination of the pre-primary and the primary stage of education. We are not very much concerned with the pre-primary education. We shall try to deal with the primary stage of education.

• This is in fact, the class from which the primary stage of education starts. The teacher may teach the various topics connected with the subject-matter of Geography in the following manner :

(a) The teacher may narrate the stories connected with the things and places seen by the students. He may also take recourse to question-answer method and acquaint the students with various things.

(b) The teacher should also go on writing the things that he is telling to his students, on the black-board. This would have a lasting value, and the knowledge of the students shall be strengthened.

(c) Text-book method should not be applied at this stage. This would make the students bored.

(d) No burden should be put on the students. Their teaching should be made quite interesting.

(e) At this stage of education, the teaching as well as the examination should be oral. The student should not be insisted upon to write things.

(f) Teaching aids, such as models, charts, maps etc., should be used as a good deal, at this stage. By and by the students should be encouraged to take to practical work and writing.

In fact, the teaching of Geography in the III class as well as IV class should be based more on observation. It is the story telling method that shall be more useful for this stage. Knowledge should be imparted more on the basis of the observation and experience of the students.

• Here an attempt should be made to strengthen the knowledge and the experiences acquired by the students in the lower classes.

Attempt should be made to give a practical basis to the teaching. Students should be encouraged to draw maps, charts etc. Use of text-books may be useful.

Even in examination, greater stress should be laid on observation and practical knowledge. Stress should not be laid on Rote Memory or writing out answers to the questions.

While using text-books, the teacher should be cautious. He should train the students in the use of text-books, but the whole of the teaching should not be based on text-books method only.

In fact, the students should be encouraged to know about the natural phenomena so that in higher classes they may be prepared to accept the things taught there.

Story telling—At this stage of education story is the best method of the teaching of Geography. Students of this age group are very much interested in listening to stories. They should be encouraged to acquire knowledge of different regions and places with the help of the stories. The stories may deal with the following—

(a) Life of people of other countries.

(b) Discovery of different lands.

(c) Natural vegetation, mineral wealth, animal wealth etc. of various regions and countries.

(d) Industry and commerce of various and countries.

Defects and their removal—Teaching of Geography and its curriculum, at the primary stage of education, suffers from various defects and drawbacks. These defects and drawbacks have to be pointed out. Without their knowledge, it is not possible to remove and cure them.

The curriculum of the subject-matter for the primary stage of education should be very scientifically drawn. The curriculum should be such that the students may really feel interested in it. On the other hand, it should be drawn with an eye on the environment, so that the teacher may finish his job well within time. Today the curriculum is not very scientifically drawn. It becomes impossible for the teacher to finish his work within time. Then it is also not possible to put his knowledge of the method of teaching into practice, while teaching Geography to the students of the primary stage of education. It happens because of the drawbacks of the curriculum.

Text-books and the syllabus laid are also not free from being cumbersome. This cumbersomeness leads to diminishing of interest in the students. Very little stress is laid on the practical work and observation. In fact, things should be properly provided for.

Interest is very important for proper learning. The subject-matter and the text-books should be organised that the student may feel interested reading the subject. Sometimes syllabus at the primary stage of education is so boring that the students lose interest in the subject. They do not feel like reading the subject. A good deal is laid on Rote Memory.

Our primary schools are ill-equipped. In fact, it is here that the teaching aids have real importance. When the primary schools do not have provision for teaching and the teaching of the subject is bound to suffer. It is also not possible for the teacher to take the students out for excursion and observation tours. The teachers themselves should have proper knowledge of the practical aspect of Geography. In primary classes, the teachers should be very well equipped.

They should be particularly trained to handle the students of this stage of education. If they are trained from this angle, they shall not be able to do justice. Unfortunately, the teachers, at this stage of education suffer from this drawback. This leads to loss of interest in the subject-matter of Geography.

As has been said more than once, in teaching of Geography tours and excursions occupy an important place. In the syllabus, tours and excursions should be properly provided for small children when taken out, should not feel unhappy. They should feel at home while going around and observing things. While tired, they should be give some refreshment. All this requires a good deal of planning. Today, we do not find provision for all of this.

In fact, teaching of Geography requires greater scientific planning. The teaching has to be so organised and planned that the students feel really interested in the subject. The teachers should also be properly trained. Unless all this is done, it is not possible to have proper teaching of the subject.

• What should be the aims and objects and methods of teaching of Geography at the Junior High School stage of education ? What should be the method of teaching of Geography at the junior High School stage of education ? How should teaching of Geography be planned for the students of Classes VI to VIII ? What are the chief defects of the system of teaching of Geography ?

• The students finish the primary education at the age of 10. After finishing the primary education, they enter the junior stage of education. Students, at this stage of education are of the age group of 10. The age is called the preamble of the adolescence. By this time, a good deal of change has taken place in their mental world. They start looking things in a realistic manner and they are also pragmatic. The students start organising their experience. They are also capable of understanding the cause and effect relationship. At this stage, they develop the capacity to analyse events. From the world of imagination, they proceed to the world of realism. It is possible for them to draw certain conclusions.

Self-regarding sentiments also start developing in them. The slightest effort on the self-respect makes them smart. They try to take a leading part in their life. All these changes in the psychology of the children require a change in the method of teaching. Method of teaching of Geography at the Junior High School stage of education should be different from the method that is employed at the primary stage of education.

By this time the students have so mentally developed that they can acquire knowledge of the subject with the help of the charts, models etc. These things shall not be used for teaching Geography to the students at this stage of education. Students of this stage have an idea of the Geography and so they should be taught Geography in its proper perspective.

This age is called the age of generalisation. Students are now anxious to know about the practical utilily of the subject. Geography should, therefore, be taught to them in the light of these requirements.

• Teaching of Geography at the Junior High School of education may be guided by the following aims and objects :

(a) An attempt should be made to strengthen the knowledge of the experiences acquired by the students in their previous stage of education. An attempt should be made to make the students understand the importance of human life and natural environment.

(b) Attempt should be make to analyse this thing or the basis of cause and effect relationship.

(e) Attempt should be made to develop the curiosity, power of imagination, learning reasoning etc. of the students.

(d) They should be trained to be able to appreciate the human life under different geographical circumstances. It shall be possible for them to have this attitude only when they have understood the importance of the geographical factors on human life.

(e) The capacity to study and understand Geography in a developed form may be inculcated in them. They should be trained to make proper use of the charts, maps, models etc. in the study of Geography.

(f) For the students at this stage of education, the Geography of the world should the whole of the country may be taught.

• While teaching Geography of the world, the teacher should keep in mind various physical divisions of the world. Geographical conditions of different countries should be explained in the light of these bigger divisions, teaching of Geography of the world should be guided by the psychological considerations. Students should be taught the subject-matter in such a way that they may be able to understand and appreciate the influence of geographical factor on human life. They should be able to know it very clearly how geographical factors have influenced the human life. By comparative method, it is possible to understand the Geography of different countries.

At this stage of education, story-telling method as well as comparative method shall be useful. In fact, both these methods-should be combined. As and when required, the narrative method or the descriptive method may be used.

While teaching Geography of different physical divisions of the world, attempt should be made to compare their climatic conditions; physical conditions, formation of the surface, vegetation, agricultural products, industry, commerce etc.

Teaching of Geography in this method shall help the students to realise the unity of the world. The unity of the world is the slogan of the day. Every attempt is made to make people realise that they are the members of one big community. When the students shall see that the geographical features of their country are similar to the geographical features of some other country they shall feel one with the people of that particular land. Such a thing will bring nearer the dream of world brotherhood.

• It should be left to the teacher of Geography to teach the Geography of the motherland of the students alongwith the Geography of the whole or to teach the two separately. In fact in the beginning, the Geography of the motherland should be taught in outline. Then it should be taught in detail. By the end of Class VIII, the Geography of the word, in general, should be finished. It should always by borne in mind that they are able to understand the relationship between their motherland and the whole world. This relationship is based on physical conditions, climate, vegetation, mineral wealth, commerce, industry etc. This thing should be very correctly explained to them. Attempt should also be made to give a comparative picture of the Geography of the motherland and other countries of the world.

• Today teaching of Geography suffers from the following defects and drawbacks. Without the removal of these defects and drawbacks, it is not possible to teach the subject in an interesting and scientific manner.

• Today the syllabus and curriculum of Geography is detailed and burdensome. It has not been planned in accordance with the psychological requirements of the students. Big and bulk text-books are prepared and the students have to read them. In fact, the subject-matter should be scientifically organised so that the students may be interested in it.

• Today Geography is not taught in scientific manner. It should be so taught that the students may be able to make use of it in their practical and actual life. It should also be so taught that the students may remain interested in it. No specific method can be laid down for the teaching of Geography. The teacher should be left free to use the method of the teaching that is suited for the psychology of the students.

• By the time the students reach the secondary classes, they have. reached adolescence, their intelligence and mental age have reached maturity. They are now able to establish the cause and effect relationship properly. Their psychological requirements are also how become different. It is, therefore, very necessary to have a properly organised and scientifically planned syllabus and method of teaching of Geography at this stage of education. The curriculum should be complete in itself and it should be capable of focussing the attention of the students on certain geographical problems. It should also be capable of developing the power of imagination, reasoning and judgment of the students. Only those topics that are capable of doing all these things should find place in the curriculum laid down for this stage of education. In short, the following principles should guide the teaching of Geography at the secondary stage of education :–

1. Attempt should be made to strengthen the previous knowledge of the students and they should be made aware of various principles and facts of Geography.

2. An attempt should be made to teach the students the geographical conditions of the people of various countries. Action and interaction of nature and man should also be explained.

3. An attempt should also be made to establish a bond of brotherhood between people of different geographical regions.

4. Attempt should also be made to develop the interest of the students of Geography and to train them to grow into useful citizens.

5. They should also be trained in the use of maps, charts, globe, atlas etc.

• Today in most of the schools, Geography is taught on regional basis. The method is quite scientific and suits the psychological requirements of the students. This method was in the beginning, introduced by Carl Riter, who is called 'Father of Modern Geography.' While studying and teaching Geography 'according to this method, an eye is kept on the influence of geographical factors on human life. This method is, therefore, based on the following two things :

(a) Analysis and explanation of cause and effect relationship; and

(b) Study of Geography from practical and utilitarian angle.

In this method students also get acquainted with the various natural factors that continue to act on human life. He also knows about the extent to which human activities have been influenced by natural factors. The students also know how they can utilise human factor in order to influence the natural conditions.

• The regional method of teaching of Geography is perfectly suited for the secondary schools. This method is based on realistic approach, which is very much suited to the psychological requirements of adolescence. Students who reach secondary classes have some background of Geography and they are also interested in the study of the subject. Their knowledge and interest has to be established properly and given a solid foundation. This method is, therefore, quite suited for this age. In this method the location and situation of a particular geographical region, its climatic condition, rainfall, mineral wealth, natural vegetation and human resources are studied. In fact, this method is quite different from the political method of teaching of Geography.

• In 1950 in Montreal, a famous city of Canada, an international seminar on the teaching of Geography was held. This seminar laid down the following subjects for the teaching of Geography at the secondary level of education :

1. General Geography of the world.
2. Intensive study of the home country or motherland.
3. Special branches and departments of Geography, such a physical, economic or political geography there should be specialised study of any of three branches of study.
4. Study of the various problem of the world. Such a study would enable the students to have a coordinate knowledge of History as well as Geography.

It was also laid down certain geographical complexes must also be studied. Study of geographical complexes involve study of certain difficult geographical conditions such as study of certain countries with more population that can be supported by the natural resources of that particular country.

Certain other Problems. The following problems are also to be studied in geography at the secondary stage of education :

(a) Means of communication and transportation in the world.

(b) Study of various geographical, political, economical and social factors that have brought about the establishment of U.N.O.

(c) Problem of giving aid by developed countries to the under developed countries of the world.

(d) Study of U.N.O. and its contribution in providing food, clothing and shelter to the people of different countries.

• The present system of teaching of Geography to the students of secondary class is brought with various defects. It has the following major defects in it :

1. The curriculum and the syllabus is not scientifically planned. It is pretty heavy.
2. The books are not scientifically written and drawn up.
3. No practical value is attached to the teaching of the subject. In other words, the students are not trained to be able to make a practical use of the subject, after they have finished their education.
4. To much of stress is laid on narration and' description. Very little scope is left for observation and scientific study.
5. The teachers are not left free to make the proper use of the teaching aids.

Due to these defects, the teaching is not made effective and interesting.

• If Geography has to be given a proper place in education and life, its subject-matter and curriculum has to be revised in a way that there may be possibility of scientific study of the subject-matter.

The curriculum and the syllabus should be so designed that the teachers may make proper use of the teaching aids and they may take the students out on excursions and educational tours.

It is the regional method of teaching of Geography or the study of Geography on the basis of physical divisions of the world that shall be really useful.

There are two methods of teaching of Geography – in one we proceed from part to the whole and in the other we proceed from whole to the part. Local Geography implies that the part shall be studied first and then the whole shall be taken up. After studying the local Geography we proceed to the whole of it, that is the World Geography. In teaching it is always wise to give concrete facts and then to proceed to abstract facts. This is natural and psychological. In fact underdeveloped minds are more capable of grasping concrete facts and then only they can grasp abstract facts. It is, therefore, wise to teach the students about local Geography first and then lo proceed to the World Geography. This would imply the study of Geography from the point of view of both the maxims, that is, proceeding from whole to part and from part to whole.

It is very neccesary to teach the students about the technical words that are used in the teaching of the subject. If a student is well aware of the technical terms he shall be able to understand the subject-matter correctly. This achievement can be made by acquainting the students with the local environments. Local environment is full of geographical facts and factors. These facts and factors can be properly understood with the help of the technical terms. For example, if the teacher wants to give the definition of the river to the students, he can very safely take them to some nearing river and explain it. It means that the teaching of Geography should start with the study of the local environment.

It is the study of the immediate environment that is called Local Geography. It is called Local Geography because it is near at hand and it is possible for the students to grasp it quickly. It is also that immediate environment influences human life very much and so it is possible for him to know about it more correctly and more easily. In the process of life we see that man tries to adjust himself with the environment and sometimes he tries to mould his environment to suit his needs. In this process he has to face various difficulties. On the other hand if man tries to escape his environment he comes across certain difficulties. These difficulties in concrete form are the Geographical factors. In local Geography we deal with mountains, rocks, forests, rivers, lands, products, minerals, means of communication, trade and its decline. In developed from these things are also studied but primarily they are studied at the local level. From this point of view it is always wise to start the study of Geography from the study of local environment.

Aims and objects. Local Geography is a part of Geography at large. It is studied in the wider perspective of the aims and objects of the teaching of Geography. It has certain immediate objects as well. The first object in this regard is to like the study of the local Geography with the Geography of the world. In fact study of local Geography is the study of the world Geography in miniature. Through this process it is possible to understand the Geography of the world in the proper manner. In short, following are the aims and objects of the study of local Geography.

1. It helps the study of the future Geography. In fact it is the local practical study of the Geography that enables the students to understand and realise the wider perspective of the Geography. Through the study of local Geography it is possible to have a clear picture of the Geographical control.

2. The Psychological principle of the teaching of a subject is to proceed from concrete to abstract. Local Geography gives the concrete knowledge of certain facts. It also helps teaching of the subject on the basis of maximum from' known to unknown. Local Geography is a known fact and the Geography of the world is unknown. It is, therefore, wise to proceed from Local Geography to the Geography of the world.

3. In order to have a clear idea of the geographical factors, it is wise to study the local Geography. In fact Local Geography is a medium of the study of Geography at large.

4. The study of the local Geography helps the imagination of the students. On the basis of the knowledge acquired it is possible for the students to have a realistic imagination about the things they have not seen. A student may have seen a hill. On the basis of this knowledge he can imagine about Himalayas.

5. Through the study of local Geography it is possible to have an idea of the study of Geography in its complete. In fact local Geography is a part of the whole of Geography. By study of the local Geography it is possible to connect it with the whole of it.

6. By seeing the local Geography, such as markets, centres of industry and trade etc. it is possible to follow easily the changes that take place and may take place in the world at large.

7. Local Geography may be studied in co-relation with History, Civics, General Science, etc. If these subjects are co-related at the local level, they can be properly understood at higher level.

8. The direct knowledge of the local Geography provides a scientific background for the study of Geography.

On the basis of these objects it can be safely said that if local Geography is neglected the education shall be marred. Without the study of the local Geographical factors, it shall be unwise to go ahead with the study of higher Geography.

Importance of excursions. We have seen it more than once that excursions occupy an important place in the study of Geography. This provides them with opportunity to come in direct contact with the Geographical factors. In excursions the students get an opportunity to see various economic and natural factors and to understand them properly. They also get an opportunity to see their influences on human life. If the students are given an opportunity to take excursions at the local level, they are able to understand the importance of geographical control and various geographical principles. If the students are to be given an idea of the fact in Agra and Kanpur, where we have rich shoe industry, it shall be wise to take them out and show it than to make them to cram it. Similarly, if the students are to be given an idea that in eastern districts of U. P. several Sugar Mills are situated, and Bombay or Ahmedabad are centres of the textile industry it shall not be wish to make them cram it. It is always wish to show the students certain things and make them imagine about certain higher and better things.

The Precautions. While the students are being taken out on excursion, in order to help the study of the local Geography the teacher must undertake the following precautions :

1. The teacher must draw an outline of the excursion. He should also explain the aims and objects of the excursion. Unless the students are clear about the objects they shall not be able to benefit by it.
2. In the classs-room the teacher should explain orally about the excursions. He should also explain its difficulties and intricacies. These may be repeated while the students are being taken out for seeing things.
3. The students should be encouraged to collect certain things that are interesting and have geographical importance. This would help development of a museum for future. It would also help them to draw maps.
4. While going out on excursions it shall be wise to take photographs of certain important scenes. These scenes shall be of lasting value. They may be hung in the Geography Room or the Geography Museum.
5. While the students are being taken out, through question-answer method all the geographical facts and seeings should be explained to them properly.
6. While on excursion, the students should be encourged to observe things by themselves. The students should be taken only when going out can be of some use.
7. The time of excursion should be suited to the local needs and requirements. The students should be taken only when going out be of some use.
8. The teacher should be very bold and efficient when he takes out the student on excursions. Unless the teacher himself is very efficient in his task he shall not be able to do anything good to the students.
9. Although it shall be too early to expect the students to take notes of the things yet they should be asked to carry

writing material with them. They should carry a notebook, a pen or a pencil, and put down the things that are of interests and importance to them.

10. In lower classes, the teacher must accompany the students, The teacher himself should be interested in excursions. In higher classes the students may be free to observe things by themselves. But in lower classes teacher must accompany the students explain everything in detail.

When should excursion begin ? Local Geography should be taught in early classes. In fact it should begin in class. Third. It is at this stage that the excursion should start. The students should be given an opportunity to observe things and put questions. Their questions should be scientifically answered. If the questions of the students are properly answered they get interested in the study of the subject. It is also wise to have a sketch of the place that is being observed.

It is wise to take the students out on excursions during various seasons of the year. This would provide the students with the opportunity to observe various changes that take place in the nature during various phases of the year. It shall also provide them with an opportunity to the changes of the season. It would also provide them with an opportunity to see the changes that take place in the rivers, in the fields and such other geographical factors. They should also be given opportunity to draw sketches and charts. These sketches and charts shall be very shabby but they are worth drawing,

In Third class various things should be shown to the students. In class Fourth students should be provided with the opportunity of nature study. Children should be shown pictures of various big buildings and places. It is always wise to link the new knowledge with the previous knowledge. This is a psychological process which strengthens the experience and the knowledge.

Along with the observation, the students should be provided with opportunity for particular work. In the class-room the students should be acquainted with the maps, sketches, etc.

By taking all these steps the teacher of Geography can provide the proper background tor the study of the subject-matter. This background shall be of great use in future life.

In Junior High school classes, the students should be given an opportunity to go out on excursions to different parts of the State or the Region. Now excursions should not be limited to local places only. By the time the students have grown and their mind are ready to receive things in the proper manner. That is why it has been suggested that in Classes VI, VII and VIII the students should be acquainted with the different branches of the Geography.

Local Geography and understanding of natural conditions and natural changes. While studying local Geography the students get an opportunity to see the various changes that take place on the face of the nature. This knowledge of the changes can be properly utilized in the study of Geography at higher stages. If the changes that take place in the nature of the world are to be studied, the changes at the local level provide with a background for proper understanding because the students have acquired some knowledge of the maps and charts. While studying local Geography, they are able to understand the maps and charts in higher classes. Having observed various things at the local level the students are able to imagine those things in better manner. It is wise to use picture of different types at this stage of education. If while teaching Geography, various charts and pictures are used, the outlook of the students get broaden. The broad outlook is very helpful in the study of Geography in higher classes.

Local Geography is helpful for the study of Geography in higher classes. Study of local Geography proves a boon in the study of Geography in secondary classes. Students in the secondary classes are mentally developed. They are able to understand things in a realistic manner. They are also be able to have proper idea of the facts. The knowledge of Geography at the local level is helpful for the study of the Geography full of geographical facts and data. Geographical facts and data are taught in higher classes. These facts and data can be properly understood if the students have the background of the local Geography: In fact local Geography provides an opportunity for observing and understanding things.

This power of observation helps the study of the maps and the charts properly. In short, it may be said that the study of Geography is very much helped by the study of local Geography.

1. Local Geography is based on the principle of studying the whole in parts. In fact it is also based on the principle of proceeding from concrete to abstract.
2. Local Geography helps the knowledge of technical terms of Geography.
3. Local Geography is studied on the basis of the following aims and object :
   (a) It is helpful in this practical study of Geography.
   (b) It gives proper idea of the geographical facts and geographical control.
   (c) It is based on the psychological principle of proceeding from concrete to abstract.
   (d) It is helped in having a clear idea of the geographical factors. It also provides the students with the power to have realistic imagination of the teaching they have not observed.
   (e) By studying the changes at the local level it is possible to study the changes that take place at higher places.
4. Excursions occupy an important place in the study of local Geography. These excursions should be scientifically conducted.
5. Excursions and study of local Geography should start at the III class.
6. The facts and the data collected while studying the local Geography are helpful in the study of Geography a higher level.

10

The Curriculum

Geography occupies an important place in the school curriculum. Till about 20-30 years back geography was taught as a turn subject history and geography under the head general knolwedge. Now we have realised the importance of teaching geography and now it occupies an honourable place in school curriculum in its own right.

The construction of curriculum of geography is a difficult task. However it would be easier to construct a syllabi in geography if we keep certain points in mind, while constructing the curriculum in geography.

Poceed from known to unknown. This means that in case of geography teaching we should start the teaching from the local geography. It we start from local geography we are following the maxims of teaching.

(i) "proceed from known to unknown."

(ii) "proceed from concrete to the abstract."

(iii) "proceed from near to far".

Subject-matter based on actual experience of the students: While constructing the curriculum of geography it should be our effort that we give a syllab in which the child can learn by actual experience. Maximum effort be made to exploit the actual experience of the child. For this, it is essential that even at elementary stage the work is of practical nature.

Use of Geographical Terminology based on home geography. An all-out effort be made to provide to the child geographical vocabulary from their surroundings. For learning islands, delta, etc. it is essential that they have ample knowledge of the geography of their area and for this the geographical vocabulary from their surrounds should be used. Thus in elementary school more emphasis be laid on 'have geography'.

Idea of human life throughout the world. The geography syllabii be such that gives the students an idea of human life throughout the world. If this aim is kept in view from early stages then the students enter the world as practical citizens.

Study in Synthetic way. Various geographical facts be given to the child in a synthetic way. Geography is a practical subject and it should not be considered as a collection of facts from geology and astronomy, etc. It should be presented as an integrated subject.

Emphasis on physical and Economic Geography. In any curriculum of geography, physical and economic geography must be given their proper place. More emphasis be placed on these branches of geography in later school years.

International understanding. We cannot make a systematic study of all the countries of world in any curriculum of geography. It makes it all the more important that we make our selection very carefully. An effort be made to put more stress on international understanding and inter-dependence of nations.

Selection of subjects. Only elementary things' of remote countries be included in syllabi so that students know their situation. Only such topics which have international significance be taught about these countries.

Primary Level

The syllabus of geography at elementary stage should be such which awaken geographical interest in the child. The children may learn geographical terminology but this terminology should be based as 'home geography'. At nursery and kindergarten levels stories having geographical meaning in them may form the basis of study of geography. The syllabus be framed in such a way that the students know their country with reference to human life and general conditions. The textbooks should tell in very simple language stories of people who live under different conditions in different parts of the world. The stories should also tell something about the geography of the country and what it looks like.

At elementary stage home geography should form the basis of curriculum. The terms such as valley, islands, bay, mountains, etc. may be taught at a latter stage. While teaching terminology at the elementary stage all efforts be made to clear their meaning by citing examples from neighbourhood. Use of pictures at this stage in desirable. Use of globe as an illustrative aid be exploited at the primary level. At primary level the syllabus should be such that through globe students may learn the names and situations of continents and oceans. Maps may also be used in primary schools. At this stage the children may be asked to draw a map of the school, the village or the locality.

Any geography syllabus will remain incomplete if it does not include the description of life of people on the globe. The syllabus be based on things of every-day use and children be encouraged to learn about children of different nations. Writing about the syllabus of geography at elementary stage an eminent writer has rightly remarked, "starting from 'home geography', surverying the whole world as a unit and looking upto the villages as their neighbours the children should learn all the broad geographical features of their country with special reference to their own state."

Many teachers are puzzled to know how to frame a syllabus for a primary school if the work is largely determined by childrens' interests and pays little attention to subjects as entities. Yet for these very reasons a syllabus is all the more necessary. As far as geographical work is concerned, the solution lies in recognising that what really matters is not the memorising of bookish facts, but the gaining of the useful background ideas and acquiring of 'tool-knowledge'. For this, suitable topics may be mentioned as examples but the topics actually studied by children of a given age will vary from year to year.

Curriculum at primary stage. At this stage the curriculum of geography may contain the following things.

Curriculum class III. In this class the curriculum may include.

(i) Our region.

(ii) Our village.

(iii) Preparation of the map of the village by the students.

(iv) Students may be asked to show the distribution of various crops of the village.

(v) Students may be given an idea of the population of the village.

(vi) Students may be given the idea of means of communication, market, etc.

(vii) Students may be encouraged to go out on excursions and to observe the things themselves.

(viii) Students be told stories on the life of the people of certain regions.

Curriculum for class IV. At this stage the students be encouraged to observe things and more stress be put on obervation. The following things be kept in mind.

(i) The outline map of the district.

(ii) General views, climate, crops, industries, etc.

(iii) Places of historical importance, means of communication, places of religious and economic importance, etc.

Students be asked to draw maps and charts. Maps of those districts may be drawn whose geography they are studying. Some practical work may be introduced at this stage which may include the following:

(i) Drawing of the map and plotting of important things in it.

(ii) To draw charts and maps of buildings, rooms, etc.

(iii) To look at the map of the country.

(iv) To look at the globe, etc.

Curriculum for class V. The student be taught the geography of the district in which he lives and of his state at this stage. He should be encouraged to draw maps, charts, etc. depicting the natural division, climatic conditions, agricultural products of the state, etc.

To statisfy the curiosity of students they may be told the stories of discoveres e.g. that of Columbus, etc.

However now-a-days elementary school course material is prepared under the following classified heads.

(i) Human geography.

(ii) Home-land or local geography.

(iii) Weather observation and physical geography.

(iv) Map work.

Human Geography. It aims at preparing the pupil for healthy citizenship. Here the aim of geography teaching is more cultural than academic. Everything is learnt and taught from human point of view. At this stage our effort is to develop the spirit of co-existence in the child. The geographical knowledge should help the child to grasp economic, racial and political problems of the world. Thus in syllabus for primary school geography such topics be included which meet the above demands of the child.

Home land and local Geography. If we have to learn only one area in detail it must be the local area which is nearest of all. Student can learn it best by direct method i.e. by exploration and observation. The students be asked to represent, what they have observed in the form of maps and diagrams to increase their power of imagination and reprdouction. The following two aims be kept in view while teaching local geography.

(i) To put emphasis on the influence of site and location on the lives of inhabitants.

(ii) To emphasise the influence of contacts made with near and distant neighbours and to advance the development of the native inhabitants.

Weather Observation and Physical Geography. Students be asked to know about compass and may be asked to read the weather clock and record the direction of the wind. They may be encouraged to construct a wind-vane. Plasticine model may be used to teach them rotation and revolution of earth. An effort be made to explain such terms as Equator, Tropics, Arctic circle, Antarctic circle, latitude and longitude.

The idea of amount of heat at various place can be conveniently given by dividing the globe into five temperature zones. State globe is a good and useful teaching aid for teaching physical geography because it will facilitate the understanding of movement of earth and even such abstract terms as axis, North pole, South pole, equator, etc. will be understood easily. After sometime when the students' power of observation has developed the teacher should illustrate the directions and kinds of wind that are prevalent in the region at different times of the year. Teacher may ask the students to maintain a weather record.

In physical geography students may be taught the causes of wind and rain, breezes, erosion of soil etc.

Map-work. Map-work forms an important part of any syllabus in geography. The drawing of maps and charts be encouraged by the teacher.

Junior High School level

The geography syllabus for this stage may be of the following pattern:

Class VI

(i) The students be encouraged and provided opportunities for strengthening the knowledge of geography gain by them in previous years.

(ii) The following areas of study be encouraged.

  (a) Importance of markets in making available the necessities of life to villages and cities.

  (b) Excursion be arranged to study the geography of the country in which they live. This should include the study of land, natural vegetation, physical divisions, agriculture, means of transportation, trade, population, etc.

(iii) The information about water regions of the world on globe.

(iv) The students be told stories of discovery of different lands such as that of Columbus, Vasco-de-gama, etc.

Some practical work which started in previous classes be further enlarged in this class. The students of class VI be asked to take up the following practical work:

(i) A study of physical map of the country on the basis of colour, scale, direction, distance, location of different physical regions, rivers, sea-shores, etc.

(ii) Various water divisions of the world be taught with the help of models and students be made to learn about contours.

(iii) Students be given due encouragement to observe weather and its changes and be asked to maintain a weather record chart, changes in seasons etc.

Class VII

(i) This is the appropriate time to take up teaching of geography of the continent (Asia). In this study we should include land, climate, natural vegetation, physical divisions, crops, means of communication, trade, commerce and population.

(ii) Means and routes of trade between different countries of the continent.

(iii) Location of various places be taught making use of latitudes and longitudes.

(iv) The study of different agricultural products be taught with reference to Asia.

(v) Students be given enough information about the natural wealth of the continent.

(vi) Means of livelihood and trade of people of different countries of the continent should also be taught in this class.

Practical work suggested for this class be of the following type.

(i) The division of the country into different parts and the study of these parts on the map. The country in which they live be taken up for this purpose.

(ii) Weather and its study including maintaining weather chart, season chart and their effect on agriculture.

(iii) Means of communication and industry in the region be studied by organising excursions. Students be encouraged to observe the effect of nature on the land and life of man.

Class VIII. The syllabus for Class VIII should include the following:

Physical Geography: The annual movement of earth, the weather, season, rays of sun, eclipse, etc. Formation of land, mountains, rocks, falls, plains, sea shores, currents, ebb and tide etc.

Geopaphy of the world: The geography of the world be taught but the basis of teaching should be the division of world on physical basis and the agricultural products of various divisions.

Study of modern life: Under this head we include the study of modern scientific inventions and the influence of natural conditions on these inventions.

Practical Work. In practical work for this class the following may be included:

(i) To keep a record of weather and seasons and to maintain charts for this purpose.

(ii) Study of physical and political divisions of the map of the world.

(iii) Various means of communication like sea routes, land routes, air roots, etc.

(iv) Trade of perishable goods

(v) Science and how it influences life.

(vi) Modern inventions.

(vii) A study of effects of works of U.N.O. on physical life, etc.

Higher Secondary Level

Geography is increasingly becoming a popular subject in secondary schools in India. It has been found that the position of geography in the school curriculam is most unsatisfactory. In secondary schools the syllabus in geography be so framed that it may be taught as a distinctive science and a planned continuity of geography teaching could be followed. The syllabus be changed and kept uptodate in confirmity with the growing demands of the developing countries. the course material at this stage should be oriented towards physical geography. Even while teaching geography on regional basis, due emphasis be placed on both human and physical factors. While teaching regional geography due emphasis be placed on local geography. The syllabus should start from immidiate surroundings and most of the time in first year of high school course be devoted to teaching of physical geography and then world geography and regional geography be taught.

We thus find that there are three components of secondary school geography.

(i) Physical geography and weather observation.

(ii) Regional geography, and

(iii) Map-work.

The curriculum of geography at the secondary stage may be sub-divided under the following headings:

(i) General study of the world other than the country in which the pupil resides.

(ii) Study of home country and its relationship with other countries of the world.

(iii) While studying the world geography the following areas be emphasised:

(a) Movement of various planets, sun, earth, etc.

(b) Formation of day and night, change of seasons, movement of earth, change of weather, longitude and latitude.

(c) Surface of the land, flow of river and its causes, various water divisions of the world, currents, ebb and tide, etc.

(d) Atmosphere, weather, climate, temperature, pressure, rainfall, bands and divisions of the world, cyclone, etc.

(e) Influence of physical conditions on human activities.

(f) Important cereals and crops of the world, raw material.

(g) Mineral wealth and power.

(h) Routes of trade and development of big cities.

While carrying out the study of home country and effort be made to acquaint the child about maximum of details of the country. For this purpose maps, atlases and other teaching aids be used freely. To acquaint the students with home country tours and excursions be organised. For this specific purpose, the regional method of teaching of geography be followed. The study of the following be included:

(i) Situations and locations of various physical divisions of the world, their longitude, latitude, etc.

(ii) Students be asked to measure the length and breadth of a specified region from the map so that they get a clear idea of physical divisions of the world.

(iii) Study of natural or physical conditions including study of mountains, rivers, peaks, etc.

(iv) To know the climate and its qualities, a study of maximum and minimum thermometer be included.

(v) Study of pressure of area and wind.

(vi) Study of rain fall in the area.

(vii) A detailed study of mineral wealth of area.

(viii) A complete study of animal wealth of area.

(ix) Study of industry, art, craft and trade.

(x) Comparative study of location of various trades and industries.

(xi) Study of industrial tours and cities.

(xii) Study of population.

While taking up the teaching of world geography, different teachers follow different order of treatment of continents. However it has now been concluded on the basis of various studies that the three southern continents should always be taught before Europe and North America.

While taking up the regional study of continents generally we teach about India. In some cases Eurasia is taken up in IXth class and Southern continents and Europe are taught in higher classes.

Map-work. Map-work be given due importance and in junior classes we should try to clarify the meaning of map and scale. Maps be used to teach relief. Before taking up the 'contour line method of showing relief, heights may be shown by shading. Various difficult topics can be taught with the help of contours.

From the above discussion it can easily be concluded that there are certain principles which should be observed while framing the syllabus of geography for different classes. The curriculum should be according to the needs of the country. The general criticism of our geography syllabus is that it is lengthy and boring and has not been planned in accordance with the psychological requirements of the child. Students are compelled to read big and bulky textbooks prepared for various classes. Thus, it is desirable if we organise the subject matter in a scientific way so that the students take keen interest in it and develop a taste for the study of geography.

From the above discussion we come to conclusion that there are certain principles which should be observed for constructing the curriculum of Geography at different stages of study. The curriculum should be according to the needs of the country. One of the greatest defects of the syllabus and the curriculum of Geography in our country is that it is detailed and burdensome. It has not been planned in accordance with the psychological requirements of the students. Big and Bulky text-books are prepared and the students have to read them. In fact, the subject-matter should be scientifically organised so that students may take keen interest in it.

1. The following principles should be kept in mind while constructing the curriculum of Geography at different stages of study :

   (i) Proceed from known to unknown.

   (ii) Subject-matter based on the actual experience of the people.

   (iii) Use of Geographical terminology based on home geography.

   (iv) Idea of human life throughout the world.

   (v) Study in synthetic way.

   (vi) Emphasis on physical and economic Geography.

   (vii) International understanding.

   (viii) Selection of Subjects.

   (ix) Syllabus for the elementary stage.

2. Syllabus of elementary stage should start from home Geography. Necessary pictures should find place according to the needs. Provision of regional studies should also be there.

3. There can be no water-tight compartment between the syllabus of elementary stage and secondary stage but the syllabus of Geography in secondary stage should be more developed that study should be systematic.

4. The curriculum at Primary, Junior High School and Secondary stage should be based on Practical work should start from the primary stage which should go on increasing.

11

Lesson Plan

It is necessary for the teacher to have a thorough preparation before he goes to the class. The teacher should not only prepare himself but also divide the topic into various sub-heads. For new teachers this thing is more important. Really speaking without a properly drawn lesson plan, a teacher cannot do justice to his students. With this point in view, there is a provision for 'practice teaching' in the training Colleges. Teachers are given practice in lesson plan drawing. For teachers of long understanding it is not necessary to draw Lesson Plans in advance. They can teach the subject without having a lesson plan before them. Even then, it shall be useful for them to draw an outline of the lesson plan. For young teachers it is more or less inevitable. Now-a-days would be teachers are given a thorough training in the lesson plan drawning. They are made to practise this work while they are preparing themselves for their future assignment. Following are the things which the pupil -teachers must bear in mind, while they are drawing up the lesson plans.

(i) Date.

(ii) Class.

(iii) Subject and topic.

(iv) Period and duration.

(v) Name of the institution.

At the top of the lesson plan these things should be put down so that the pupil-teacher as well as the students should know the duration in which the topic has to be finished. Name of the class, topic and institution give an idea of the whole situation. After it the following things are to be put down.

General aims. In these aims and objects, the mental age of the circumstances and other requirements of the student are kept in mind. These general principles are generally the same for several subjects.

Heading of the chapters. These should be put down in brief as far as possible. It is never wise to take up a long heading.

While giving out this heading, it is always wise to narrate the general principle of the teaching of the Geography, which is, Study of the influence of Geographical environment on the human life, This is also called Geogrophical Control.'

Sub-heads or topics. If the whole lesson is to be taught at the same time it is not possible to divide the time properly. It is, therefore, useful to divide the whole chapter or subject-matter into smaller heads or topics.

Specific aims and objects. This head is a special thing for the teaching of the particular topic and should be laid down clearly so that the student is able to know what shall he achieve by reading a particular subject or topic. He shall then be more attentive towards it. Proper background for the study of the subject is to be created. It is also wise to link that particular topic with the life. Suppose Trade is to be taught. If this is explained to the students that India needs expansion of trade then the students shall feel more inclined to read about that particular chapter or topic. It shall also be wise to explain the effect of trade on human life. It provides the means of livelihood and students may take it up after finishing their education.

Teaching aids. In order to make the teaching interesting, it is useful to have certain aids. These aids should be scientifically handled and used. For example, if the teacher teaches the Sugar Industry, he should show the charts and pictures depicting the Mills and Sugarcane crops etc.

Steps of the process of the teaching. Although teaching is a day-to-day activity and it is not possible to lay down all the steps of its process, yet it should be wise to put down certain steps. This would save the disgression. Following things maybe put down :

(i) Writing of substance. (ii) Method of Teaching. (iii) Teaching aids etc.

Background. This subject implies the utilisation of previous knowledge of the students. The teacher knows about the previous knowledge of the students. He has to start his teaching in such a way that the present topic may be linked with the previous knowledge of the students. If the teacher succeeds in linking the present with the past, in the field of the knowledge, he succeeds. Suppose teacher has to teach the 'trade' or 'industry', it shall be wise to ascertain as to what extent do the students know about the physical conditions, climates, products, means of communications, handicraft etc. With the help of the previous knowledge the present subject-matter may be linked and the result shall be useful.

Introduction. This subject has an important place in the teaching. It is at this stage that a teacher prepares student for studying the subject or the topic. He puts certain questions to the students and with the help of these questions prepares a proper back-ground. There may be various methods of preparing the back-ground but the best method is *Question Answer Method.* In the concluding questions of this step the topic and subject-matter which is to be taught, may be made perfetcly clear.

Statement of objects. After the 'Introdcution' the teacher must explain the students the subject which is to be taught.

Main lesson. Under this heading the topic is actually presented. Teaching is properly organised and the lesson is divided into various sub-heads. While doing all this, it should be kept in mind that certain geographical factors may be included in them.

In order to keep the interest of the students alive it shall be wise for the teacher to put certain questions to the students while the process of teaching is going on. With the help of these questions, it shall be possible to develop the lesson.

Recapitulate. When the lesson has been taught, it shall be wise to put certain questions to the students, in order to ascertain if the students have followed the subject-matter. This can be done with the help of certain questions and other devices. Suppose the subject 'Trade' has been taught, it shall be wise to put certain question concerning tail topic.

Blackboard Work. When the teacher has taught the whole of the lesson he should write the substance on the blackboard. He may also draw certain charts and maps on the Blackboard.

LESSON PLAN NO. 1

Name of Institution : DAV School

Date—12-9-2002 Class V. Duration of period—40 Minutes

Period I

Topics—Products of Uttar Pradesh

Subject—Geography. Initial Works

(1) Plains

(2) North Western Mountains area. The things may be put down on the blackboard

(3) Southern Parts

General Aims

(1) Through the knowledge of Geography it is possible to know about various places.

(2) It is possible to know about the geographical conditions and its influence on human life especially products.

(3) By studying Geography, it is possible to know about physical conditions and their influence on the products and population.

Specific aims. Study of products of Uttar Pradesh on the basis of the knowledge acquired through the observation of local products.

This observation may be carried out with the help of the excursions and travels. The teacher may present the samples in the class-room. He may also take help from the charts and pictures.

Teaching Aids. The teacher may carry the followings with him :

(1) Physical Map of Uttar Pradesh.

(2) Atlas, sketches etc.

(3) Samples of the grains produced in the various parts of Uttar Pradesh.

(4) Pictures depicting the farmers working on the field and certain parts showing the work on the farms.

(5) Picture of the means of irrigation.

(6) Black-board, coloured chalk stick.

The student has the knowledge about the physical conditions, situation climate, vegetation etc. of U.P. He has also seen the field in the neighbourhood of the school and has seen the things that are grown in them.

Introduction. The teacher may put the following questions to the students, in order to prepare proper background :

(1) What things do you eat in Food ?

(2) With what things clothes are made ?

(3) Which grain is produced in the field situated in the West of your school ? "From where do you get the wood that the wood are used in your house ?

(4) Do you take tea in winter ?

(5) With what the Sugar is made ?

With these questions it shall be possible to bring the topic of agricultural products.

Method of Teaching. In order to make the teaching convenient it shall be wise to divide the whole topic into two. In the first part the product of the plains may be taught and in the second part the products of the mountain regions may be taught.

With the help of the questions, the lesson should be started on the basis of the previous knowledge of the students. Relevant questions well help the development of the knowledge and the lesson.

Part One

The following questions shall be helpful.

(1) When does the work of agriculture begin in your village ?

(2) When are houses built, during winter or summer ?

(3) Where from the wood that is used for house-building is obtained ? (From the trees of Sal, Neem, or mangoes).

Statement of Object. Now having created the proper background the teacher shall state that we shall study about the products of our State.

Main Lesson. This may be developed with the help of the following questions :

(1) Which are the main crops in your village or district ?

(2) When is the crop of Kharif sown and harvested ?

(3) Why do the crops get dried or spoiled ?

(4) How is the crop saved when there is no proper rainfall ?

With the help of these questions an idea about general products may be given. Then the students may be directed to the principal and main topic of the product of the plain.

(5) What is the condition of land ?

On the basis of the answers furnished to these questions, the students may be told that there are a good number of forests at low lying area of tarai plains. There is only nominal agriculture. Mostly people take to cattle grazing and breeding. It is in the plains that agriculture is the main industry.

Then the following questions may also be put forward.

(1) What are the main agricultural products of your State ? (Wheat, rice, sugarcane, etc.)

(2) In which part and why is wheat produced in huge quantity ?

(3) In which part and why does rice grow in such a large quantity ?

(4) Where does the sugarcane grow in huge quantity and why ?

With the help of the answers that are put forward by the students, to these questions, it may be explained that in the western parts, there is soil and climate suited for producing wheat. In that part the soil is good and there is proper arrangement for irrigation and so in the western districts of the State wheat is produced in large quantity. In the eastern part of Uttar Pradesh, there is good crop of rice and paddy. The reason for it is that the soil is suited for the cultivation of paddy. There is good deal of rainfall also. Other crops such as that of oilseeds, pulses etc. are found on almost all the part of the State. Agriculture is the main source of the livelihood of the plains of the State.

Part Two

The following questions may put to the students :

(1) What is the main product of the Western part of Western mountainous parts of the State ?

(2) Why do people of the area take to cattle feeding and grazing ? What is their chief food or diet ?

(3) Why do they like milk and other milk products ?

Answers to these questions shall bring it out clearly that in that area a good deal of forests are available, people of these areas are able to lead their life with the help of the products of wood. There are some small fields where some grains are produced. In places where agriculture is possible paddy is produced. There is facility of pastures and so people take to cattle grazing. Rice, meat, milk etc. form their main diet or chief items of food.

Then the teacher may put forward the following questions :

(1) What is the chief product of the southern part of the land and why ?

(2) How is it that agriculture as well as cattle grazing are carried out side ?

(3) Does some wheat grow in the southern part of U. P. or not ?

On the basis of the answers to these questions it must be made clear to the students that southern part there is dearth of water and so the land is not fertile. Even then barley, maize and some wheat is grown in that area. Where irrigation facilities are available agriculture is carried on but in other places only pasture are available.

Recapitulation and revision. The teacher may carry out the recapitulation and revision of the lesson taught with the help of the following questions :—

(1) What are the chief products of Uttar Pradash and where are they grown ?

(2) Why is so much sugar produced in Uttar Pradesh ?

(3) What is the influence of these things in human life ?

Black-board work and practice. The teacher should write out the substance of the lesson on the black-board and then he should direct the students to copy it out on the exercise book.

The students should be encouraged and made to practice to show the various products on the map.

The influence of the agricultural products on human life should also be explained to the students. A comparison should be made with other agricultural States of India.

Various products may be shown on the maps in colours.

LESSON PLAN NO. 2

ABM High School (Moradabad)

Lesson Plan of Story Method

Dated 9-10-2002 ClassVI Time 35 Minutes Subject

Geography (Cane industry in Uttar Pradesh)

General Aims

(1) To make the students understand that the following things are required to run an industry :

(a) Raw material; (b) labour; and (c) means of communication and transport.

(2) To acquaint the students with the industry through Story Method.

Specific Aims

To make the students aware of the process of sugar industry, Teaching Aids :

The following things may be utilised by the teacher in teaching the lesson :

(a) Map of U. P. (b) Sketch of a mill. (c) If possible, a picture showing the crushing of the sugar-cane.

Previous Knowledge

(1) The students shall be aware of the small centres of home and cottage industry where jaggery (gur) is prepared.

(2) The students shall also be well aware of the process of sugarcane production and its harvesting etc.

Introduction. This may be put forward in the form of the following questions:

(1) What is the taste of sugar ? (Sweet)

(2) Where is it procured from ? (From the market)

(3) Where does it come from to the market ? (From mills)

Statement of the Teacher. Today I am intending to narrate before you the story of the industry of sugar. This is one of the main industries of our country.

Main Lesson. There was a person by the name of Rameshwar Prasad. He tried thrice to pass, High School examination but failed. After that he told goodbye to the book and left home. After three days of wandering here and there, he reached Captainganj in Gorakhpur Destrict. In the market he heard that he could get work in a sugar mill. Since Rameshwar Prasad had been starving for two days, he enjoyed the hospitality of a generous person and started thinking about his future. There was no difficulty at home. He could go there and lead a happy life, but he was afraid of books. He was also ashamed of his action. However, he was carried up to the mill gate by the generous person who had provided him with food. There he was engaged as a labourer for carring the bricks. On Friday and Saturday he worked there and in the evening of Saturday he received Rs. 2/- as his wages. The mason with whom he was working took pity on him. Rameshwar Prasad was, in fact, a Brahman, but he gave himself as a Kurmi. Even then he was not prepared to eat the food touched by anyone else. The mason came to know of the fact that Rameshwar Prasad was a Brahman and so he introduced him to an engineer. This seemed to be the opening of his future.

On Monday morning Mr. Singh, the engineer, recommended the case of Rameshwar Prasad to the Attendance Clerk and got him appointed as a labour to the Fitter. He was put under the charge of the Fitter generally known as *Bhagat Ji*. Bhagat Ji as a competent workman. He was a sympathetic person also and suited treating Rameshwar Prasad nicely. It was the time of crushing season and so the work was going on at top speed. Bhagat Ji could reach any part of the mill and with him Rameshwar Prasad also got the opportunity to visit various sections of the mill.

First of all the cart loads of sugarcane arrived and they were put to test. From the third day the work of the crushing started. In the meanwhile, the Panman, Sardar Ranvir Singh, lost his Pan Labour or 'Pan Coolie'. The Pan Coolie had run away and so he made a damand for a compensation for dependable Pan Labourer.

Now Rameshwar Prasad was put in the charge of Sardar Ranvir Singh and he became a Pan Coolie.

Rameshwar Prasad continued to work there for two years. One, Mr. Ram Singh went to Captainganj, Gorakhpur. He was a friend of Rameshwar Prasad and met him. Rameshwar Prasad took him around the mill and showed him various sections of the sugar mill.

First of all, Mr. Ram Singh was taken to the yard, outside the mill. There hundreds of carts loaded with sugarcane were standing. Many more carts were arriving from the different directions. After that yard, Rameshwar Prasad took his friend inside the mill. Just after entering the gate. Ram singh saw a big tank like thing. Sugarcane was dumped into it. From there it was mechanically carried forward. Later on, it was crushed by heavy crushers and about a foot thick sugarcane juice was coming out of it.

Process in the Pan

In the Pan the juice was converted into thick jaggery or gur. There mechanically the molasses part of the juice was separated. The Jaggery or thick juice here looked black and dirty. It did not look like white sugar, as we see, but like black manure.

There again it was mixed with juice and heated again. It was heated thrice in the pan. When it had been heated thrice, the molasses got separated and now the white sugar started pouring in. This was dropped out of the filter of a machine located at a height of 30' to 40'. From that hilght the sugar was dropped. Then its temperature was brought down mechanically and so it fell in the filter.

There were three types of crystals—small, medium and big. All these three types of crystals were filled in separate bags.

When Ram Singh had seen all this, he enquired from Rameshwar Prasad, "Where shall it now go ?"

Rameshwar Prasad explained that after putting the labels and the number on the bags, it would be lodged in the godown, from where it would be sent to the market to be sold. After explaining all these things, Rameshwar Prasad took Ram Singh to the godown.

Ram Singh saw that at the gate of the godown several wagons of goods train were standing. Ram Singh again enquired, "Rameshwar, what it going on there ?" Rameshwar replied that the wagons were being loaded with the bags of sugar. Then Ram Singh saw that those wagons were being driven to the station. When he enquired of the clerk, who was looking after the loading of the bags on the wagons, he was informed that the sugar bags had been purchased by a trader of Calcutta whose firm was known as "*Sagarmal and Sons*". He also explained that certain other orders were also with him. After loading 2,200 bags of Sagarmal and Sons the clerk explained that he would load the orders of others firms.

Statement of the Teacher

Children, you may be surprised to listen that 2,200 Bags were purchased by one man. You may ask a question—"What shall he do of these 2,200 bags?"

Ram Singh was anxious and curious to know about the whole of the sugar industry and so from the sugar mill he came to the railway station. There he saw that clerk of *'M/S Sagarmal and Sons'* was present. Ram Singh enquired of him, "You are a Marwari how did you come to this part of U. P. ?

"Boy," the old man replied, "I am from Calcutta and had come here to purchase 2,200 bags of sugar for my firm, M/S Sagarmal and Sons. I actually wanted 3, 000 bags of sugar but the Manager is giving only 2,200 bags."

Surprised Ram Singh asked, "What will you do of 2,200 bags ?" The old man explained, "Some bags we have to send to other countries while the others shall be sold in the market. Various wholesale dealers have placed orders with us. Unless all this is done, we shall have to suffer loss ?"

Since the old man seemed to be annoyed, he left Rameshwar and Ram Singh with these words and went away. Rameshwar

Prasad and Ram Singh also come back. Ram Singh left the place by the evening train and came home.

Questions

The teachers may use the following questions for revision work :

(1) Why is sugar manufactured in Captainganj, Gorakhpur ?

(2) Where from is so much of sugarcane procured ?

(3) Where does so much of sugar go ? Why does it go to the market ?

(4) Why so much of sugarcane is produced in the eastern part of India ?

(5) What are the various means ot transport and communication ?

These questions shall make it clear to the students that the land of the eastern part of India is good for the crop of sugarcane and so a good deal of sugarcane is produced in eastern U. P. It shall also be clear to the students that sugarcane is transported to the mills by bullock-carts. Sugar is sent to distant countries where it is not manufactured. Sugar is exported by rail and ship, trucks and such other means of communication. It occupies an important place in the industry of our country.

12
Examinations System

Examination system is the test of the knowledge acquired. In the present set-up of education it is this very system which helps us to ascertain the efficiency of a student in a particular subject. Examinations are of two types :

(a) Written or theoretical ; and

(b) Oral.

Written tests are also called essay type of test. It is the tests that are even today applied for testing the knowledge. Probably it is this type of test, which makes the students feel unhappy and nervous about their examination days. Sometimes they are not able to answer questions properly and so it becomes difficult for them to get through.

Students are not able to answer questions properly because they are not trained in this particular art. There are definite methods of answering questions. Those who learn this art get very good marks. The teacher has to train the students in the art of answering questions.

Questions Papers

Questions of Geography are slightly different from questions of other subjects. In Geography a student has to be told about the fact that questions should be accompanied by sketches, maps, etc. In Geography greater emphasis is laid on the power of thinking. It is not possible to learn certain things by heart and reproduce them in the subject-matter of Geography. He cannot solely depend upon the bookish knowledge. He is to apply his independent thinking and common sense.

Examination of Geography is oral as well as written. In lower classes it is the oral examination which is more useful. This oral testing can go on along with the teaching as well. The teacher may ask the students to answer questions having bearing on the lesson which was-taught in the class-room. He may also ask the students about certain things on the map. He may also ask them to draw certain maps and charts at home.

The teacher of Geography must provide home task to the students. Teaching of Geography cannot be completed in the classroom. The students have to be told to draw maps and charts at home and only then they shall be able to keep in mind what they have learnt in the class-room. While answering questions on Geography, human element must always be kept in mind. Geography is, in fact, the study of the influence of geographical factors on human life and so it should always be kept in mind.

(1) Oral test—In the elementary classes it is the oral test which is useful. The students should be asked certain oral questions and they should be made to answer them. These questions should be psychologically designed. Only psychologically designed questions can elicit proper information and test the knowledge and efficiency of the students.

Oral questions have one difficulty. It is not possible for all the students to take part in this type of testing. Only a few students get an opportunity to answer questions. It is on account of this reason that written tests are employed.

(2) Written test—Written test may be of several types. The teacher may examine his students everyday in the class-room. Then, after a certain period of time, a test of longer duration may be given to the students. This duration may be of an hour or three hours. The questions in this test should be based on the subject or the topics taught to the students. Later on, terminal or annual examinations may be held. In these tests the students should be asked to write out their answers to the questions.

Reform in old system of examination : Essay type of examination or old system of examination has been criticised for long. People do not like this system of examination. A demand has been going on that the system of examination should be amended and changed. The arguments that are advanced against this system of examination are the following :

(a) The students have to write a lot and they have to depend upon their rote memory.

(b) The students do not get an opportunity to answer questions independently. Their power of thinking and reasoning does not get an opportunity for expression.

(c) Writing power and the handwriting of the students influences the award of the marks.

(d) Sometimes individual consideration also influence the marking.

(e) Certain other arguments of this nature are also advanced against this method of examination.

New type of test. The examination reform has been the long desired need. Educationists have started realising that no change in the education system can be effected unless the examination system is changed. It is also not possible to do away completely with the system of examination and so reform is the only way out. With this aim in view certain researches were carried on and conducted. Now certain new types of tests have been devised. It is claimed that they are more objective and help the examiner to keep away the subjective considerations. These tests are also helpful for the development of the independent thinking and reasoning of the students. Rote memory does not find an important place in these tests. These tests are also connected with the syllabus and curriculum. In fact, it is claimed that new types of tests and the old types of tests should be so combined that the result may be good and helpful.

Geography and new types of tests. For a pretty long time teachers of Geography continued to lay stress on the rote memory. They encouraged the students to learn certain geographical facts by heart and reproduce them the geographical problems that are presented before the students and they are encouraged to answer them in such a way that the knowledge acquired may prove to be of practical use.

Certain new types of tests. The new system of examination has put forward the following types of tests :

(1) True-false Tests,

(2) Recall Test,

(3) Multiple Choice Test,

(4) Matching Test.

True-false test. In this type of test certain statements are given. Before the statement, the words true/false are written. If the statement is true, student has to tick 'true' and if the statement is false, he has to tick the 'false'. An example is given below :

(i) There is more of rainfall in Delhi as compared to Calcutta. (True/False)

(ii) Major part of Southern India is made of alluvial soil. (True/False)

(iii) In Assam more tea is produced as compared to Bengal. (True/False)

(iv) In Bengal most of the factories consume coal. (True/False)

(v) Singapore is one of the most important towns of the Equatorial region. (True/False)

(vi) The people of the Equatorial region have made a great progress in industry. (True/False)

(vii) Rubber is produced in the forests of the Mediterranean region. (True/False)

(viii) The Ganges is the largest river of the Equatorial region. (True/False)

(ix) The staple food of the people of the Equatorial region consists of rice. (True/False)

(x) The countries of the Monsoon region are very productive. (True/False)

Recall test. In this type of test the knowledge of facts is tested. Teacher ascertains whether the students still remember certain facts or not. In this type of Test simple questions are asked whose answers are limited in a word or two. Here, we are giving the examples :

(1) What is the average temperature in the Equtorial region ? (.........)

(2) Name of the natural region where cinchona is produced in the largest quantity. (.........)

(3) Which mineral product is found in the largest quantity in countries. (.........)

(4) Which region exports ivory. (.........)

(5) In which region do we find fruits such as grapes, organges and figs? (.........)

(6) Name the main industry of Java. (.........)

Completion test. In this type of test the students are asked to fill in certain blanks, such as :

(i) ....is the biggest cone producing country of the world.

(ii) The name of the highest mountain peak of the world is.........

(iii) On 21st June the sun rays are straight on.........

(iv) The place which has the highest rainfall lies in the.........State of India.

(v) The most populated town of the Monsoon region is.........

(vi) The town of.........in Indonesia is famous for its sugar mills.

(vii) Citrus fruits are the special gift of the.........region.

(viii) Tea is produced in the.........region.

(ix) Most of the countries of the Equatorial region lie in the south-east of the continent of.........

Multiple choice test. In this type of test, certain statements are given. Before every statement, there are certain reasons assigned. Out of these reasons, only one is correct. The student is asked to mark the correct one. Examples are given here :

(i) Lancashire is the most famous textile producing centre on account of the following reasons :

(a) There people are expert in textile production.

(b) Cheap labour is available for the job.

(c) The climate is soiled for the industry.

(ii) In Eastern U. P. there are sugar mills because :

(a) Rich people live there.

(b) Land is suitable for sugarcane production.

(c) Cheap labour is available.

(iii) The Equatorial region is well-known for the following agricultural and natural projects :

(1) Wheat.

(2) Rubber.

(3) Tobacco.

(4) Rice.

(iv) The climate of the following natural regions is the most pleasant for human beings :

(1) The Equatorial region

(2) The Monsoon region.

(3) The Tundras.

(4) The Mediterranean region.

(v) The Monsoon region exports the following commodities to other parts of the world :

(i) Tea. (ii) Jute. (iii) Rice. (iv) Citrus Fruits.

(vi) Extensive areas in the following natural region covered with thick, dense forests :

(i) The Tundras. (ii) The Hot Deserts. (iii) The Mediterannean region. (iv) The Equatorial region.

Matching test. In this type of Test some facts are given in one column and other facts are given in another column. Every facts in the first column is related to one of the facts in the second column. The students are required to pick-up the corresponding facts from the second column and give their numbers in the front of the facts related to some in the first column.

Town

1. Bhilai
2. Jagadhari
3. Kolkatta
4. Surajpur (Punjab)
5. Visakhapatnam
6. Raniganj
7. Sindri

Countries

1. India
2. Malaya
3. Arab Countries
4. Ethiopia
5. Indonesia
6. Australia
7. Greece

Industries

1. Petroleum Refinery Plants

2. Jute Mill
3. Paper Mill
4. Ship-building
5. Cement Industry
6. Coal Mining
7. Fertilizers
8. Steel manufacture
9. SafetyMatches Industry

Products exported

1. Rubber
2. Dry fruits
3. Petroleum
4. Sugar
5. Steel
6. Coffee
7. Coal
8. Tea
9. Wheat.

Factual test. In this type of test certain things are written before one statement. Out of the several things written, only one is the fact. The student has to mark out the word or thing which is actual and correct. An example is given below :

(i) The basin of Ganges is famous for producing wheat, rubber, tea, apple, cotton.

(ii) Egypt is famous for coco, rice, cotton, tea, wheat.

(iii) In Pampas there are grape vines, cattle wealth, potatoes bears, oranges.

Summary

1. Today examination is as important as it was in olden days. No change has taken place in the concept of examination.
2. Examination is a method of testing the knowledge and the efficiency of the students.
3. In Geography examination occupies an important place. Examination in Geography his to be more scientific as compared to other subjects.
4. Oral test is useful for lower classes. For higher classes it is the essay type test which is at present used.
5. Essay type of examination has been criticised since long.
6. Now new type of tests have been designed. They are more objective and useful for the students. Given below are a few objective type of tests :

   (1) True-false Test, (2) Recall-Test. (3) Completion Test. (4) Multiple Choice Test, (5) Matching Test, & (6) Factual Test.

13
Textbooks

Text-books occupy a very important place in the teaching of Geography. They form part of the traditional teaching aids. In fact it would be wrong to call them teaching aids. They are a means of important knowledge. It is through text-books that the knowledge is imparted to students. They serve as a guide and means for the teachers as well as the students. Through the help of the text-books the teacher can impart knowledge to the students and can help them to revise the lesson learnt in the class-room. With the help of the text-books it is also possible to give home task to the students. If properly used text-books can go a long way in the teaching of Geography in a successful manner.

It is possible to teach regional Geography without using textbooks but it is not possible to teach Geography of larger areas, such as country, sub-continent, or the world, without the use of the Geography. These text-books are written with a specific purpose of serving the needs of the students and so it is very necessary for them to be useful and good. These text-books should be so designed that they may serve the purpose of the students of the standard for which they are used. They should neither be very bulky nor very small. There should be enough material to serve the purpose of the students.

Utility of text-books in primary classes—In the primary classes the students are not very matured. They require text-books that may serve the undeveloped mind. In fact text-book should not be used a lot in the primary classes. Text-books should be sparingly used.

Text-books in the secondary classes – Here the students require text-books. Students of this stage of education are properly developed. They try to learn things in a realistic manner. They can benefit a good deal from the text-books. In fact, the method of teaching that should be question-answer method. The students may be asked to read the text-books silently and then question may be put on the subject-matter. For some difficult subject-matter, the students may be asked to refer to text-books.

Text-books in order to be useful should contain the following qualities –

1. Text-books that are intended to be used should be useful for the students as well as teachers. They should be so designed that on the one hand they may be written according to the psychological requirements of the students and on the other they should serve the purpose of the teacher who wish to impart knowledge to the students in a successful and interesting manner.
2. The size of the book should be handy. It should be possible for the students to carry them properly. They should not be bulky. This is specially true about books intended for the primary classes.
3. Printing and get-up of the books should be interesting and attractive. They should be printed in the letters that they do not require strain on the eyes of the students. On the other hand they should be correctly and neatly printed.
4. The exterior of the picture should be attractive. If the exterior is attractive, students would like to carry them and keep them. This is true of the books intended for primary classes.
5. They should serve the purpose of the subject-matter as well as the aims and objects of teaching. They should be written with a view on the aims and objects of the teaching.
6. The text-books should be accurately written. They should present the subject-matter in such a manner that there is

no fault in them. The subject-matter presented there in should be upto date.

7. The style of the books should also serve the psychological requirements of the students of different stages. Text-books intended for the students of the primary classes should be written in a story form. In the text-books meant for higher classes the author may use the regional method or some other method that is useful for the students of the stage.

8. The text-books should continue to keep the interests of the students alive in the subject-matter. The subject-matter should be presented in a simple and lucid style and clear form.

9. The text-books should contain all the necessary and relative material required for a particular stage of education.

10. The text-books of different stages should be complimentary to each other. Text-books that are used in primary classes should have some bearing and connection with the textbooks that shall be used by the students in the Junior High School classes. Similarly text-books that are to be used by the students of the secondary classes should keep in mind the books that have been used by the students in the Junior High School classes.

11. Text-books should be free from prejudice. The presentation of the subject-matter should be unbiased. There should be no material which can injure the susceptibility of any class or category of people. They should contain objective description of the people and conditions *of* different countries.

12. The text-books should contain charts, maps, diagrams, etc. as and where required. Without the charts, maps and diagrams etc. the subject-matter of Geography cannot be taught properly. It is, therefore, necessary to give place to all these things in the text-books.

13. Geography is a developing subject. Every day we find that new researches have been made in the field of Geography;

Upto date knowledge of Geography must be given place in the text-books.

14. At the end of every chapter of the text-book there should be certain questions that may be used for the revision of the subject-matter. Without these questions the text-books shall not be useful.

15. If required the text-books may give a substance of the chapter at the end of each lesson. Such a provision will help the students to grasp the subject-matter properly

Supplementary Books

Other than the text-books we have certain other kinds of books that are also used in the teaching of Geography. They are of the following types—

(a) Help Books, and (b) Reference Books.

Help books. Help books are very necessary for the students as well as teacher. There should be good collection of such books in the library of every school. These books help the students to acquire further knowledge of the subject. They are in fact written in an interesting form of a story or description of the travels. Students read them not as text-books but as interesting reading material. This interesting reading material encourages them to learn more about geographical facts.

Reference books. Reference books are big standard books that are used by the teachers and grown-up children. Annual Geographical Reports, Government Reports, Dictionaries and Encyclopaedia, Magazines etc. form this category of books. These books should be kept in the library for the use of the teachers and grown up students. There should also be rich collection of reference books in the school.

Precautions in regard to use of text-books. While the teacher is teaching the students in the class should not use the text-books very much. Text-books should be used for revising the lesson or for writing out the home task. The teacher may ask the students to read the book at home or in the class and then put questions in order to ascertain whether the students have grasped the subject-matter or not While teaching, the teacher must put down the substance of the chapter taught on the black-board.

1. Text-books are essential of the scheme of education. They are treated as teaching aids but in the fact they are more than that.
2. In primary classes text-books should not be very much used.
3. In secondary classes text-books should be used. Even here the text-books should not be used very much.
4. In secondary classes the text-books should be used for preparing the home task or the lesson already taught in the class-room.
5. Text-books should have the following questions in them—
   (a) They should not be very bulky. In fact they should handy.
   (b) They should be properly written, keeping in view the psychological requirements of the students.
   (c) Printing and get-up should be nice and attractive.
   (d) The subject-matter of the text-book should be upto date and accurate.
   (e) The text-books should be properly illustrated. They should contain charts, maps, etc.
   (f) There are also other qualities that are required for the text-books.
6. Other than text-books, Help Books and Reference Books are also needed for the teaching of Geography.

"No geography teacher will question the value of maps in Geography teaching. Maps are in fact indispensable. They are required in the study of most topics of regional Geography, such as position relief, climate, natural vegetation, minerals, the distribution of population, towns, industries, communications."

—Prof. *E A. Macnee*

Maps and their importance. We have already seen the quotation from Prof. E. A. Macnee in his book entitled, "The Teacher of Geography." He has laid a good deal of stress on maps. These maps, as we have already seen, from a part of the teaching aids and the scheme of the teaching of Geography. In fact maps and charts are very important and it is very necessary to treat them separately in a chapter.

Maps are very useful in giving a realistic picture of the subject-matter to the students. Geographical facts and geographical factors cannot be explained properly without the help of the maps. In the maps we have the geographical factors such as situation, climate, produce, agricultural products, population etc. Maps help the explanation of all these factors in a concrete form. Maps and charts are concrete methods of explaining abstract facts.

These maps and charts add to the educational value of the room and make the subject interesting and attractive. With the help of the maps and charts the teacher can explain the things easily and quickly. It is also possible to teach the subject with these maps in a more Scientific and Psychological manner. In fact maps form an integral part of the teaching of Geography. It is therefore necessary to have a clear idea about them as well.

Kinds of maps : Maps may be of the following types :

(1) Wall maps, (2) Sketch maps, (3) Atlases and (4) Charts and Indexes.

Requisites of understanding and studying the maps: Since maps form an integral part of the teaching of Geography it is necessary to understand certain factors that influence the proper understanding of maps and charts. They are enumerated below—

1. It is difficult to draw maps correctly on the black-board. Sometimes boundary lines are wrong. It is wise to have drawn maps. Such maps present the boundary lines in a correct manner. If such maps are available the students shall be able to fill in the things properly. Maps with the correct boundary lines are more necessary for the students of the lower classes. They have to be taught things very

correctly so that things do not go wrong. Once a student commits a mistake he perpetuates it.

2. It is necessary to give practice to the students to use maps. Every student must have an Atlas. In the Atlas he can see the rivers, dirctions of their flow etc. Similarly he can watch a mountain and have an idea about it. He can also see the location of the city and other things.
3. On the basis of memory it is difficult to drawmaps and sketches correctly. It is all the more difficult for the students who are learners in the field. They should be given proper practice and opportunity to draw maps.
4. Student should have the correct idea of the things about which they have to draw maps. Unless there is clarity of knowledge, it is not possible to draw maps properly. The outlines of the maps should be given correctly and properly. In other words, the students should have exact knowledge of the outlines about which the maps have to-be drawn.
5. It shall be useful to encourage the students to fill in the maps with colour. Colour-filling in the maps develop the aesthetic sense of the students. It also makes them interested in the drawing of the maps. Use of coloured pencils helps to distinguish and discriminate between the various things. It is, therefore, useful to encourage the students to use coloured pencils.
6. Unless the students are given an opportunity to study the maps properly it shall not be possible for them to interpret these maps in a correct manner. Proper study of the maps means that the students should have perfect idea of whole country whose map they are studying. It is wise to repeat the use of the maps and globes so that the doubts of the students may be removed and they may have correct idea of the things. In fact the students should be encouraged to make friendship with the maps. Such a practice would encourage them to know things properly and have details about it.

7. *Fairgrieve* has said that 99% of Geography is taught through maps. It is through the maps that it is possible to have proper interpretation of the subject-matter of Geography. On the other hand if the students are not made to practise the. use of the maps properly,, it may have disastrous results. It is quite possible that they may have a wrong idea of the whole thing and their knowledge of Geography may be incomplete.

Really speaking maps are a very important aid for the teaching of Geograpy. It is with the help of these maps and sketches that it is possible to draw a proper picture of the geographical factors on the minds of the students. After some time these factors become a part of the memory of the students. They may repeat the things like various events of a film. Once the student has learnt the things with the help of the maps, it can strengthen the knowledge with the help the sense organs.

In fact the knowledge acquired by a student with the help of the maps becomes thorough. The student becomes well aware of the knowledge of the country whose Geography he has read with the help of the maps.

Maps and their teaching. It is necessary to teach the use of the maps in a proper manner. Really speaking every lesson requires illustration. This illustration may be presented with the help of the maps. The teacher may himself draw the maps on the blackboard or illustrate the things with the help of the maps already present. If the maps are ready in hand they save a lot of time.

"While the maps are drawn on the black-board it is necessary to have a correct outline. Here also an outline may be prepared in advance. However, this does not rule out the possibility of giving practice to the students to draw maps.

Atlases are essential and every student must possess one. In this regard the teacher of Geography must be slightly strict. He should insist on the fact that every student must carry an Atlas with him.

Stage of the study of the maps and sketches. There are three stages of the study of the map. In fact these stages are equally important and useful for the study of maps as well.

First Stage. This is the stage when the student starts getting acquainted with the things of his environment. He tries to observe things of the nature that is around him. He continues to do it consciously. While going to school from his home he observes various things on the way. If he lives in a village he sees the fields and the process of sowing and harvesting that is going on in them. He also sees the change of the weather and the season. If he lives in the city he sees the various industries that come across him. Similarly it is possible for him to get acquainted with the geographical. factors with the help of maps. It is, therefore, necessary for the teacher to strengthen his experiences. It is also his duty to widen his experiences. These experiences that he acquires while in coming in contact with the local environments can be used for furthering the knowledge of Geography. This knowledge can serve us background for the understanding of the various principles. In the class the teacher of Geography should use the maps in such a manner that the knowledge of the local Geography may be strengthened and this knowledge may form the basis of furthering the knowledge.

Second Stage. This is the stage when the real responsibility and the work of the students begins. Now it is not sufficient only to hint at or indicate the maps. It is necessary to provide the solid knowledge to the students. This solid knowledge requires that various geographical facts should be actually shown on the maps. Students should be so equipped that they may acquire the knowledge of the various geographical facts on the basis of their presentation on the maps. The teacher should attempt and try to make students capable of realising that the maps present certain natural facts. It is possible that this process may take some time but it is essential for the proper understanding and realisation of Geography. Then the students should also start drawing maps of their own.

Third Stage. At this stage the students come to realise that maps are nothing but symbolic presentation of the realities of life. Now he starts furthering his knowledge with the help of the symbolic knowledge already acquired. With the help of these symbols he starts getting acquainted with new things. No doubt he is well aware of these symbols and hints. It is, therefore, necessary to have a scientific and proper study of the maps.

Properly organised and scientific study of the maps. It is necessary to have a properly organised and scientific study of the maps. If the study of the maps is carried out in a haphazard and ill manner, it shall be of very little use. It shall also not help to organize the development of the minds of the students. Infact maps are a means to bring about planned and scientific development of the mind. They train the students to take up things in a planned and organised manner. Students also learn to present the things with the help of the maps. Their knowledge is strengthened.

It is not wise to teach the study of the maps independently. In other words it means that the maps should be studied while the subject is being taught. Such a co-relation with bring about the proper understanding of the maps as well as the subject-matter.

Practice of showing of the charts and the maps. Students should be given thorough practice of drawing the charts accurately. They shall not be able to draw the maps and the charts accurately, they shall not be able to have the proper knowledge of the subject-matter. The maps should be selected according to the Psychological requirements of the age and stage of the students. Unless this factor is borne in mind it shall not be possible for the students to study them properly. The maps should be such as to attract the interests of the students. Unless the maps are attractive and interesting the students shall not be able to draw benefit out of it. In the maps, things should be plotted properly and correctly. The students should be encouraged to present things in a proper form on the maps.

The students should not be given vague instructions in regard to the drawing of the map. In fact they should be told thing exactly.

Use of Charts and Indexes. Use of Charts and Indexes is very necessary for the teaching of Geography. In fact these indexes and charts should be used to secondary and higher classes. They should not be used in elementary classes and Junior High School classes. If such a thing is done it shall not be of any educational use.

In lower classes there should be very simple maps. Too much of accuracy should not be insisted upon. Students may take to colouring the maps.

In Junior High School and Middle classes more accuracy should be insisted upon. Students may be explained the use of the sketches ar d preparation of the maps etc. Too much of time should not be spent on it.

Students should be encouraged to draw sketches and maps.

In Secondary classes and Higher classes maps should be used with all properly and also to use them in an accurate manner. It is at this stage of education that use of maps has its real importance.

1. Maps and Charts are very important for the teaching of Geography.
2. Maps and Charts include the following :

   (a) Wall Maps, (b) Atlases, (c) Sketch maps, and (d) Charts and Indexes
3. Charts and Maps should be taught separately. They should be taught along with the subject-matter. In fact these maps and charts should be an agency to clarify the abstract facts of Geography.
4. Students should be given a good deal of practice in drawing the maps and sketches.
5. In lower classes outline of the maps may be taught. In junior classes some accurate teaching of the maps may be takenup and in secondary and higher classes the use of the maps should be made thoroughly correct and in accurate manner. Students should also be encouraged to colour the maps and charts.
6. Indexes and Charts are more useful for secondary classes and higher classes.

Geography is taught with an eye on human life. In fact the teaching of the subject begins at early stages of the primary classes. Here the students are expected to learn about the life and Geographical conditions of different countries. The teaching of the subject has to be so modified and arranged that the Psychological requirements of the students may be made. In the students of primary classes the teacher has to adopt the method of story telling. This method can be very useful.

Story Telling and Teaching of Geography. Students of primary classes are very fond of listening to stories. These children are of the age group between 8 to 11, and so they listen to stories. Listening to stories is an essential part of their Psychology. It is also possible for them to remember stories. If the subject of Geography is imparted to them through the medium ol stories it shall have a lasting effect on their mind. Their mental set up shall have been so arranged that they shall be able to make the use of their knowledge in their future life. Through stories it is also possible to acquaint the students with the various physical divisions of the world and teach them about various other geographical factors.

Stories are generally based on imagination. It does not mean that do not have the element of realism in them. They have realism in them and so at later stages it is possible to teach the student the subject of Geography in a realistic manner, of course basing on the knowledge acquired through stories. Story method serves as a base for establishing the proper knowledge of the subject.

Through story method it is possible to explain the control and effect of various geographical factors of human life. Life of one man can serve as a guiding principle for understanding the general effect of the factors that influence human life from the point of view of Geography.

Through story method it is possible to bring out clearly the influence of various geographical factors on human life in a very interesting manner. This thing cannot be done so easily with the help of other methods and specially for the students of tender age.

While employing the method of story telling the teacher of Geography must keep the following things in mind :

1. The story should be specially designed to serve the psychological requirements of the students.
2. They should be written in a simple language and lucid style. This would enable the students to grasp them properly.
3. They should be intended with the purpose of teaching certain topics of Geography. The teacher should always aim at proper teaching of the subject.
4. The story should also try to establish proper foundation for the future knowledge of the subject.

In short, it may be said that story method is an ideal method for teaching of Geography to the students of lower classes.

Excursions and travels in the teaching of Geography. Excursions and travels provide practical knowledge of the subject. While the students are taken out for travels and excursions, they get an opportunity to learn things directly. Knowledge so acquired is stable and useful. Prof. E. A. Macnee has rightly remarked :

"It is essential that the foundations of Geographical knowledge shall be laid in the field. No amount of reading from books can make up for a practical knowledge gained by looking at the earth which the child is studying. It follows that from the very early stages expedition should form part of the Geography course. In the lower schools there is usually plenty of time and many simple excursions can be made."

Beginning from limited area and going to vaster field. These excursions should start from a limited area. First of all the students should be asked to go round the school compound. Then they may be taken round the village and afterwards to places where they may get some geographical data. In higher classes they may also be taken to markets and places of industrial importance. While the students are going round on excursions and travels the teacher may explain the things properly to them.

The students must have the idea of the travels and excursions. While taking out the students on geographical tours and excursions they may be explained the purpose very clearly. Unless they are very clear in their minds about the purpose of their going out, they shall not be able to acquire the knowledge in the proper manner. In early stages this clarity of the thought may not be so important but in higher classes it is necessary.

In Junior High School or middle stage of education, ambitious expeditions and excursions may be undertaken. At this stage of education erosion of the soil, deposition and such other things may be taught.

After the excursion has finished the students should be asked to write out what they have seen. This would strengthen their knowledge and experience. They may also be asked to draw models, charts, pictures, etc.

In higher classes the students should be taken out to places of industrial and agricultural importance. Such places can provide knowledge to the students. After coming back from the travels and excursions the students should be asked and encouraged to write down what they have seen and draw maps.

. ***The requisites of travels and excursions.*** While taking out the students for travels and excursions the teacher should keep the following in his mind :

1. Discipline should be maintained while the students are going out. It can be very safely done if the teacher continues to direct them properly and gives them an opportunity to see things in the proper perspective. If the students get interested in their observation they shall not be indisciplined.

2. While the students are being taken out to excursions they should be made comfortable. It means that they should be lodged properly and given proper food. Unless the students are physically comfortable their mind shall not work properly and it shall not be possible for them to acquire knowledge in the proper manner.

3. The teacher should continue to direct the students in proper manner. He should continue to explain the importance of each and everything that the students have seen. He may also explain which things are used for map drawing and which things are useful for charts etc.

4. When the excursions or travels have ended the teacher should point out the particular chapter which may have bearing on the excursion or the travel. Such a reading will strengthen the experience and give a solid foundation to the knowledge.

5. Students should invariably be asked and encouraged to carry a note-book with them while they are on excursions. They should also be encouraged to write out important things. Such things shall be useful in the class-room and proper study of the subject.

6. While on excursion the students should be encouraged to collect things that are of geographical importance. This collection should be lodged in the Geography museum. Such a collection by the students would develop in them the love for museum. They would try to collect things in the proper manner and preservation in the museum which is an essential part of the teaching of the subject.

In short, it means that travels and excursions are an important means of the teaching of Geography.

Salient Features

1. The method of story telling can be very useful for the teaching of Geography to the students of lower classes.

2. This method should be used in a scientific and psychological manner. In other words it means that stories should be written in a psychological and scientific manner.

3. Travels and excursions also provide a practical basis to the learning of Geography. These travels and excursions should start from limited area and proceed to vaster ones.

4. These travels and excursions should be scientifically planned so that the things observed may be utilized for the teaching work in the class-room.
5. The students should be encouraged to observe things properly and take notes. These notes may later on be developed and the students encouraged to read the relevant chapters from the textbooks and compare them with their notes. Such a knowledge would be stable and useful.

For every subject a separate room is essential. For teaching literary subjects ordinary rooms may serve the purpose, but for the teaching of subject like Geography, a separate room is essential. Geography is also a science and so the need for a separate room is greater than for the other subjects. In the year 1950 in Montreal (Canada), a seminar was organised in which the representatives of 23 nations participated and all of them agreed to the point that a separate Geography room is the most essential thing. The teaching of Geography cannot be effective without a room. If we will not use the maps and charts, how can we teach in effective way ? As in Chemistry, Physics, Botany and Geology, various apparatuses are used, so is the case of Geography Maps, Globes, Graph, Sketches and different other things are necessary to teach the subject. If we will not have a separate Geography room it will be difficult for us to collect all these things at a place and even if we collect these things, it will be practically impossible to take away all the things from one place to the other. Secondly, without particular room it will be difficult for a teacher to get the congenial atmosphere to put himself in a better form and so the well equipped separate Geography room is the most essential thing, in order to make the teaching of Geography more effective.

The Geography room should be at least 40' x 30' for thirty students. Its height should be at least 8'. In short, we can say that it should be twice of the ordinary room. There should be two gates and two windows on the northern wall of the room. On the eastern wall there should be two doors and one window. There should be adequate arrangement for the light and the air. There should be enough space so that every student may have separate desk. On the southern wall of the room there should be almirah and on the western wall the black-board. It should be constructed in such a way that whenever needed, the lights may be put off so that the teacher may show the different scenes.

Every room must have at least four black-boards, one for the graph work, other for the sketch work and maps and the rest for writing the gist etc.

Maps. Map is the most essential thing for a Geography room. These maps should be kept in the almirahs so that they may be used conveniently. There should be adequate arrangement for drawing the maps. A thin 2" long stick should be there to point out the students the various aspects and places. For sketching a good map, the following things are essential:

(1) Tape, (2) Chain, (3) Pole, (4) Drawing boards, (5) Spirit Level, (6) Plain table (7) Alidate, (8) Compass, (9) Plumpol.

Pictures. To show the various aspects of life there should be a large number of pictures. Without these pictures we connot put before the students the human feelings in better form. These pictures should be set in such a way that the students may see them properly.

Globes. Globes are also essential for a Geography room. Without these globes how can we put before the students the various things ? The globes may be of two types—

(1) Black and white globes, and

(2) Natural globes.

Various types of thermometers and other meterological instruments etc. Various types of thermometers are also essential in order to make the teaching more effective. In teaching the temperature, humidity, etc., they serve a great purpose.

The following types of thermometers and other apparatuses are used in the Geography room :

(1) Fahrenhei Thermometer,

(2) Centigrade Thermometer,

(3) Barometer,

(4) Main and Max Thermometer,

(5) Wind vane,

(6) Rain Gauge,

(7) Dry and Wet Thermometer.

Paintings. Various types of paintings can also be used for the teaching of Geography. The paintings of the villages, cities and human dresses may serve the useful purpose in this direction. The teacher should make these paintings according to the need.

Astronomical apparatuses. These astronomical apparatuses are used to give a hint of the astronomy to the students of Geography. Without astronomy the teaching of Geography is incomplete and so these apparatuses are used. The teacher should make these paintings according to the need.

Various types of slides, parts of the rock etc. These slides and parts of the rock are essential in order to give the students the complete knowledge of the subject.

Film projection. Film projection and epidiascope are really valuable equipments in a Geography room. The windows should be equipped with blark blinders for the proper functioning of the projection.

Library. Library plays an important part in each and every institution. So is the case with the Geography room. There should be a separate library in the Geography room where the students may go and consult the books. Various geographical magazines and reports of the Government should be kept in this library.

Other rooms attached to Geography room. In addition to the well-equipped Geography room, few more rooms should be attached to it for the convenience of the teacher and the students. At least three rooms are essential.

Clay room. This room should be the half of the main Geographical room. It should be 20' × 15". There should be adequate arrangement of light and air in the room. The floor of the room should be smooth and water supply should also be adequate. The following apparatuses are necessary for this :

(a) A box for keeping the mud,

(b) A long table,

(c) Drawing boards,

(d) A water tank,

(e) The open floor, and

(f) Other things.

Equipment room. This room should be well decorated and there should be different places to keep the different things. There should be almirahs to keep the various chemicals used for photography etc. There should be dry place for keeping Plaster of Paris and Lead etc.

Dark room. This room should be a smaller one. In this room there should be a passage so that the light of different colour may enter the room. Artificial light is also essential for the room. There should be few almirahs and tables in the room.

Geography museum. It is very difficult to have a geographical museum in each Geography room. But this type of museum may serve the useful purpose. To have this museum is an expensive job but we can spend less and gain more if we keep the museum in the smaller form. The students will come in direct contact with the nature and with the things they are taught in the class with the help of the museum. Only those things should be kept in the museum which are essential for the students. For the students, specially in the higher classes, more expensive things will be required but for the students studying in the lower classes, only few important things will serve the purpose. For an ordinary Geographical museum the following things are necessary :

1. Pictures showing the life of different countries.
2. The models of mud which reflect upon the geographical aspects of the life of different countries.

3. Few paintings, clothes, utensils and other things reflecting upon the geographical aspects.

4. Various types of stones and rocks.

5. Stamps and coins of different nations.

In order to equip the Geography room, it should be kept in mind that it is the room for the students and not for the teachers. Only those things which are essential for the students should be there in the room. If the room will not serve the purpose of the students it will be futile. Though it is true that every teacher is also a student of the subject but while purchasing the various equipment for the room, it should be kept in mind that only those thing should be purchased which are for the benefit of the students. For the students studying in the lower classes it is also essential to see that the apparatuses and the equipment are of their standard only.

1. It is necessary to have a separate room for teaching of every subject. For subjects involving some practical work is all the more important.

2. There should be a separate room for the teaching of Geography. This room should be properly equipped.

3. Geography room must have the following things in it:

   (a) Maps, (b) Pictures, (c) Globes, (d) Thermometer of different types, (e) Pictures and paintings, (f) Astronomical apparatus, (g) Slides, (h) Pieces of rocks, stones etc.

4. There should be a library attached to the Geography room.

5. Attached to the Geography room there should be a Clay Room for keeping clay for the models.

6. There should also be an Equipment Room properly decorated.

7. There should also be a Dark Room attached to the Geography room.

8. It shall be good to have a Geographical Museum or a Museum lodged in the Geography room.

14

Relationship with other Subjects

The major aim of education is the unification of knowledge existing in different branches of learning. To achieve such a unification, a conscious effort has to be made by teachers teaching various subjects. It is only in such joint ventures that we will be able to achieve the goal of unification of knowledge and bridge the gap that separates them.

The Significance

This is an age of correlationship and no subject can be taught in isolation. It is only for convenience of study that we have splitted the knowledge into different subjects but no subject is completely aloof from others and it has to be correlated with other subjects.

Modern educationist have no doubt in their mind about the fact that the teaching of a particular subject should be carried out in correlation with other subjects. The correlation is more between those subjects that have a common bearing. There are various types of correlationships 'and every type of correlationship has its importance in the education in different ways.

The two important types of correlation are:

(i) correlation with daily life.

(ii) correlation of geography with other subjects.

Role in Routine Life

For fostering a love for study of geography in his students the geography teacher should bring home to his students the useful and interesting applications of knowledge of geography in daily life. It is likely to make his lesson more interesting, stimulating and realistic. Teacher is free to include such phenomenon which are matters of every-day life even if these are not prescribed in the syllabus. Teacher should make a conscious effort to arouse the interest of his students in such applications of geography in every-day life. A good geography teacher can fmd many applications of geography in daily life and it would be much better if he quotes examples with rural background in rural schools and examples having urban background while teaching in urban schools. For correlating geography with every-day life an effort be made to make use of available community resources. For example a teacher can plan a visit to some dam while teaching about dams or to some mountaineous resort while teaching about mountains. Geography is a science as well as an art and aims at preparing ideal and successful citizens. No aspect of human life remains untouched by geography and every human activity has some geographical importance.

Relationship and Coordination

Geography and History. Geography is intimately correlated to history and in the 50's the two subjects were taught together. In fact they are twins, one stresses time and the other spaces. History studies people of different times and geography deals with the people of different places.

The two subjects are now studied separately for convenience of study but we cannot completely separate the two subjects. Geography is the stage on which drama of history is enacted and it is the geography which determines the historical events and can offer explanation for historical actions of mankind. Similarly historical facts can serve as a good basis for arousing interest in geographical studies. In explanation of historical facts the geographical factors that are taken into consideration are physical conditions of the life of man, climate, produce, means of communication, etc. All these factors determine the direction of human life and history is created by human life and activities. History of each and every country is governed by these factors.

Truely speaking," historical studies devoid of geographical background would be inaccurate and unscientific.

In past ages if some countries had succeeded in invading some other countries, it had been possible because of geographical factors. The Himalayas was considered unvoilable again because of geographical factors. Germany had to face defeat in Russia because of severe winter in that part of the world.

Thus, for a proper understanding of historical events, geographical factors have to be taken into consideration. Many a historical map has been drawn on the basis of geographical factors. Geographical factors were the sole cause of the downfall of many empires. The growth of England into a first rate sea power can be explained if we consider the geographical factors and geographical location of England.

We can quote a number of historical events which could be explained if we consider the geographical factors, e.g. why was Aurangzeb not able to keep South India under his control for long? Expansion of French and English Colonies in North America, why French settled among the line of St. Lawrence? The growth of Delhi, Lahore or London can be better understood by taking into con-sideration various geographical factors. The hostility between France and Germany can be explained because this is due to the existence of river Rhine and Lorrain Coal fields.

The correlation between history and geography is self evident if we look at the equipments/apparatus used for teaching these subjects. For teaching these we make use of maps, pictures and atlases.

Geography and Political Science. In the study of political science the most important thing is the study of administration of a particular unit and the problems associated with it. There are wide differences in administration in different lands. These differences may be attributed to difference in geographical conditions. In some countries we find that democracy has survived for very long years which has been possible only because of geographical factors (e.g. as in Switzerland).

Not only the political system but even the traditions, culture, etc. are also guided by geographical factors of a land. In the present-day world when we are moving towards world citizenship and world government we have to remember the part played by geography. One of the basic aims of geography, as pointed out earlier, is the establishment of world citizenship. To achieve this objective we have to give prominence to various common geographical factors.

To understand the different political set-ups in different countries we have to understand the differences in geographical factors in those countries. The role of America and Russia and their present position in world polity is also due to certain geographical factors. The main point of contention between world powers has been there anxiety to have control over oil-rich South-East Asian region.

In many instances a proper knowledge of geographical factors can be of much use in solving some political problems. Thus we find there is much of correlation between geography and political science.

Geography and Economics. Geography is very intimately related to Economics. This interelationship has led to the branches such as *Economic-geography.* Agriculture, industry and other economic activities depend, to a large extent, on the various geographical factors prevailing in a region. e.g. the industrial unit is generally established in an area where the raw material are available in abundance. The wealth of a country, to a large extent, depend upon various geographical factors because the wealth-generating activities, industry and agriculture depend on various geographical factors. Thus to achieve good economic results we must have a good geographical background. Actually speaking in Economic geography we study various principles which help us in the study of economic aspects of various geographical factors. It is not only the availability of raw material and the production but the means of transport and communication, etc. have also to be taken into consideration while studying the economics of a project. Thus we find that geography and economics are highly correlated.

Geography and Language. Literature is much influenced by the geographical factors prevailing in a region. To learn a language we must acquaint ourselves with the geography of the area. The description of nature and other geographical conditions of area can be easily found to the existing literature of the area. The description of various character in novels, dramas, stories, etc. are influenced by the prevailing geographical conditions. Even the dress, the dressing style, etc. of a region are also governed by various geographical factors. All such descriptions are available in literature which provide us much information about the geographical factors of a region. Thus we find that for the proper study of geography a proper knowledge of language is essential. Only a limited and preliminary knowledge of a language is sufficient for study of geography in primary schools but at higher stages of learning of geography a good knowledge of language is desirable. The correlation of geography to languages should be clearly brought about in higher classes. Thus we find that there is a lot of correlation between geography and language and literature.

Geography and Art. Art includes (i) useful art and *(ii)* fine art. In useful art we make some thing that is useful and in fine art we make a thing having a quality. Fine art develops the aesthetic sense. To correlate useful art with geography the students in a manual class may be asked to prepare almirahs, map holders, map stands etc.

A good hand at art can draw fine maps, charts and models. In such charts and maps the heights of mountains, formation of lands etc. can be depicted nicely and a fine hand at art can depict these things aesthetically. In this way art can be used to generate students interest for geography. Geography provides a good material for the students of art and fine art. Thus there exists a lot of correlation between geography and art.

Geography and Hand Work. In the present day curriculum hand work occupies an important place. The hand work has been included in geography mainly is to train the eye to accuracy and rapidity in observation. It also helps in the development of latent powers of mind and inculcates habits of neatness etc. At time; geography provides subject matter for hand work and sometimes hand work provides subject matter for geography. The school garden provides various opportunities for the study of geography.

Geography and Mathematics. Mathematics is considered the mother of all subjects. Thus mathematics is highly correlated to various other subjects and so there is a lot of correlation between mathematics and geography. For giving a practice in various mathematical formulas about measurement of height, depth, area etc. the mathematics teacher can choose data from geography. The quantitative aspects in mathematics can be explained by taking the data from population, production, crops etc. Similar use of geographical problems can be made in Algebra and geometry classes. To understand geographical charts, geographical survey maps and cartographical works in geography the knowledge of mathematics is essential. In comparative method of teaching geography mathematics is quite useful and helpful. Writing about correlation between mathematics and geography an eminent writer observes, "Geography and mathematics have much in common. Mathematics deals with number and measurements. But numbers and measurements are based on environment. Through geography we try to understand environment. Therefore we can understand it better with the help of mathematics.

Children must be able to read the thermometers and barometers. They must be able to keep meterological records and also they should be able to draw graphs and diagrams. This knowledge can be obtained through the study of mathematics alone. If we correlate the subjects of mathematics and geography on the basis of craft and physical and social environment of the child, we can give him the real and useful knowledge of both of the subjects".

Thus we find that geography and mathematics are highly correlated to each other.

Geography and Natural Sciences. Geography is so highly correlated to natural sciences that it is considered as one of the subjects that maybe included in sciences. We find that a large number of geographical facts are included in the subject matter of atural sciences such as physics, chemistry, agriculture, botany, zoology etc. The cause and effect relationship that is emphasised in the study of geography is a gift of science to geography. For a correct understanding of various geographical facts we have to make use of many a scientific rules and formulas. Thus we find a close correlation between science and geography.

Geography and Geology. Geology is the study of the surface of the earth and so geology is highly correlated to geography. The knowledge of geology can be quite helpful in the study of earth quacks, volcanoes etc. Thus these two are considered as twin subjects.

Geography and Agriculture. These two are deeply correlated because the agricultural products are influenced by the geographical factors. A geography teacher can make a good contribution in the study of agriculture and so there exists a correlation between geography and agriculture.

Geography and Religion. In recent times there is an increasing trend for including the study of religion in geography. A close relationship exists between geography and religion because geography emphasises the influence of environments on the religion of a country. We find that a large number of beliefs in a religion are closely associated to the geographical factors.

Geography and Social Studies. In primary classes geography forms part of nature study. It can also form a part of social studies. We have already considered a close correlation between geography and history which is an important subject forming a part of the social studies. The social studies includes history, civics and politics.

Thus we find that geography is highly correlated to a number of other school subjects and sometimes such a correlation may lead to overlapping and it involves the danger of repetition and waste of time. This repetition and wastage of time should be avoided and for this purpose it would be better if the teachers teaching various subjects remain in touch with each other.

This is an age of co-relationship. No subject can be taught in isolation. Every subject has bearing on the other subject. For the convenience of study, no doubt, the field of knowledge has been split up into different subjects but no subjects is away from the other. Every subject cannot be treated as a watertight compartment. It has to be co-related with other subjects. The success of a teacher of Geography lies in teaching Geography in co-relation with other subject.

In olden days, Geography was essentially a descriptive subject. It was considered to be a description of the world and its inhabitants. It was the ideal Geography that was considered to be an important part of the subject, ports, bays, cities, islands, rivers, mountains, forests etc. and their description was supposed to be the whole of Geography. Later on, it was realised that even these things cannot be taught away from each other. All these things also have bearing upon each other.

Modern educationists are convinced that the teaching of a particular subject should be carried out in co-relation with other subjects. This co-relation is generally between the subjects that have common bearing. When a particular subject is taught in co-relation with other subjects, then the knowledge acquired is stable and permanent. We have seen at various other places that this relationship is of several types. These several types of co-relation have their importance in the education in different ways. In attempting to establish co-relationship we co-relate the knowledge of Geography with the knowledge of other subjects. We have also to co-relate this knowledge with the life in general. Without it, it would not be the labour spent.

Geography is a subject which has the elements of science as well as an art. It aims at preparing ideal and successful citizens. It attempts to impart practical knowledge to the students to grow into successful citizens. On the other hand, it tries to study the subjects in a scientific manner. From this point of view, it serves as a lin between natural sciences and the social sciences.

No aspect of human life remains untouched by Geography. Every human activity has some Geographical importance or the other. Therefore, the teaching of Geography has a two fold co-relationship. On the one hand, it is related to social sciences or humanities such as History, Economics, Political Science, Literature, Art etc. while on the other it is co-related with natural sciences such as Chemistry, Geology, Mathematics, Physics etc.

The teacher has to have a very clear attitude in this regard. He must know the relation of Geography with other subjects and try to bear this thing in mind. If he does not do so, he will not be able to succeed in his task. He should be a broad minded person. He should refer the subject-matter of other subjects as and when he has an opportunity or the reference permits. Let us now try to examine the co-relation of Geography with other subjects.

There was a time when these two subjects were taught together. Till very recently, they were treated as one subject. Now they are treated separately for the convenience of study. But, in fact, of the two cannot be separated. They are the two sides of one coin. Geography is the stage on which the drama of History is enacted. It is the Geography which determines the historical events of a particular country. Geographical factors mean the physical conditions of the life of man, climate, produce, means of communication etc. and all these factors determine the direction of human life. It is the human life and activities that create History. History of each and very country is governed by all these factors.

In past ages, if certain countries had succeeded in invading certain countries, it had been possible only on account of geographical factors. If in past ages Himalayas was supposed to be inviolable, it was so on account of geographical factors. If Germany had to face defeat in Russia, it was only on account of the cruelties of geographical factors, which expressed this in the form of severe winter.

We have seen that historical maps are drawn on the basis of Geographical factors, Various social, religious, economic and historical events have taken place on account of Geographical factors. Without knowing Geography, it is not possible to know history in a proper manner. Downfall of various empires took place solely on account of these geographical factors. If England grew into a first rate sea power, it could be so only on account of its Geographical situation and Geographical location.

Sometimes it is not possible to explain certain historical facts without having proper knowledge of geographical factors. We hear that Aurangzab cold not succeed in holding the southern part of India under his control for a very long time. It could be so only on account of geographical condition of South India. South India is full of mountains and land is also not even. Thes geographical conditions provided opportunities for guerilla war and the people of South did employ these tactics.

Political Science is the subject that studies the administration of a particular unit and certain allied problems. Sometimes political administrations differ from land to land. This difference is on account of geographical conditions. In Switzerland even today direct democracy is practised. It has been possible only on account of geographical factors. Traditions, political principles and certain other things are also guided by geographical factors.

Today world citizenship and world government have become the ideals of Political Science and Practical Politics. Geography can play a vital role in this direction. Geography also aims at establishing world citizenship. It does so by explaining the common geographical features of different countries.

Sometimes it is possible to solve various political problems with the help of the knowledge of geographical factors. Once we know about the geographical background of a particular political problem, it shall not be very difficult for us to solve it. All these factors very clearly indicate that there is close relationship between Geographical and Political Science.

These two subjects are very intimately related. They are so intimately related that there is a branch of Geography which is known as Economic Geography. Agriculture, industry and economic activities are subordinate to geographical factors. Wherever we find the location of coal iron ore, it is possible to establish industries. Economics, which is called the science of wealth, cannot make proper progress without the knowledge of geographical factors. It is the geographical factors that govern the wealth of a particular person or a country. Various agricultural and economic products are the results of geographical factors. In fact, Geography provides a background to the Economics.

In Economic Geography we have the description of various principles on the basis of which it is possible to study the economic aspect of the geographical factors. While discussing certain departments of Geography, we have also to take into consideration various factors of Geography. For example, when we discuss about the production, we cannot discuss it without taking into consideration the geographical factors. In fact, these two subjects are interdependent.

Although there does not seem to be a relationship of subject matter between the two but they are certainly inter-related. Literatures are very much influenced by geographical conditions. In order to learn a language, we have to know about geographical conditions. Science ages, literature has been full of the description of the nature. Poets and writers could not have described nature successfully and they do not known the geographical facts properly. Various aspects of literature, namely stories, novel, drama, epic, etc are to a great extent, influenced by geographical factors. Characters are delineated with an eye on geographical environment. No character can be treated without giving due regard to the Geographical environment in which he or she has to live. Ways of living, dress, ways of talking are very much influenced by geographical factors. Oral as well as written forms of the languages are also influenced by the geographical factor. In various stories we find the description of geographical facts and discoveries. We also find literature dealing with various aspects of human life.

If on the one hand Geography provides the subject-matter to the literature, on the other language and literature are also helpful for the study of Geography. Without thorough and proper knowledge of language, it is not possible to study Geography properly. In lower classes or primary classes very little knowledge of the Languages and vocabulary is sufficient to meet the requirements of the study of Geography. But in higher classes good knowledge of language adds to the thorough study of the subject-matter. If language facilitates the studies of Geography, Geograyhy also adds to the vocabulary of the language and literature.

In teaching Geography to higher classes, it will be worthwhile to correlate the teaching of the subject of Geography with language and literature the subject-matter of Geography can add to the richness of the literature as well. It can open new avenues of subject-matter. In short, it can be said that Geography and language and literature are inter-related.

Art is of two types – (i) the useful art; and (ii) the fine art. Any attempt that is made to make the thing useful and beautiful is termed as an art. When the thing is made useful, it is through practical art and when some aesthetic sense is developed in a particular thing, it brings about fineness in it and so it is termed as Fine Art. Art brings about the development of the aesthetic sense of the students and also helps them to express their ideas independently. Art is useful for the study of Geography. A good hand at art can draw fine maps, charts and models. Through these charts and maps it is possible to express the ideas successfully and nicely. In these maps and charts, we depict the height of the surface, the height of the mountains, the formation of the land and the span of the rivers etc. A fine hand at art can depict these things successfully, aesthetically and nicely. This can make the teaching of Geography interesting and simple. The interest of the students can be generated in Geography through art. If beautiful maps are presented before the students, they may feel interested in studying and reading Geography.

On the other hand, Geography also provides with interesting subject material for art. Various facts of the subject-matter of Geography can inspire a student of art to draw pictures and scenery. In short, it may be said that art and Geography are inter-related.

Geography has still not gone out of the field of social sciences. Ways of living of people and their thoughts are very much governed by geographical factors. It is generally seen that people living in countries with rich geographical background are liberal and progressive in outlook. On the other hand, people living in the countries with poor geographical background are neither liberal nor progressive. It is all due to difficult conditions of living. In countries with difficult circumstrnces it is difficult to expect people to have a high sense of morality. Social sciences deal with various aspects of social life of man. In other words, these social sciences study man as a social being. Since social life of man is very much influenced by the geographical conditions, it is natural for Geography to have intimate relationship with other social sciences.

Graft is also a kind of art. In craft, with the help of the material, we try to draw models, charts etc. It is now considered to be necessary to teach art and craft to the students for the proper development of their personality and mind. In fact, craft is the useful part of the art. Today for the successful teaching of Geography, craft is necessary.

In our system of education Mathematics occupies an important place. Since long, it has been occupying that place and it shall continue to do so. In our education main include the teaching of Arithmetic. In fact, various, problems of our life are solved with the help of Mathematics. If we want to have proper account of the agricultural produce, export and import, production etc. we have to take the help of Arithmetics. In fact, Arithmetic or Mathematics gives the language of figures to the geographical data. It is also helpful in drawing the maps, contours, charts, etc. It is in these charts and graphs that we depict the population, area and other things. The teacher of Geography can very safely employ various principles of Mathematics and make the teaching of Geography exact and useful. In Comparative Method of Teaching of Geography, Mathematics, is very useful and helpful. Regarding the correlation of Geography with Mathematics, an eminent writer has written "Geography and Mathematics have much in common. Mathematics deals with number and measurements. But numbers and measurements are based on environment. Through geography we try to understand the environment. Therefore, we can understand it better with the help of Mathematics. Children must be able to read the thermometers and barometers. They must be able to keep meteorological record and also they should be able to draw graphs and diagrams. This knowledge can be obtained through the study of Mathematics alone. If we correlate the subjects of Mathematics and Geography on the basis of craft and physical and social environment of the child, we can give him the real and useful knowledge of both of the subjects."

If we have to measure the distances of the width or the depth of the river, we have to take help from Arithmetic. In lower primary classes, the relationship between the two is not of much importance and consequence. In Junior High School or High School Classes this relationship becomes more pertinent and important. In higher classes Geometry, which is a part of Mathematics, proves very useful. In having an idea of the longitude and the latitude and finding out time, we have to take help from Mathematics. This very clearly indicates that the two are deeply related.

Today Geography is coming out of the field of social sciences and entering the field of natural sciences. Natural include Physics, Chemistry, Agriculture, Botany, Zoology, Geology, etc. Various. facts of Geography are included within the subject-matter of these natural sciences. In teaching of Geography we try to base our study on cause and effect relationship. This cause and effect relationship is the gift of science to the field of Geography. In this manner we have to keep in mind the bearing, and the importance of the two.

In order to have correct understanding of various geographical facts and principles, we have to take help of the principles of science. The natural Geography or physical Geography, which studies the climate, pressure of the wind and its velocity, currents, weather, mineral wealth etc. takes a good deal of help of natural sciences.

Geology deals with the study of the surface of earth, has a very intimate relationship with Geography. If we want to have a correct idea about the earthquakes, volcanoes etc. we have to take help from the knowledge of Geology.

Study of Geography involves handling of various apparatuses such as Barometer, Rain gauge, Thermometer, etc. All these apparatuses cannot be handled properly unless we have some knowledge of the principles of Physics.

All these things indicate that natural science and Geography are very much correlated.

Agriculture have a very deep relationship with local Geography. Agricultural products are very much influenced by geographical factors. The teacher of Geography can contribute a lot to the field of agriculture.

In primary classes Geography forms the part of nature study. It can also form the part of social studies. In higher classes these two subjects are taught separately, but their relationship continues to be the same.

1. Geography is a subject which is correlated with social sciences as well as natural sciences. It is, in fact, passing out of the field of social sciences and entering the field of natural sciences.

2. History of Geography are intimately related. Geography provides the stage on which the drama of History is enacted. In fact, History and Geography are two sides of a coin.

3. Geography and Political Science are also correlated. Political Science deals with the administration of a particular Political unit. The administration cannot be run successfully unless the administrators have an idea of the geographical background of that land.

4. Geography and Economics are also inter-related. Economics studies the economic life of man. Economic life cannot be studied without having an idea of the geographical background.

5. Geography and Language and Literature-Geography, Language and Literature are correlated. Geography provides subject-matter for literature and language. On the other hand, language and literature are helpful for the proper study of Geography.

6. Geography is helped by art and craft. Art and craft are useful in the drawing of maps and charts. On the other hand, art and craft can benefit by the subject-matter of Geography.

7. Geography is also related to other social-sciences. Social sciences deal with the life of man as a social being. This social life of man cannot be studied without proper background of geographical factors.

8. Geography is also related to Mathematics or Arithematic. Mathematics provides the language of figures to the geographical facts.

9. Geography is also related to natural sciences such as Physics, Chemistry, Botany, Zoology, Agriculture, Geology, etc. These sciences help the proper study of the subject-matter of Geography.

Additional Reading

Bhaskara Rao, Digumarti (1994). *Scientific Aptitude,* New Delhi: Ashish Publishing House. ISBN 81-7024-658-X.

Bhaskara Rao, Digumarti (1995). *Animal Kingdom.* New Delhi: Discovery Publishing House. ISBN 81-7141-274-2.

Bhaskara Rao, Digumarti (1995). *Batracology.* New Delhi: Discovery Publishing House. ISBN 81-7141-279-3.

Bhaskara Rao, Digumarti (1997), *Scientific Attitude.* New Delhi: Discovery Publishing House. ISBN 81-7141-308-0.

Bhaskara Rao, Digumarti (1996). *Scientific Attitude vis-à-vis Scientific Aptitude.* New Delhi: Discovery Publishing House. ISBN 81-7141-308-0.

Bhaskara Rao, Digumarti, Editor (1996). *Encyclopaedia of Education for All,* 5 Volumes. New Delhi: APH Publishing Corporation. ISBN 81-7024-759-4 (set).

Vol. I *Education for All: The World Conference.* ISBN 81-7024-760-8.

Vol. II *Education for All: The EPA-9 Summit.* ISBN 81-7024-761-6.

Vol. III *Education for All: Quality Education for All.* ISBN 81-7024-762-6.

Vol. IV *Education for All: Planning and Monitoring.* ISBN 81-7024-763-4.

Vol. V *Education for All: The Indian Scenario.* ISBN 81-7024-764-0.

Bhaskara Rao, Digumarti, Editor (1996). *Global Perceptions on Peace Education,* 3 Volumes. New Delhi: Discovery Publishing House. ISBN 81-7141-319-6.

Bhaskara Rao, Digumarti, Editor (1996). *National Policy on Education*. 2 Volumes. New Delhi: Anmol Publications Pvt. Ltd. ISBN 81-7488-323-1.

Bhaskara Rao, Digumarti, Editor (1997). *Care the Child*, 2 Volumes. New Delhi: Discovery Publishing House. ISBN 81-7141-394-3.

Bhaskara Rao, Digumarti, Editor (1997). *Education for the 21st Century*. New Delhi: Discovery Publishing House. ISBN 81-7141-389-7.

Bhaskara Rao, Digumarti, Editor (1997). *Reflections on Scientific Attitude*. New Delhi: Discovery Publishing House, ISBN 81-7141-319-6.

Bhaskara Rao, Digumarti, Editor (1997). *Success Story of a Primary Education Project*. New Delhi: APH Publishing Corporation. ISBN 81-7024-850-7.

Bhaskara Rao, Digumarti, Editor (1997). *World Food Summit*. New Delhi: Discovery Publishing House. ISBN 81-7141-386-2.

Bhaskara Rao, Digumarti, Editor (1998). *Adolescence Education*. New Delhi: Discovery Publishing House. ISBN 81-7141-432-X.

Bhaskara Rao, Digumarti, Editor (1998). *Community and School Nutrition Education*. New Delhi: Discovery Publishing House. ISBN 81-7141-435-4.

Bhaskara Rao, Digumarti, Editor (1998). *District Primary Education Programme*. New Delhi: Discovery Publishing House. ISBN 81-7141-396-X.

Bhaskara Rao, Digumarti, Editor (1998). *Earth Summit*, 2 Volumes. New Delhi: Discovery Publishing House. ISBN 81-7141-435-4.

Bhaskara Rao, Digumarti, Editor (1998). *National Policy on Education: Towards an Enlightened and Humane Society*, New Delhi: Discovery Publishing House. ISBN 81-7141-426-5.

Bhaskara Rao, Digumarti, Editor (1998). *Reforming School Education*. New Delhi: Discovery Publishing House. ISBN 81-7141-403-6.

Bhaskara Rao, Digumarti, Editor (1998). *Teacher Education in India*. New Delhi: Discovery Publishing House. ISBN 81-7141-406-0.

Bhaskara Rao, Digumarti, Editor (1998). *World Summit for Social Development*. New Delhi: Discovery Publishing House. ISBN 81-7141-420-6.

Bhaskara Rao, Digumarti, Editor (2000). *Education for All: Achieving the Goal*, 3 Volumes, New Delhi: APH Publishing Corporation. ISBN 81-7648-152-1.

Vol. I *The Global Consensus*. ISBN 81-7648-155-6.

Vol. II *Mid-Decade Review Reports of Regional Seminars*. ISBN 81-7648-154-8.

Vol. III *Issues and Trends*. ISBN 81-7648-155-6.

Bhaskara Rao, Digumarti, Editor (2000), *International Encyclopaedia of AIDS*, 11 Volumes in 13 Parts. New Delhi: Discovery Publishing House. ISBN 81-7141-6 (Set).

Vol. 1 *Introduction to HIV/AIDS*. ISBN 81-7141-523-7.

Vol. 2 *HIV/AIDS—Issues and Challenges*, 2 Parts. ISBN 81-7141-524-5.

Vol. 3 *HIV/AIDS—Socio Economic Realities*. ISBN 81-7141-524-3.

Vol. 4 *HIV/AIDS—Law Ethics and Human Rights*, 2 Parts. ISBN 81-7141-526-1.

Vol. 5 *AIDS and NGOs*. ISBN 81-7141-527-X.

Vol. 6 *AIDS and Home Care*. ISBN 81-7141-528-8.

Vol. 7 *STD Case Management*. ISBN 81-7141-529-6.

Vol. 8 *HIV/AIDS Prevention and Care—Teaching Modules for Nurses and Midwives*. ISBN 81-7141-530-X.

Vol. 9 *HIV Prevention Education for Education for Educational Institutions*. ISBN 81-7141-531-8.

Vol. 10 *Instructional Modules for AIDS Education*. ISBN 81-7141-532-6.

Vol. 11 *School Health Education to Prevent AIDS and STD—A Package for Curriculum Planners*. ISBN 81-7141-5338-4.

Bhaskara Rao, Digumarti, Editor (2000). *International Encyclopaedia of Science and Technology Education*, 11 Volumes. New Delhi: Discovery Publishing House. ISBN 81-7141-548-2 (Set).

Vol. 1 *Science and Technology Education.* ISBN 81-7141-568-7.

Vol. 2 *Science Education in Developing Countries.* ISBN 81-7141-570-9.

Vol. 3 *Organisational Structure of Science.* ISBN 81-7141-570-9.

Vol. 4 *Science Education in Asia and the Pacific.* ISBN 81-7141-571-7.

Vol. 5 *Science and Technology Education for All.* ISBN 81-7141-572-5.

Vol. 6 *Values, Ethics, Talent and Girls in Science and Technology Education.* ISBN 81-7141-573-3.

Vol. 7 *Popularization of Science and Technology Education.* ISBN 81-7141-574-1.

Vol. 8 *Science, Power and Society.* ISBN 81-7141-575-X.

Vol. 9 *Information Technology.* ISBN 81-7141-576-8.

Vol. 10 *Teacher Training in Science and Technology Education.* ISBN 81-7141-577-6.

Vol. 11 *Teacher Training in Science and Technology: A Curriculum Framework.* ISBN 81-7141-578-4.

Bhaskara Rao, Digumarti, Editor (2001). *Distance Education in Different Countries.* New Delhi: APH Publishing Corporation. ISBN 81-7648-229-3.

Bhaskara Rao, Digumarti, Editor (2001). *Decentralised Management of Education (Management of Education in Panchayati Raj and Municipal Bodies).* New Delhi: Discovery Publishing House. ISBN 81-7141-617-9.

Bhaskara Rao, Digumarti, Editor (2001). *Electrochemistry for Environmental Protection.* New Delhi: Discovery Publishing House. ISBN 81-7141-619-5.

Bhaskara Rao, Digumarti, Editor (2001). *Global Educational Studies.* New Delhi: Discovery Publishing House. ISBN 81-7141-616-0.

Bhaskara Rao, Digumarti, Editor (2001). *Global Synthesis of Educational Assessment.* New Delhi: Discovery Publishing House. ISBN 81-7141-613-6.

Bhaskara Rao, Digumarti, Editor (2000). *International Encyclopaedia of Human Rights*. 7 Volumes in 13 Parts. New Delhi: Discovery Publishing House. (Royal Size). ISBN 81-7141-567-9 (Set).

Vol. 1 *International Instruments of Human Rights*, 2 Parts. ISBN 81-7141-595-4.

Vol. 2 *Regional Instruments of Human Rights*. ISBN 81-7141-604-7.

Vol. 3 *Human Rights and the United Nations*, 2 Parts. ISBN 81-7141-605-5.

Vol. 4 *Fact Files of Human Rights*, 3 Parts. ISBN 81-7141-605-3.

Vol. 5 *Study Stories of Human Rights*, 3 Parts. ISBN 81-7141-607-3.

Vol. 6 *International Meetings on Human Rights*, 2 Parts. ISBN 81-7141-608-X.

Vol. 7 *Professional Training in Human Rights*. ISBN 81-7141-609-8.

Bhaskara Rao, Digumarti, Editor (2001). *Jomtein Decade of Education*. New Delhi: Discovery Publishing House. ISBN 81-7141-618-7.

Bhaskara Rao, Digumarti, Editor (2001). *Nuclear Materials: Issues and Concerns*, 2 Volumes. New Delhi: Discovery Publishing House. ISBN 81-7141-611-X.

Bhaskara Rao, Digumarti, Editor (2001). *World Conference on Education for All*. New Delhi: APH Publishing Corporation. ISBN 81-7141-274-9.

Bhaskara Rao, Digumarti, Editor (2001). *World Conference on Higher Education*, New Delhi: Discovery Publishing House. ISBN 81-7141-610-1.

Bhaskara Rao, Digumarti, Editor (2001). *World Conference on Science*. New Delhi: Discovery Publishing House. ISBN 81-7141-612-8.

Bhaskara Rao, Digumarti, Editor (2003). *Inspiring Experience in Teacher Education*. New Delhi: Discovery Publishing House. ISBN 81-7141-656-X.

Bhaskara Rao, Digumarti, Editor (2003). *International Studies in Education*, 3 Volumes, New Delhi: Discovery Publishing House. ISBN 81-7141-647-0.

Bhaskara Rao, Digumarti, Editor (2003). *Military Conversion: Impact on Science and Technology*, New Delhi: Discovery Publishing House. ISBN 81-7141-578-4.

Bhaskara Rao, Digumarti, Editor (2003). *United Nations Millennium Summit*. New Delhi: Discovery Publishing House. ISBN 81-7141-632-2.

Bhaskara Rao, Digumarti, Editor (2003). *World Assembly on Aging*. New Delhi: Discovery Publishing House. ISBN 81-7141-637-3.

Bhaskara Rao, Digumarti, Editor (2004). *World Conference on Human Rights*. New Delhi: Discovery Publishing House. ISBN 81-7141-661-6.

Bhaskara Rao, Digumarti, Editor (2003). *World Education Forum*. New Delhi: Discovery Publishing House. ISBN 81-7141-639-X.

Bhaskara Rao, Digumarti, Editor (2004). *Education Employment and Human Resource Development*. New Delhi: Discovery Publishing House. ISBN 81-7141-681-0.

Bhaskara Rao, Digumarti, Editor (2004). *Successfully Schooling*. New Delhi: Discovery Publishing House. ISBN 81-7141-677-2.

Bhaskara Rao, Digumarti, Editor (2004). *European Education and Teachers*. New Delhi: Discovery Publishing House. ISBN 81-7141-702-7.

Bhaskara Rao, Digumarti, Editor (2004). *Teachers in a Changing World*. New Delhi: Discovery Publishing House. ISBN 81-7141-694-2.

Bhaskara Rao, Digumarti, Editor (2004). *Learning to Live Together*, 4 Volumes. New Delhi: Discovery Publishing House.

Vol. 1 *International Conference on Learning to Live Together.*

Vol. 2 *Globalisation and Living Together.*

Vol. 3 *Curriculum for Learning to Live Together.*

Vol. 4 *Science Education for the Contemporary Society.*

Bhaskara Rao, Digumarti (2004). *International Guidelines on Open and Distance Education*, New Delhi: Discovery Publishing House.

Bhaskara Rao, Digumarti, Editor (2004). *Adult Learning in the 21st Century*. New Delhi: Discovery Publishing House.

Bhaskara Rao, Digumarti, Editor (2004). *Educational Practices: Research and Recommendations*. New Delhi: Discovery Publishing House.

Bhaskara Rao, Digumarti, Editor (2004). *Chernobyl: Never Again*. New Delhi: APH Publishing Corporation.

Bhaskara Rao, Digumarti, Editor (2004). *Virology and Immunology*. New Delhi: APH Publishing Corporation.

Bhaskara Rao, Digumarti, C.A.P. Swami and B.S.V. Dutt (1997). *Self-Evaluation in Student Teaching*. New Delhi: Discovery Publishing House. ISBN 81-7141-374-9.

Bhaskara Rao, Digumarti and B.S.V. Dutt, Editors (2003). *Education: Programmes and Policies*. New Delhi: APH Publishing Corporation. ISBN 81-7648-470-9.

Bhaskara Rao, Digumarti and D. Naresh Kumar (2004). *School Teacher Effectiveness*. New Delhi: Discovery Publishing House.

Bhaskara Rao, Digumarti and D. Sridhar (2002). *Job Satisfaction of School Teachers*. New Delhi: Discovery Publishing House. ISBN 81-7141-652-7.

Bhaskara Rao, Digumarti and Digumarti Pushpa Latha (1994). *Achievement in Biology*. New Delhi: Discovery Publishing House. ISBN 81-7141-264-5.

Bhaskara Rao, Digumarti, C. Sridevi and K. Vijaya (1995). *Achievement in Social Studies*. New Delhi: Discovery Publishing House. ISBN 81-7141-281-5.

Bhaskara Rao, Digumarti and Digumarti Pushpa Latha (1995). *Achievement in English*. New Delhi: Discovery Publishing House. ISBN 81-7141-283-1.

Bhaskara Rao, Digumarti and Digumarti Pushpa Latha (1994). *Achievement in Science*. New Delhi: Discovery Publishing House. ISBN 81-7141-280-70.

Bhaskara Rao, Digumarti and Digumarti Pushpa Latha (1995). *Achievement in Mathematics*. New Delhi: Discovery Publishing House. ISBN 81-7141-278-5.

Bhaskara Rao, Digumarti and Digumarti Pushpa Latha, Editors (1998). *International Encyclopaedia of Women*. 5 Volumes. New Delhi: Discovery Publishing House. ISBN 81-7141-410-9.

Vol. 1 *Status of World's Women*. ISBN 81-7141-494-X.

Vol. 2 *Women, Education and Empowerment*. ISBN 81-7141-498-1.

Vol. 3 *Women Challenges and Advancement*. ISBN 81-7141-497-4.

Vol. 4 *Women and Family Health*. ISBN 81-7141-497-4.

Vol. 5 *Women and International Action*. ISBN 81-7141-498-2.

Bhaskara Rao, Digumarti, Digumarti Pushpa Latha and Digumarti Harshitha, Editors (2001). *Biological Warfare*. New Delhi: Discovery Publishing House. ISBN 81-7141-597-0.

Bhaskara Rao, Digumarti, Digumarti Pushpa Latha and Digumarti Harshitha, Editors (2001). *Women as Educators*. New Delhi: Discovery Publishing House. ISBN 81-7141-602-0.

Bhaskara Rao, Digumarti and Digumarti Harshitha, Editors (2001). *Education in India*. New Delhi: APH Publishing Corporation. ISBN 81-7141-207-2.

Bhaskara Rao, Digumarti, Digumarti Pushpa Latha and Digumarti Harshitha, Editors (2001). *Assessing Learning Achievement*. New Delhi: Discovery Publishing House. ISBN 81-7141-601-2.

Bhaskara Rao, Digumarti, Digumarti Pushpa Latha and Digumarti Harshitha, Editors (2001). *Energy Security*. New Delhi: Discovery Publishing House. ISBN 81-7141-598-9.

Bhaskara Rao, Digumarti, Digumarti Harshitha and K.R.S.S. Rao, Editors (1999). *Advanced Biotechnology*. New Delhi: Discovery Publishing House. ISBN 81-7141-516-4.

Bhaskara Rao, Digumarti and K.R.S. Sambhasiva Rao, Editors (1996). *Current Trends in Indian Education*. New Delhi: Discovery Publishing House. ISBN 81-7141-311-0.

Bhaskara Rao, Digumarti and K. Vijaya (1995). *A Text Book of Evaluation*. Ambala Cantt: The Associated Publishers.

Bhaskara Rao, Digumarti and N.V.M. Mohana Rao (2002). *Problems of Mentally Handicapped Children*. New Delhi: Discovery Publishing House. ISBN 81-7141-645-4.

Bhaskara Rao, Digumarti and S. Chandra Mohan (2002). *Sports Management*. New Delhi: APH Publishing Corporation. ISBN 81-7648-467-9.

Bhaskara Rao, Digumarti and Sk. Johni Basha (2004). *Teachers' Population Education Awareness*. New Delhi: APH Publishing Corporation.

Bhaskara Rao, Digumarti, V.V. Rao, V.V. Lakshmi and V.V. Krishna, Editors (1999). *Status and Advancement of Women*. New Delhi: APH Publishing Corporation. ISBN 81-7648-169-6.

Babu, P.C., Author and Digumarti Bhaskara Rao, Editor (2004). *Flowers of Wisdom*. New Delhi: Discovery Publishing House. ISBN 81-7141-695-0.

Bhagya Lakshmi, Lingineni, Author and Digumarti Bhaskara Rao, Editor (2000). *Reading and Comprehension*. New Delhi: Discovery Publishing House. ISBN 81-7141-543-1.

Bhuvaneswara Lakshmi, Gadde, Author and Digumarti Bhaskara Rao, Editor (2000). *Attitude Towards Science*. New Delhi: Discovery Publishing House. ISBN 81-7141-541-6.

Devraj, T.A.S., Author and Digumarti Bhaskara Rao, Editor (1997). *Trace Analysis of Uranium and Thorium*. New Delhi: Discovery Publishing House. ISBN 81-7141-375-7.

Durga Rani, K., Author and Digumarti Bhaskara Rao, Editor (2000). *Educational Aspirations and Scientific Attitudes*. New Delhi: Discovery Publishing House. ISBN 81-7141-555-55.

Dutt, B.S.V. and Digumarti Bhaskara Rao (2001). *Empowering Primary Teachers*. New Delhi: Discovery Publishing House. ISBN 81-7141-615.2.

Ediger, Marlow and Digumarti Bhaskara Rao (1996). *Science Curriculum*. New Delhi: Discovery Publishing House. ISBN 81-7141-321-8.

Ediger, Marlow and Digumarti Bhaskara Rao (2000). *Teaching Mathematics Successfully*. New Delhi: Discovery Publishing House. ISBN 81-7141-552-0.

Ediger, Marlow and Digumarti Bhaskara Rao (2001). *Teaching Science Successfully.* New Delhi: Discovery Publishing House. ISBN 81-7141-600-4.

Ediger, Marlow and Digumarti Bhaskara Rao (2001). *Teaching Social Studies Successfully.* New Delhi: Discovery Publishing House. ISBN 81-7141-596-2.

Ediger, Marlow and Digumarti Bhaskara Rao (2002). *Philosophy and Curriculum.* New Delhi: Discovery Publishing House. ISBN 81-7141-631-4.

Ediger, Marlow and Digumarti Bhaskara Rao (2002). *Improving School Administration.* New Delhi: Discovery Publishing House. ISBN 81-7141-633-0.

Ediger, Marlow and Digumarti Bhaskara Rao (2002). *Elementary Curriculum.* New Delhi: Discovery Publishing House. ISBN 81-7141-658-6.

Ediger, Marlow and Digumarti Bhaskara Rao (2003). *Language Arts Curriculum.* New Delhi: Discovery Publishing House. ISBN 81-7141-657-8.

Ediger, Marlow and Digumarti Bhaskara Rao (2004). *Teaching Language Arts Successfully.* New Delhi: Discovery Publishing House. ISBN 81-7141-678-0.

Ediger, Marlow and Digumarti Bhaskara Rao (2004). *Teaching Mathematics in Elementary Schools.* New Delhi: Discovery Publishing House. ISBN 81-7141-687-X.

Ediger, Marlow and Digumarti Bhaskara Rao (2004). *Teaching Science in Elementary Schools.* New Delhi: Discovery Publishing House. ISBN 81-7141-709-4.

Ediger, Marlow and Digumarti Bhaskara Rao (2004). *School Curriculum and Administration.* New Delhi: Discovery Publishing House. ISBN 81-7141-709-4.

Ediger, Marlow and Digumarti Bhaskara Rao (2004). *Modern Elementary School.* New Delhi: Discovery Publishing House.

Ediger, Marlow and Digumarti Bhaskara Rao (2004): *Relevancy in Elementary Curriculum.* New Delhi: Discovery Publishing House. ISBN 81-7141-751-5.

Ediger, Marlow and Digumarti Bhaskara Rao, (2004). *Teaching Social Studies in Elementary Schools*. New Delhi: Discovery Publishing House.

Ediger Marlow, B.S.V. Dutt and Digumarti Bhaskara Rao (2004). *Teaching English Successfully*. New Delhi: Discovery Publishing House. ISBN 81-7141-707-8.

Harshitha, Digumarti and Digumarti Bhaskara Rao, Editors (2004). *Educational Innovations*. New Delhi: Discovery Publishing House.

Indira Devi, Author and J. Prasanth Kumar and Digumarti Bhaskara Rao, Editors (2004). *Values in Language Text Books*. New Delhi: Discovery Publishing House.

Jayasree, Kandi, Author and Digumarti Bhaskara Rao, Editor (1999). *Correlates of Socialisation*. New Delhi: Discovery Publishing House. ISBN 81-7141-517-2.

John Babu, Chikati, Author and T.J.R. Prasad, G.M. Madhukar and Digumarti Bhaskara Rao, Editors (1996). *Problem Solving in Mathematics*. New Delhi: APH Publishing Corporation. ISBN 81-7648-273-0.

Lalitha, T., Author and K.S. Prabhakaram, D.S.N. Sastry and Digumarti Bhaskara Rao, Editors (2004). *Educational Philosophic Beliefs*. New Delhi: Discovery Publishing House. ISBN 81-7141-765-5.

Madhu Bala, Jampala, Author and Digumarti Bhaskara Rao, Editor (2004). *Adjustment Problems of Hearing Impaired*. New Delhi: Discovery Publishing House.

Marja, Talvi and Digumarti Bhaskara Rao, Editors (1996). *Educational Leadership and Social Changes*. New Delhi: Discovery Publishing House. ISBN 81-7141-320-X.

Nirmala Jyothi, M., Author and Digumarti Bhaskara Rao, Editor (2003). *Non-detention Systems in School Education*. New Delhi: Discovery Publishing House. ISBN 81-7141-654-3.

Prabhakaram, K.S., Author and Digumarti Bhaskara Rao, Editor (1998). *Concept Attainment Model in Mathematics Teaching*. New Delhi: Discovery Publishing House. ISBN 81-7141-424-9.

Prasanth Kumar, J., Author and Digumarti Bhaskara Rao, Editor (1998). *Effectiveness of Distance Education System*. New Delhi: Discovery Publishing House. ISBN 81-7141-437-0.

Prasanth Kumar, J., Author and G. Sundara Rao and Digumarti Bhaskara Rao, Editors (2000). *Open University Student Support Services*. New Delhi: Discovery Publishing House. ISBN 81-7141-550-4.

Ramatulasamma, K., Author and Digumarti Bhaskara Rao, Editor (2002). *Job Satisfaction of Teacher Educators*, New Delhi: Discovery Publishing House. ISBN 81-7141-655-1.

Rama Krishnaiah, D., Author and Digumarti Bhaskara Rao, Editor (1998). *Job Satisfaction of College Teachers*, New Delhi: Discovery Publishing House. ISBN 81-7141-438-9.

Rama Kumar Ratnam, M., Author and Digumarti Bhaskara Rao, Editor (1998). *Dukka: Suffering in Early Buddhism*. New Delhi: Discovery Publishing House. ISBN 81-7141-653-5.

Rathaiah, Lavu and Digumarti Bhaskara Rao, Editors (1996). *International Innovations in Education*. New Delhi: Discovery Publishing House. ISBN 81-7141-359-5.

Ramesh, Ganta and Digumarti Bhaskara Rao, Editors (1998). *Environmental Education: Problems and Prospects*. New Delhi: Discovery Publishing House. ISBN 81-7141-423-0.

Rathaiah, Lavu and Digumarti Bhaskara Rao (1997). *Achievement Correlates*. New Delhi: Discovery Publishing House. ISBN 81-7141-385-4.

Reddy, Sudhakar Y., Author, and Digumarti Bhaskara Rao, Editor (2003). *Creativity in Adolescents*. New Delhi: Discovery Publishing House. ISBN 81-7141-659-4.

Reddy, M.S., Author and Digumarti Bhaskara Rao, Editor (2004). *Creativity in College Students*. New Delhi: Discovery Publishing House. ISBN 81-7141-697-7.

Radramamba, B., Author and Digumarti Bhaskara Rao, Editor (2003). *Problems of Teaching*. New Delhi: APH Publishing Corporation. ISBN 81-7648-462-8.

Sanjeeva Rao, P.C., Author and Digumarti Bhaskara Rao, Editor (1996). *A Text Book of Geology*. New Delhi: Discovery Publishing House. ISBN 81-7141-313-7.

Satya Narayana V., Author and Digumarti Bhaskara Rao, Editor (2001). *Physical Education, Social Attitudes and Leadership Qualities*. New Delhi: Discovery Publishing House. ISBN 81-7141-593-8.

Srinivasulu Reddy, M., and K.R.S. Sambasiva Rao, Authors and Digumarti Bhaskara Rao, Editor (1999). *A Text Book of Aquaculture*. New Delhi: Discovery Publishing House. ISBN 81-7141-482-6.

Srinivasa Rao, Mandalapu, Author and Digumarti Bhaskara Rao, Editor (2004). *Achievement Motivation and Achievement in Mathematics*. New Delhi: Discovery Publishing House. ISBN 81-7141-674-8.

Vanaja, M. Author and Digumarti Bhaskara Rao, Editor (1999). *Inquiry Training Model*. New Delhi: Discovery Publishing House. ISBN 81-7141-515-6.

Vanaja. M. and N. Sneha Latha, Authors and Digumarti Bhaskara Rao, Editor (2004). *Student Shyness*. New Delhi: APH Publishing Corporation.

Valeri V. Koustiouk, Author and Digumarti Bhaskara Rao, Editor (2002). *A Text Book of Cryogenics*. New Delhi: Discovery Publishing House. ISBN 81-7141-642-X.

Valeri V. Koustiouk, Author and Digumarti Bhaskara Rao, Editor (2004). *Refrigeration and Environment*. New Delhi: APH Publishing Corporation.

Veena Kumari, Balusu and Digumarti Bhaskara Rao (1996). *Operation Black Board*. New Delhi: Ashish Publishing Corporation. ISBN 81-7024-711-X.

Veena Kumari, Balusu, Author and Digumarti Bhaskara Rao, Editor (2000). *Psycho-Social Correlates of Achievement*, New Delhi: Discovery Publishing House. ISBN 81-7141-547-4.

Vanaja, M., Author and Digumarti Bhaskara Rao, Editor (1999). *Inquiry Training Model*. New Delhi: Discovery Publishing House. ISBN 81-7141-515-6.

Venkata Rao, P. and Digumarti Bhaskara Rao (1989). *A Text Book of Zoology—Junior Intermediate*. Guntur: Vignan Publishers.

Venkata Rao, P. and Digumarti Bhaskara Rao (1989). *A Text Book of Zoology—Senior Intermediate*. Guntur: Vignan Publishers.

Venugopala Rao, K., Author and Digumarti Bhaskara Rao, Editor (2000). *Teacher Morale in Secondary Schools*. New Delhi: Discovery Publishing House. ISBN 81-7141-551-2.

Vidya, C., Author and Digumarti Bhaskara Rao. Editor (1996). *A Text Book of Nutrition*. New Delhi: Discovery Publishing House. ISBN 81-7141-309-9.

Vidya Bharathi, D., Author and Digumarti Bhaskara Rao, Editor (2000). *Educational Philosophies of Swami Vivekananda and John Dewey*. New Delhi: APH Publishing Corporation. ISBN 81-7648-309-9.

Books in Telugu Language

Bhaskara Rao, Digumarti (1986). *Dhrushya Sravana Bodhanapakaranalu* (Audio Visual Teaching Aids). Guntur: Nagarjuna Publishers.

Bhaskara Rao, Digumarti (1993). *Jeevasashtra Bodhana* (Teaching of Biology). Guntur: Nagarjuna Publishers.

Bhaskara Rao, Digumarti (1995). *Vignanasasthra Bodhana* (Teaching of Science) Guntur: Nagarjuna Publishers.

Bhaskara Rao, Digumarti (1997). *Vidya Manovignana Seshtram* (Educational Psychology). Guntur: Creative Press.

Bhaskara Rao, Digumarti (1998). *DSC Study Material*. Guntur: Nagarjuna Publishers.

Bhaskara Rao, Digumarti (1998). *Upadhyayudu Vidya*. (Teacher and Education). Guntur: Nagarjuna Publishers.

Bhaskara Rao, Digumarti (1998). *Vidya Drukpadalu* (Prespectives of Education). Guntur: Nagarjuna Publishers.

Bhaskara Rao, Digumarti (1999). *EdCET Teaching Aptitude*. Guntur: Nagarjuna Publishers.

Bhaskara Rao, Digumarti (2001). *Bharata Samajamulo Upadyayudu Vidya* (Teacher and Education in Emerging Indian Society). Guntur: Nagarjuna Publishers.

Bhaskara Rao, Digumarti (2001). *Bhoutika Sastra Bodhana Paddathulu* (Methods of Teaching Physical Science). Guntur: Nagarjuna Publishers.

Bhaskara Rao, Digumarti (2001). *Jeeva Sastra Bodhana Padhathulu* (Methods of Teaching Biology). Guntur: Nagarjuna Publishers.

Bhaskara Rao, Digumarti (2001). *Vidya Manovignana Sastram* (Educational Psychology). Guntur: Nagarjuna Publishers.

Bhaskara Rao, Digumarti (2003). *Patsala Yajamanyam/Paripalana* (School Management and Administration). Guntur: Nagarjuna Publishers.

Bhaskara Rao, Digumarti (2004). *Vidya Sanketika Sastram mariyu Computer Vidya* (Educational Technology and Computer Education). Guntur: Nagarjuna Publishers.